21185
1091

£15.00

REASONING WITH ARBITRARY OBJECTS

Aristotelian Society Series

Volume 1
COLIN MCGINN
Wittgenstein on Meaning:
An Interpretation and Evaluation

Volume 2
BARRY TAYLOR
Modes of Occurrence:
Verbs, Adverbs and Events

Aristotelian Society Monographs Committee:
Anthony Savile (Monographs Editor)
Martin Davies
Jennifer Hornsby

*This volume edited for the Aristotelian Society
by Martin Davies.*

Kit Fine

Reasoning With Arbitrary Objects

Aristotelian Society Series

Volume 3

Basil Blackwell · Oxford

© Kit Fine 1985

First published 1985
in cooperation with The Aristotelian Society
King's College, London WC2R 2LS

Basil Blackwell Publisher Ltd
108 Cowley Road, Oxford OX4 1JF, England

Basil Blackwell Inc.
432 Park Avenue South, Suite 1505
New York, NY 10016, USA

All rights reserved. Except for the quotation of short passages for the purposes of criticism and review, no part of this publication may be reproduced, stored in a retrieval system, or transmitted, in any form or by any means, electronic, mechanical, photocopying, recording or otherwise, without the prior permission of the publisher

British Library Cataloguing in Publication Data

Fine, Kit
Reasoning with arbitrary objects.
1. Logic
I. Title
160   BC51

ISBN 0-631-13844-7

Library of Congress Cataloging in Publication Data

Fine, Kit.
Reasoning with arbitrary objects.

Bibliography: p.
Includes index.
1. Reasoning.   2. Logic.   I. Title.
BC177.F56 1985   160   85-6045
ISBN 0-631-13844-7

Printed in Great Britain by
Photobooks (Bristol) Ltd

Contents

Preface   vii

Introduction   1

I   The General Framework
1. Arbitrary Objects Defended   5
2. The Models   22
3. Conditions   31
4. Existence   36
5. Truth   41
6. Validity   48
7. Definitions   53

II   Some Standard Systems
8. Hilbert and Gentzen   61
9. Quine   81
10. Copi   104
11. Why Go Generic?   122
12. Accord with Ordinary Reasoning   127

III   Systems in General
13. The General Notion of a System   147
14. Soundness   150
15. Completeness   161
16. Further Conditions   167
17. Genericity Generalized   171

IV Non-Standard Systems
  18. Restricted C   177
  19. Variants   183
  20. Connections   195
  21. Inclusive and Intuitionistic Systems   205

Bibliography   210

General Index   215

Index of Symbols   219

Preface

This book had its origin in the classroom. I was teaching natural deduction to a group of students and had come to the point at which the rule of universal generalization is introduced. I had wanted to give an explanation of the rule in terms of arbitrary objects. But my sense of rigour got in the way, and I gave instead an explanation in terms of schematic names.

When I left the classroom, I gave the matter some more thought. I hold it as a general methodological principle that when there is a clash between intuition and rigour, when one's sense of rigour prevents one from saying what, from an intuitive point of view, it seems that one can say, then it is rigour and not intuition that should give way. Applying this principle to the case at hand, it seemed that there should be an account of arbitrary objects upon the basis of which a satisfactory explanation of the rule of universal generalization could be given. It was the attempt to develop such an account that led to the present work.

I appreciate that there are many philosophers to whom the whole idea of arbitrary objects will appear abhorrent: very few things are proved in philosophy; but did not Frege show, once and for all, that generality was to be explained in terms of the quantifiers and not by reference to a special kind of generic object? It should therefore be mentioned that I myself was once a firm adherent to the Fregean position and that it was only with the greatest struggle that I was able to see the advantages of the opposing view.

In terms of that struggle, the present work represents a transitional stage. I have broken away from the Fregean tradition to the extent of allowing arbitrary objects to be the referents of certain singular terms. But I have stayed within that tradition in that the standard symbolism and semantics of the quantifiers have been retained. I now think that the true potential of the generic approach is only fully realised when the quantifiers, as standardly conceived, are dropped altogether and the arbitrary objects themselves are made the sole vehicle of generality.

There are several people who, in one way or another, helped me with the book. Alice Gannt and Peggy Coonagh did all of the typing. Ran Lahar assisted in the proof reading. David McCarty, Tim McCarthy, David Over, Barry Richards, Neil Tennant and Peter Woodruff discussed various of the ideas with me. Timothy Smiley read through the whole manuscript and made many valuable suggestions. Martin Davies prepared the manuscript for publication. I am very grateful to all these people and, most of all, to my wife.

Introduction

This book deals with certain problems in understanding natural deduction and ordinary reasoning. As is well known, there exist certain informal procedures for arguing to a universal conclusion and from an existential premiss. We may establish that all objects of a certain kind have a given property by showing that an arbitrary object of that kind has that property; and having shown that there exists an object with a given property, we feel entitled to give it a name and declare that it has the property. So we may establish that all triangles have interior angles summing to 180° by showing of an arbitrary triangle that its interior angles sum to 180°; and having established that there exists a bisector to an angle, we feel entitled to give it a name and declare that it *is* a bisector to the angle.

These informal procedures correspond to certain of the quantificational rules in systems of natural deduction. Corresponding to the first is the rule of universal generalization, which allows us to infer $\forall x \phi(x)$ from $\phi(a)$ under suitable restrictions. Corresponding to the second is the rule of existential instantiation, which allows us to infer $\phi(a)$ from $\exists x \phi(x)$, again under suitable restrictions.

In these inferences, certain terms play a crucial role; and it is natural to ask how they are to be understood. What role is to be attributed to the term a in the inferences from natural deduction? What is to be made of our talk of arbitrary triangles or indefinite bisectors in ordinary reasoning?

The present work is based upon the hypothesis that these critical terms refer to arbitrary or representative objects. The term a in the inferences from natural deduction functions as a name of a suitable arbitrary object. And our talk of arbitrary triangles or of indefinite bisectors is to be taken at its face value as also evincing reference to arbitrary objects.

The core of the work will be taken up with applying this hypothesis to two main systems of natural deduction: the one of Quine's *Methods of Logic* [52]; and the other of Copi [54], as amended by Kalish [67] and Prawitz [67]. In the case of each of these systems, we shall propose a generic semantics and then, by reference to that semantics, both establish soundness and motivate the restrictions on the rules.

We shall also be concerned to cover certain other topics. We develop the pure theory of arbitrary objects somewhat beyond the needs of the present application, partly because of its intrinsic interest and partly with a view to other applications. We embark on a general study of systems containing a rule of existential instantiation and prove some general results on what form satisfactory systems of this sort can take. Finally, on the basis of an alternative generic semantics, we develop certain presuppositional systems and relate them to existing systems in the literature. The book is divided into parts according to the topic treated, with the first part dealing with the pure theory, the second with the application to the systems of Copi and Quine, the third with systems in general that contain a rule of existential instantiation, and the last with the presuppositional systems.

The work here is part of a much larger project, one in which the theory of arbitrary objects is to be applied to the use of pronouns in natural language and to the use of variables in informal mathematics and programming languages. These other topics have been altogether ignored, although the perceptive reader may pick up on certain intended points of contact. The closely related topic of developing a generic semantics for the ε- and η-calculi of Hilbert and Bernays [34] and Hailperin [57] has also not been considered; and my hope is that I shall be able to deal with it thoroughly elsewhere.

The book does not need to be read from beginning to end and the first part, in particular, may be consulted according to the demands from the other parts. The reader who is having difficulties may find my 'Natural Deduction and Arbitrary Objects' [85] helpful as a somewhat gentler introduction to the subject.

PART I

THE GENERAL FRAMEWORK

In this part, I present a brief account of the theory of arbitrary objects. My main concern has been to expound those parts of the theory that are most relevant to the application to natural deduction. But I have also tried to indicate, as we go along, some of the other features of the theory and some of the different ways in which it may be modified.

The part is in seven chapters. The first chapter is a philosophical defence both of the coherence and of the value of a theory of arbitrary objects. It is extracted substantially from my paper 'A Defence of Arbitrary Objects' and may be omitted by those who have read the paper or have no interest in philosophical matters. The other chapters give a more rigorous account of the generic approach. Chapter 2 introduces the models that contain arbitrary objects, the so-called A-models. Chapter 3 presents some conditions of interest on A-models and Chapter 4 establishes some results on the existence of A-models. Chapters 5 and 6 define the notions of truth and validity for statements or inferences concerning arbitrary objects. And Chapter 7 provides a theory of definitions for arbitrary objects.

1
Arbitrary Objects Defended

There is the following view. In addition to individual objects, there are arbitrary objects: in addition to individual numbers, arbitrary numbers; in addition to individual men, arbitrary men. With each arbitrary object is associated an appropriate range of individual objects, its values: with each arbitrary number, the range of individual numbers; with each arbitrary man, the range of individual men. An arbitrary object has those properties common to the individual objects in its range. So an arbitrary number is odd or even, an arbitrary man is mortal, since each individual number is odd or even, each individual man is mortal. On the other hand, an arbitrary number fails to be prime, an arbitrary man fails to be a philosopher, since some individual number is not prime, some individual man is not a philosopher.

Such a view used to be quite common, but has now fallen into complete disrepute. As with so many things, Frege led the way. Given his own theory of quantification, it was unnecessary to interpret the variables of mathematics as designating variable numbers; and given the absurdities in the notion of a variable number, it was also unwise. It was with characteristic irony that he wrote: 'Perhaps there is a seminal ideal here which we could also find of value outside mathematics' ([79], p. 160).

Where Frege led, others have been glad to follow. Among the many subsequent philosophers who have spoken against arbitrary objects, we might mention Russell ([03], pp. 90–91), Lesniewski (see Luschei [62], pp. 22–3, 27), Tarski ([65], p. 4), Church ([56], p. 13), Quine

([52], pp. 127–8), Rescher ([68], pp. 134–7) and Lewis ([72], p. 203). If more philosophers of the present day have not added their voices to the protest, it is probably because they have not thought it worth the bother. As Menger says ([79], p. 144), the thesis that there are no variable numbers is 'today one of the few propositions about which logicians as well as mathematicians are in general agreement'.

In the face of such united opposition, it might appear rash to defend any form of the theory of arbitrary objects. But that is precisely what I intend to do. Indeed, I would want to claim, not only that a form of the theory is defensible, but also that it is extremely valuable. In application to a wide variety of topics – the logic of generality, the use of variables in mathematics, the role of pronouns in natural language – the theory provides explanations that are as good as those of standard quantification theory, and sometimes better.

Rather than present the finished theory at the outset, we may see it as the outgrowth of the criticisms that have been directed against its cruder formulations. Each criticism, if not deflected, will lead to an appropriate change of formulation. The finished form of the theory will then emerge as the cumulative result of these various criticisms; it will be, if you like, the prize that the proponent of the naive view can carry off with him in the contest with his critics. This is not how I myself came to the theory; but it is perhaps the most congenial approach for those who are already sceptical.

Three kinds of objections will be considered in all. Bluntly put, they might be stated as follows: there are no arbitrary objects; the principles governing them are incoherent; and the theory leads to questions without answers.

Let us consider each objection in turn, with the ontological worry first. Is it seriously to be supposed that, in addition to individual numbers, there are arbitrary numbers and that, in addition to individual men, there are arbitrary men? What strange sorts of objects are these? Can I count with arbitrary numbers or have tea with an arbitrary man?

Two questions may be discerned here: are there any arbitrary objects?; and, what are they like? To deal with the first, it is necessary to distinguish, in a way that is familiar from the philosophical literature, between two uses of the phrase 'there are'. The opinions of the nominalist will serve as an illustration. In one use of the phrase, he is concerned to deny that there are numbers; for that is just his position. But in the other use, he may be prepared to admit that there are numbers; for he may be prepared to speak with the mathematician or the common man and say that there is a solution to the equation '$x + 5 = 12$' or that there are prime numbers greater than 5.

If now I am asked whether there are arbitrary objects, I will answer according to the intended use of 'there are'. If it is the ontologically significant use, then I am happy to agree with my opponent and say 'no'. I have a sufficiently robust sense of reality not to want to people my world with arbitrary numbers or arbitrary men. Indeed, I may be sufficiently robust not even to want individual numbers or individual men in my world. But if the intended sense is ontologically neutral, then my answer is a decided 'yes'. I have, it seems to me, as much reason to affirm that there are arbitrary objects in this sense as the nominalist has to affirm that there are numbers.

If this is right, then our ontological scruples should not tell against the development of a theory of arbitrary objects. The nominalist is not against number theory, but only against a certain construal of it, one that sees its acceptability as resting on the existence of numbers. In the same way, our critic should not be against arbitrary object theory, but only against its realistic construal.

Of course, anyone who accepts a theory yet disputes its realist commitment must give some other account of what its acceptability consists in. But here I am happy to go along with the most ardent reductionist and have him reduce the whole theory of arbitrary objects to one that trades in more respectable entities. Indeed, the final formulation of the theory will make it clear how just such a reduction might go. My only concern, at this stage, is to insist on the legitimacy of an intermediate level of theorizing, one that provisionally accepts the ontology of arbitrary objects.

The other ontological worry concerns, not the existence of arbitrary objects, but their nature: what are arbitrary objects? The two worries are connected, though; for despairing of a satisfactory answer to the question 'what are they?', philosophers have concluded that they are not.

The question 'what are they?' may be taken, in an ordinary, non-philosophical way, as a request for an explanation of what objects one is talking about. One can then do no better, I think, than refer to the kind of role that arbitrary objects are intended to play. One says much what was said at the beginning of the paper, that each arbitrary object is associated with a range of values, that it possesses those properties common to its values and so on. Of course, any attempt to pin down the role of the objects more exactly may result in an inconsistent theory. But an inconsistent theory need not be entirely useless in helping us to understand what objects are being talked about; for it may point in the direction of their intended role, without actually giving it. We can all get a pretty good idea of what sets are meant to be from the axioms of naive set theory, even though those axioms turn out to be inconsistent.

The question 'what are they?' may also be taken, in a philosophical way, as a request for a category or kind to which the objects can be assigned. We may then supply the quite reasonable answer that arbitrary objects belong, like sets of propositions, to the category of abstractions. To be sure, it is hard to say what in general an abstraction is or what is distinctive about arbitrary objects as a kind of abstraction; but these are difficulties that arise for all abstractions.

There may be thought to be a special problem with arbitrary objects; for it seems that they must somehow be on an ontological par with the corresponding individuals. An arbitrary number is just another number, an arbitrary man just another man. It therefore appears that one can say the same sorts of things about each. So one is led to the absurd conclusion that one might count with arbitrary numbers or have tea with an arbitrary man.

This supposition of ontological parity has perhaps two main sources. The first is a certain metaphysical or psychological picture that may have been suggested by the more zealous advocates of arbitrary objects. It is as if an arbitrary man were merely a defective man, one shorn of his peculiar features; and, in the same way, it is as if a general idea were merely a defective version of a particular idea. So behind every individual man is an arbitrary man, behind every particular idea a general idea. The second source is a certain argument: membership in a particular category is a common property of all the individuals; it would therefore appear that the arbitrary object should have the property and so also be in the category.

This picture and argument have had their hold, but there is nothing in the theory that requires us to accept either. The picture is an idle adjunct to the theory and may simply be dropped. The argument is more serious but, on a proper formulation of the theory, turns out to be defective.

The second objection we wish to consider is to the effect that the theory of arbitrary objects is logically incoherent. It may be granted that there is no ontological absurdity in the mere supposition that there are arbitrary objects. But, it will be argued, there is a logical absurdity in the principles that are meant to govern such objects. For the key principle, without which a theory would be unthinkable, is that each arbitrary object should have the properties common to the individuals in its range. But formulate such a principle properly and it will be seen to lead, either on its own or in conjunction with innocuous premises, to contradictory conclusions.

There are two forms this line of argument can take. One uses a logically complex property as a counter-example to the principle. The other uses a property that is not logically complex, but is otherwise special.

The first line of argument goes back to Berkeley (Intro., X) and, in one form or another, has been resurrected by many subsequent philosophers. A typical version goes as follows. Take an arbitrary number. Then it is odd or even, since each individual number is odd or even. But it is not odd, since some individual number is not odd; and it is not even since some individual number is not even. Therefore it is odd or even, yet not odd and not even. A contradiction.

This particular version of the argument uses the complex property of being odd or even. Other versions of the argument use other complex properties. However, it will be clear from the treatment of this case how the treatment of the other cases should go.

Crucial to this argument is a certain formulation of what I shall call the *principle of generic attribution*, the principle that any arbitrary object has those properties common to the individuals in its range. Let us ignore the reference to properties as not essential to our present purposes, and deal instead with conditions or open sentences. Let $\phi(x)$ be any condition with free variable x; let a be the name of an arbitrary object a; and let i be a variable that ranges over the individuals in the range of a. (We here follow a general convention whereby a names a.) Then the required formulation of the principle is:

(G1) $\phi(a) \equiv \forall i \phi(i)$ (a ϕ's iff every individual ϕ's)

Upon letting a name the arbitrary number of the argument, the various claims made about that number can be obtained by making appropriate substitutions for the condition $\phi(x)$. For example, upon substituting Ex (x is even), we obtain:

(G1)′ $Ea \equiv \forall i Ei$;

and the claim that a is not even ($-$Ea) then follows from the evident truth that not all numbers are even ($-\forall$iEi).

It must be granted that, once this formulation of the principle is accepted, the argument goes through. But it may be doubted whether the formulation should be accepted. For look at its consequence (G1)' and ask whether the arbitrary number a satisfies the condition (Ex $\equiv \forall$iEi) of being even iff all individual numbers are even. What the intuitive principle of generic attribution seems to tell us is that an arbitrary number a should satisfy the condition iff all individual numbers do. But not all individual numbers satisfy it; no even number does. So far from being a correct formulation of the intuitive principle, (G1) is something that the principle requires us to judge false.

Of course, we may have here a further sign that the intuitive principle is contradictory. But another possibility is that it is only intended that the intuitive principle apply to the whole context in which the name of the arbitrary object appears. Under this proviso, the correct formulation of the principle is:

(G2) The sentence ϕ(a) is true iff the sentence $\forall$iϕ(i) is true.

Or using satisfaction in place of truth, the formulation becomes

(G2)' a satisfies the condition ϕ(x) iff each individual i in the range of a satisfies the condition ϕ(x).

From this perspective, the original formulation (G1) rests on the fallacy of applying the principle internally, to only a part of the context in which the name of an arbitrary object appears. For although we may affirm $\forall$iϕ(i) $\equiv \forall$iϕ(i), we cannot correctly infer ϕ(a) $\equiv \forall$iϕ(i).

In such a way, the argument from complex properties can be stymied. It has always been thought that we have in this, and related, arguments a knockdown case against the whole theory of arbitrary objects. But if I am right, such arguments depend upon the failure to distinguish between two basically different formulations of the principle of generic attribution: one is merely a rule of *equivalence* and is stated in the material mode; the other is a rule of *truth* and is stated in the formal mode. Once the distinction is made, the arguments are seen to be without foundation.

But even if the traditional argument against the theory of arbitrary objects breaks down, may there not be more sophisticated variants of the argument that succeed? Consider again the statement Oa ∨ Ea ('a is odd or a is even'). From the modified formulation (G2), it follows that this statement is true and yet that neither disjunct is true. So the semantical rule for disjunction fails. Or consider the statements Oa and −Oa. From G2, it follows that neither Oa nor −Oa is true. So the semantical rule for negation fails. Suppose now Oa is false only when −Oa is true. Then the Law of Bivalence also fails.

Yet why should these consequences be thought to be unacceptable? There are other cases in which we are prepared to admit similar consequences. One is provided by vague language. Consider a blob, whose colour is a borderline case of both red and orange. Then it is true that the blob is red or orange, yet not true that it is red or that it is orange; and it is not true that the blob is red or that it is not red.

Also, it is not as if, in the absence of the classical semantic rules, we are left in the dark as to what the truth-conditions of statements concerning arbitrary objects should be. The statement $\phi(a)$, regardless of its inner complexity, simply has the same truth-conditions as $\forall i \phi(i)$.

But perhaps the worry is not so much about indeterminacy in the truth-conditions as inconstancy in the use of the logical constants. When '∨', let us say, occurs between statements concerning only individuals, we evaluate the result according to the classical truth-tables; when '∨' occurs between statements concerning arbitrary objects, we evaluate the result according to the rule of generic attribution. Is not this to use '∨' in two radically different ways?

I do not see that the theory demands that there be no shift in the sense of the logical constants, though it is certainly convenient, should there be a shift of sense, that there be no corresponding shift of symbol. But there is, in any case, a way in which we can see the theory as leaving the sense of '∨' intact. For in evaluating a disjunction $\psi(a) \lor \chi(a)$, we first apply the rule of generic attribution. This tells us that $\psi(a) \lor \chi(a)$ is true iff each of the statements $\psi(i) \lor \chi(i)$ is true for i an individual in the range of a. We then apply the standard rule of disjunction to each of the statements $\psi(i) \lor \chi(i)$. Thus at the only point at which we evaluate a disjunction, we evaluate it according to the classical rule. Thus it is not as if there are two rules of disjunction, differently activated according to the subject-matter of the statement. There is only one rule, appropriately activated according to the stage of the evaluation.

But is it not disturbing that the statement $\psi(a) \lor \chi(a)$ should be apparently disjunctive in form and yet not *immediately* evaluated according to the rule of disjunction? It seems that we must either deny that $\psi(a) \vee \chi(a)$ is a genuine disjunction or else give up the principle that disjunctions are evaluated directly by a disjunction rule.

I, for one, am happy to accept the second alternative. But for those who are not, there is an acceptable way of holding to the first alternative. For we may suppose that the statement $\psi(a) \vee \chi(a)$ is syntactically ambiguous. It may either be formed by disjoining $\psi(a)$ and $\chi(a)$ or by applying the property abstract $\lambda x(\psi(x) \vee \chi(x))$ to a. In the first case we have a genuine disjunction, in the second case not. A more perspicuous notation would use $[\lambda x(\psi(x) \vee \chi(x))]a$ for the second case, thereby making it clear that the statement is not genuinely disjunctive in form.

We may now evaluate genuine disjunctions directly in accordance with the classical rule. The extensions of property abstracts $\lambda x\phi(x)$ may be evaluated in the usual way for individuals and in a way analogous to (G2) for arbitrary objects. Thus the effect of the principle (G2) is achieved without any damage to the principle of direct evaluation.

However, there is still a price to pay; for the principle of property abstraction, $[\lambda x\phi(x)]a \equiv \phi(a)$, will fail. This principle too might be retained, if the expression $\lambda x\phi(x)$ were not regarded as denoting a property. But then other principles would have to be given up.

In general, it is impossible to achieve complete logical parity between individual and arbitrary objects; the difference in their logical, or rather meta-logical, behaviour must show up somewhere. But depending upon how exactly the generic attributions are expressed and interpreted, the difference may be made to show up now in this principle, now in that. It is only the most adamant logical purist who could not find one formulation to his liking.

Another logical objection to the principle remains, the argument from special properties. A typical version goes as follows. Take the property of being an individual number. Then each individual number has this property. So from the principle of generic attribution, it follows that any arbitrary number has this property, which is absurd.

There is no point in appealing here to our metalinguistic formulation (G2) of the intuitive principle. The statement 'all individual numbers are individual numbers' is true. It therefore follows from (G2) that the statement 'a is an individual number' is also true.

Indeed, the reformulation (G2)′ itself provides a counter-example. For the reformulation reads:

(G2)′ a satisfies $\phi(x)$ iff each individual i in the range of a satisfies $\phi(x)$.

Now this statement itself is a rather complex condition $\psi(x)$ on the arbitrary object a. So applying (G2) to $\psi(a)$, we see that (G2)′ is true iff:

> for every individual j (in the range of a), j satisfies $\phi(x)$ iff each individual i in the range of j satisfies $\phi(x)$.

But this is absurd.

It must be recognised, I think, that this objection requires us to make yet another modification in the formulation of our principle. We must distinguish between two kinds of condition or predicate. There are first of all the *generic* conditions and predicates. These include all of the ordinary predicates, such as 'being odd' or 'being mortal', and all of the conditions obtainable from them by means of the classical operations of quantification and truth-functional composition. To these conditions, the principle of generic attribution, in its revised form (G2), is applicable. There are then the *classical* conditions or predicates. These include certain special predicates, such as 'being an individual number' of 'being in the range of', and the various conditions obtained with their help. To these, the principle (G2) is not applicable.

The principle of generic attribution should therefore now receive the following formulation:

(G3) for any *generic* condition $\phi(x)$, $\phi(a)$ is true iff $\forall i \phi(i)$ is true;

and similarly for the version (G2)′ in terms of satisfaction. Given that the predicate 'is an individual number' is not generic, the previous argument then breaks down.

This answer to the objection might appear to be excessively weak. Certain counter-examples are provided to the principle of generic attribution. It is then claimed that the principle does not hold for all conditions. But for which? Presumably only those for which it holds.

But the status of the revised principle is not as trivial as this caricature of my response would have it. First, it is not as if the principle had no application. Call a language *generic* if all of the conditions obtainable by its use are themselves generic. Then many languages, of natural and independent interest, will be generic; and so the principle (G3) will have wide application to all such languages. But even when a language is not itself generic, it will correspond to one that is. For we may re-interpret its predicates or other non-logical constants so that they are classically evaluated in their application to individuals but 'generically' evaluated in their application to arbitrary objects. The new language will then be generic by definition and, over the domain of individuals, will be in semantic agreement with the original language.

Second, even in those cases in which the principle is not applicable, it will always be clear what the conditions for generic attribution should be – or rather, if there is any lack of clarity here, it will have its source in the reference to arbitrary objects. Take the conditions that figured in the previous arguments. Then we may suppose that it is just given when an object is to be an individual number or when an individual is to be in the range of an arbitrary object. In a formal development of the theory, these relations will just be specified as part of the structure of arbitrary objects. So it is not as if we are left in the dark here. There may no longer be any *general* procedure for evaluating the statements about arbitrary objects; but it will always be clear, from case to case, how the evaluation is to proceed.

Of course, there may be cases in which a predicate is ambiguous as between a generic and a classical reading. The predicate 'is a number' is a good example. On a generic reading, it is inclusive of all arbitrary numbers; on a classical reading, it is exclusive of them. So if it is asked whether an arbitrary number is a number, the answer will be 'yes' or 'no', according to whether a generic or a classical reading is intended.

It is this ambiguity that may explain why the argument for the ontological parity of individual and arbitrary objects has been seen to be so compelling. For it depends upon the failure to distinguish between the generic and classical readings of the predicate 'is a number'. Attend to the generic reading and it follows that each arbitrary number is a number; switch to the classical reading, and it then appears to follow that each arbitrary number is an individual number.

Finally, we may note, in support of the distinction between generic and classical conditions, that it corresponds to an intuitive distinction in the way that the names for arbitrary objects can be used. Applied to a generic condition $\phi(x)$, the name a plays a merely *representative* role; it serves to represent the individuals in the range of the arbitrary object. Applied to a classical condition $\phi(x)$, the name a plays an essentially *referential* role; it serves to pick out the arbitrary object itself. So if we wish to know whether a condition $\phi(x)$ is generic or classical, we may ask: is the name a in $\phi(a)$ being used in a merely representative or an essentially referential capacity?

We see therefore that a satisfactory version of the principle of generic attribution can be maintained. In response to the argument from complex predicates, we may insist on a metalinguistic formulation of the intuitive principle, one that makes explicit reference to truth or satisfaction. In response to the argument from special predicates, we may restrict the application of the metalinguistic formulation to generic conditions. Once these two changes are made, the principle is seen to be impervious to the logical objections that have usually been directed against it.

We turn now to the third objection. We have so far concentrated on a single principle, the principle of generic attribution, and have shown how a coherent formulation of it may be given. But this is a far cry from having a *theory* of arbitrary objects. A host of questions remain; and unless they can be answered, it is doubtful whether anything approaching a satisfactory theory can be obtained.

In considering this objection, we can perhaps do no better than to consider some of the detailed points raised by Frege. In arguing against the mathematician Czuber, Frege writes ([79], p. 160):

> This [Czuber's account] gives rise to a host of questions. The author obviously distinguishes two classes of numbers: the determinate and the indeterminate. We may then ask, say, to which of these classes the primes belong, or whether maybe some primes are determinate numbers and others indeterminate. We may ask further whether in the case of indeterminate numbers we must distinguish between the rational and the irrational, or whether this distinction can only be applied to determinate numbers. How many indeterminate numbers are there? How are they distinguished from one another? Can you add two indeterminate numbers, and if so, how? How do you find the number that is to be regarded as their sum? The same questions arise for adding a determinate number to an indeterminate one. To which class does the sum belong? Or maybe it belongs to a third?

Let us treat these questions in turn. First, 'to which of these classes [of the determinate and indeterminate numbers] do the primes belong?' Some of the determinate (individual) numbers are prime. But what of the indeterminate (arbitrary) numbers? Suppose 'prime' is taken, in its classical reading, to mean 'individual prime'. Then no arbitrary number is prime. Suppose now that 'prime' is taken in its generic reading. Then the statement 'a is prime', for *a* an arbitrary number, will not be true, since some individual numbers are not prime. Of course, neither will it be false, since some individual numbers *are* prime.

There is, however, a complication. We have so far taken an arbitrary number to have an unrestricted range, one that includes all individual numbers as values. But it also seems reasonable that there should be arbitrary numbers with a restricted range, one that includes only some of the individual numbers as values. Suppose we now ask, of these arbitrary numbers, whether any of them are prime. Then we should say: the statement 'a is prime' is true iff all of the individual numbers in the range of *a* are prime. So an arbitrary prime is prime, but not an arbitrary (and unrestricted) even number or an arbitrary (and unrestricted) factor of 12.

Frege's second question is of the same nature as the first and so need not be considered separately. This takes us to the next question: 'How are they [the indeterminate numbers] to be distinguished from one another?' But why should there be a nontrivial difference between any two arbitrary objects? In Euclidean space, for example, there is, in the absence of a coordinate system, no non-trivial way of distinguishing between any two points.

A theory does not require an identity criterion for its objects. But still, the present theory is able to provide one – not as it stands, but upon the introduction of two new elements. The first is the simultaneous assignment of values. We have so far explained which individuals can be assigned to arbitrary objects in a very simple manner. Each arbitrary object has been endowed with a range of values. The individuals $i, j, \ldots$ are then assignable to the objects $a, b,$ ... iff each individual is in the range of its arbitrary object. This simple idea must now be given up; for we must allow an interdependence among the values assigned to the arbitrary objects, so that what individuals are assignable to one object may be constrained by the values assigned to others. We must therefore be told, not merely what ranges the arbitrary objects have, but also what combinations of values from those ranges are admissible. It may be, for example that i, j are assignable to the two arbitrary numbers $a, b,$ iff $j = i^2$.

We must now think of the arbitrary objects as working in harness. A single arbitrary object will be representative of a class of individuals, as before. But a pair of arbitrary objects will be representative of a relation between individuals; and similarly for sequences of greater length. The principle of generic attribution must accordingly be modified so as to apply to all of the arbitrary objects that might be mentioned.

(G4) If $\phi(x_1, x_2, \ldots, x_n)$ is a generic condition containing no names for arbitrary objects, then $\phi(a_1, a_2, \ldots, a_n)$ is true iff $\phi(a_1, a_2, \ldots, a_n)$ is true for all admissible assignments of individuals $i_1, i_2, \ldots, i_n$ to the objects $a_1, a_2, \ldots, a_n$.

We could think of the previous principle (G3) as applying to the objects $a_1, a_2, \ldots, a_n$ one at a time. But we must think of the present principle (G4) as applying to those objects simultaneously.

The second component of the new apparatus is the relation of dependence among arbitrary objects or what may be called *object* dependence. This corresponds exactly to what mathematicians have in mind when they distinguish between dependent and independent variables. The two components are connected; for any value dependence must be sustained, in one way or another, by relations of object dependence. More exactly, when b is an arbitrary object that depends only upon the arbitrary objects $a_1, a_2, \ldots,$ then the values assignable to b must be determinable upon the basis of the values assigned to $a_1, a_2, \ldots$ Thus the relation of object dependence provides a principle for the *local* determination of admissible value assignments. Despite their connection, it is important to keep the two notions of dependence apart. Let a be an arbitrary real; its values are all the individual reals. Two distinct arbitrary reals that are dependent upon a may be distinguished. There is first the cube a^3 of a; this depends upon (stands in the relation of object-dependence to) a and assumes the value j when and only when a assumes the value $\sqrt[3]{j}$. There is then the cube root $\sqrt[3]{a}$ of a; this likewise depends upon a and assumes the real value j when and only when a assumes the value j^3. Now the value dependency between each of the pairs (a, a^3) and $(\sqrt[3]{a}, a)$ is the same; the components can take the real values i, j when and only when $j = i^3$. However, the object-dependency between each of the pairs is different; for a^3 depends upon a, while $\sqrt[3]{a}$ depends upon a. Mathematicians sometimes talk as if, given a pair of arbitrary reals (c, d) that stand in an indicated relation of value dependence, we can decide which is to be the dependent and which the independent variable. But on the view being put forward here, we are not free to decide, *given* the objects c and d, which way the relation of dependency goes. Rather we are free to decide, compatibly with the indicated value dependence, what objects we are talking about, whether it is, let us say, the pair (a, a^3) or the pair $(\sqrt[3]{a}, a)$.

The problem of providing identity criteria for arbitrary objects can now be solved. Say that an arbitrary object is *independent* if it depends upon no other objects and that otherwise it is *dependent*. We distinguish two cases, according to whether the objects are independent or dependent. Suppose first that a and b are independent objects. Then we say that $a = b$ iff their ranges are the same. This is pretty much Czuber's account. (See Frege [79], p. 161 and [70], p. 110.) We have taken the ranges to be sets, but we could have equally well taken them in a more intensional sense.

Suppose now that a and b are dependent objects. Then we shall say that $a = b$ iff two conditions are satisfied. The first is that they should depend upon the same arbitrary objects; their 'dependency range' should be the same. The second is that they should depend upon these objects in the same way. Suppose that a and b each depend upon the objects $c_1, c_2, \ldots$. With a may be associated the relation R_a that holds of $i, j_1, j_2, \ldots$ iff $i, j_1, j_2, \ldots$ may simultaneously be assigned as values to $a, c_1, c_2, \ldots$; and similarly for b. The second condition is then that the relations R_a and R_b should be the same. Again, the relations have been taken in extension, but may equally well be construed intensionally.

Let us make the reasonable assumption that the relation of dependence is well-founded: any sequence of arbitrary objects $a_1, a_2, a_3, \ldots$, with a_1 depending upon a_2, a_2 upon a_3, and so on, must eventually come to an end. The above two criteria then enable us to distinguish any two arbitrary objects a and b. First suppose that a and b are independent. Then they may be distinguished by the first criterion. Now suppose that one is dependent and the other independent. Then they are already distinguished by the fact that the one depends upon another object and the other does not. Finally, suppose that both a and b are dependent. If they depend upon the same objects, they can be distinguished by the second criterion in terms of the way they depend upon those objects (the relations R_a and R_b). So suppose that a and b depend upon different arbitrary objects. There is then an arbitrary object c upon which a depends, let us say, but not b. We can then distinguish a and b if we can distinguish c from all of the objects $d_1, d_2, \ldots$, upon which b depends. But the whole of the previous argument may be repeated for the pairs $(c, d_1), (c, d_2), \ldots$. Of course, this may lead to yet further pairs of objects that stand in need of distinction. But the well-foundedness of the dependency relation will guarantee that the process eventually comes to an end.

In such a way, we may answer Frege's question about identity. But a doubt may remain. Although the theory does not require it, we will want to make an application to the variable-signs of mathematics. In a sentence such as 'Let x and y be two arbitrary reals', we will want to say that the symbols 'x' and 'y' refer to two arbitrary reals. But to which? It is natural to suppose that 'x' and 'y' refer to two unrestricted and independent arbitrary reals. But by the first criterion there is only one such real. So do either of the symbols refer to it and, if so, to what does the other refer?

Frege ([70], p. 109) makes a similar point in arguing *against* the view that these letters designate arbitrary objects:

> This way of speaking is certainly employed; but these letters are not proper names of variable numbers in the way that '2' and '3' are proper names of constant numbers; for the numbers 2 and 3 differ in a specified way, but what is the difference between the variables that are said to be designated by 'x' and 'y'? We cannot say. We cannot specify what properties x has and what differing properties y has. If we associate anything with these letters at all, it is the same vague image for both of them. When apparent differences do show themselves, it is a matter of application; but we are not here talking about these. Since we cannot conceive of each variable in its individual being, we cannot attach any proper names to variables.

There are various ingenious solutions to this problem. But perhaps the most natural is one that makes x and y not be independent at all. There is a unique arbitrary pair of reals, p; it is the independent arbitrary object whose values are all the pairs of reals. We may then take x and y to be the first and second components of this arbitrary pair. More exactly: x and y will each depend upon p and upon p alone: when p takes the value (i, j), then and only then will x take the value i and y the value j. By the identity criteria, x and y, as so defined, will be unique.

It has to be admitted that on this account the reference of the symbols 'x' and 'y' may vary with the context. If 'y' is mentioned first, then 'y' will designate what 'x' would designate if *it* were mentioned first. Also, we must either suppose that there is implicit an arbitrary ω-sequence or we must let the length of the sequence vary with the number of arbitrary reals referred to. In this respect the use of the variable-symbols 'x' and 'y' is different from the use of the numerals

'2' and '3'. But in the crucial respect of designating a particular object, the use of the two kinds of symbol will be the same.

Frege's next question concerns cardinality: 'How many indeterminate numbers are there?' We may sink this into the more general question: what arbitrary objects are there? Consider first the arbitrary objects that take their values from a given set I of individuals. Such objects may be generated in stages, according to their 'degree' of independence. At the first stage are the independent objects. Since there are no essential constraints on the existence of arbitrary objects, we should expect that to each set of individuals from I there will be an arbitrary object with that set as its range. At the second stage are the arbitrary objects that depend upon the objects generated at the first stage, but not on anything else. We should now expect that, for each set X of independent objects and each suitable relation R, there will be an arbitrary object that has X as the set of objects upon which it depends and that has R as the way it depends upon them. At the other stages, both finite and transfinite, the arbitrary objects will be determined in a similar manner.

For each set I of individuals, we thereby obtain a 'system' A_I of arbitrary objects. Now the choice of I here is completely free. In particular, it may contain arbitrary objects, so that these may now figure as values to other arbitrary objects. Let us suppose that as the systems A_I are generated, the base sets I are expanded with the objects so obtained. Then with this understanding, we may take the arbitrary objects to be those objects that belong to one of the systems A_I.

The question of cardinality may now be considered. The general system A of arbitrary objects and, indeed, each of the individual systems A_1 is a proper class. Therefore the class of arbitrary objects has no cardinality or, if one likes, it has the same cardinality as the universe. However, for each I of given cardinality and each ordinal α, we may determine, by a simple combinatorial calculation, how many objects of A_1 are generated by the stage α. Thus we are in as good a position to answer questions concerning cardinality in the case of arbitrary objects as in the case of sets.

Frege's final questions concern the application of arithmetical operations to arbitrary numbers: 'Can you add two indeterminate numbers and, if so, how?' Now the theory does not require that the sum of two arbitrary numbers be defined. Consider the equation '$a+b=b+a$'. Then the principle of generic attribution (G4) tells us that the equation is true iff '$i+j=j+i$' is true for each i and j that can be assigned to a and b. Thus at no point, in the evaluation of the sentence, need we consider a denotation for the complex terms.

However, this argument rests on the identity context 'x = y' being generic. If, as in other parts of mathematics, a complex term is to be applied to classical conditions, then a denotation should be supplied. What then is a suitable denotation c for '$a+b$'? First, we would like i, j, k to be admissible values of a, b, c, iff i, j are admissible values for a, b and $k = i+j$. Second, we would like c to depend just upon a and b and upon whatever a or b depend upon. Now it follows from our discussion of cardinality, that such an object c exists; and it follows, from our discussion of identity, that c is unique. Therefore the problem of finding a suitable sum is solved.

Frege's supplementary queries are readily met: 'The same questions arise for adding a determinate number to an indeterminate one. To which class does the sum belong? Or maybe it belongs to a third?' The sum of a and i, for a and arbitrary and i an individual number, is the unique arbitrary object b such that (1) k, j are admissible values for b, a iff $k = i+j$ and j is an admissible value for a, (2) b just depends upon a and upon whatever a depends upon. There is no need of a third category of objects here and so no danger of a proliferation of categories.

This takes care of all of Frege's questions. Crucial to our answers has been the apparatus of dependence: a class of admissible assignments suitably circumscribed by a relation. We may safely say that if it is the metalinguistic formulation of the principle of generic attribution that makes the theory of arbitrary objects possible, it is the introduction of this apparatus that gives it life.

2

The Models

Let us now attempt to make the previously outlined theory of arbitrary objects more precise.

At the heart of the theory are three notions. One is the notion of an arbitrary object itself. It is supposed that, in addition to the individuals of a given kind, there are arbitrary or generic objects of that kind: in addition to individual numbers, arbitrary numbers; in addition to individual men, arbitrary men.

The second notion is that of dependence. This is a relation between arbitrary objects. Intuitively, it holds when the value of one arbitrary object (what it 'is') depends upon the value of the other arbitrary object. Accept that x and x^2 are arbitrary numbers. Then x^2 will depend upon x, since what x^2 is (*e.g.*, 1, 4, or 9) will depend upon what x is (1, 2, or 3).

The last notion is that of a value assignment. Arbitrary objects receive values. An arbitrary number takes as its values all individual numbers, an arbitrary man all individual men. Moreover, what value one arbitrary object receives may constrain the values that other arbitrary objects receive. The value assignments tell us what values the arbitrary objects can simultaneously receive.

These notions receive their formal expression in the notion of a generic or A-model. We suppose ourselves to be working with a first-order language $\mathfrak{L}$. This must contain at least one predicate, and it may also contain individual constants, function symbols, and a predicate of identity.

Let $\mathfrak{M}$ be a classical model for $\mathfrak{L}$. So $\mathfrak{M}$ will be of the form $(I, \ldots)$, where I (the domain) is a non-empty set and ... indicates the interpretation for the non-logical constants of the language. We use the prefix 'I' (for 'individual') in connection with the model $\mathfrak{M}$ and its components. So $\mathfrak{M}$ itself is an *I-model*, I is an *I-domain*, and the members of I are *individuals* or *I-objects*.

$\mathfrak{M}$ may then be expanded to a generic model $\mathfrak{M}^+$. Any such model $\mathfrak{M}^+$ is of the form $(I, \ldots, A, \prec, V)$, where:

(i) $(I, \ldots)$ is the model $\mathfrak{M}$;

(ii) A is a set of objects disjoint from I;

(iii) $\prec$ is a relation on A;

(iv) V is a non-empty set of partial functions from A into I, i.e. functions v for which $\mathrm{Dm}(v) \subseteq A$ and $\mathrm{Rg}(v) \subseteq I$.

The three components A, $\prec$ and V correspond to our three notions. A is the set of arbitrary or variable objects. It is assumed that these are disjoint from the set of individuals. $\prec$ is the relation of dependence between arbitrary objects. '$a \prec b$' indicates that the value of a (what a is) depends upon the value of b (what b is). When the relationship $a \prec b$ holds, we call a the *dependent* object and, for want of a better word, we call b the *dependee*. V is the family of value assignments. The presence of v in V indicates that the arbitrary objects $a_1, a_2, \ldots$ in the domain of v can simultaneously assume the respective values $v(a_1), v(a_2), \ldots$. This may be pictured as follows:

$$v: \frac{a_1 a_2 \ldots a_n}{i_1 i_2 \ldots i_n}.$$

The members of V are called the *admissible* value-assignments. An arbitrary partial function from A into I might, by contrast, be called a *possible* value-assignment.

Just as we use the prefix 'I' for classical or individual-related terms, so we use the prefix 'A' for generic or arbitrary-object-related terms. $\mathfrak{M}^+$ itself is called a *possible A-model*, A an *A-domain*, and the members of A *A-objects*. The variables 'i', 'j', 'k' are used for I-objects, and the variables 'a', 'b', 'c' for A-objects.

We find it helpful to adopt the following terminology. With $\mathfrak{M}$ and $\mathfrak{M}^+$ as above, $\mathfrak{M}^+$ is said to be *based on* $\mathfrak{M}$ or $\mathfrak{M}$ to *underly* $\mathfrak{M}^+$. We follow the convention that '$\mathfrak{M}^+$' is used to denote an A-model based on $\mathfrak{M}$. An A-model $(I, \ldots, A, \prec, V)$ shorn of its structural component ... is called an *A-structure;* and an A-structure $(I, A, \prec, V)$ shorn of its value-theoretic component V is called an *A-frame.* For $a \in A$, the *value-range* $\text{VR}(a)$ of a is $\{v(a) : v \in V\}$. Thus the value-range of an A-object consists of all the values it can assume. If $\text{VR}(a) \neq I$, then a is said to be *value-restricted* and otherwise to be *universal* or *value-unrestricted.* In the special case in which $\text{VR}(a) = \Lambda$, we say a is *null.* An A-object $a \in A$ is *dependent* if $a \prec b$ for some $b \in A$, and otherwise it is *independent.* An A-object is *restricted* if it is either value-restricted or dependent and otherwise it is *unrestricted.*

A subset B of A is *closed* if whenever $a \in B$ and $a \prec b$ then $b \in B$. A closed set therefore contains the dependees of any member. We use $[B]$ for the closure of B, *i.e.* the smallest closed set to contain B; and we use $|B|$ for $[B] - B$. In case $B = \{a\}$, we use $[a]$ and $|a|$ for $[B]$ and $|B|$ respectively.

We say that a value-assignment $v \in V$ is *defined on* $B \subseteq A$ if $\text{Dm}(v) = B$ and *defined over* B if $\text{Dm}(v) \supseteq B$. For $B \subseteq A$, we let V_B be the set of value-assignments of V defined on B; and in case $B = [a]$, we write V_B as V_a.

For $a \in A$, the *value dependence* $\text{VD}(a, B)$ *of a upon B* is the function f defined, for $v \in V_B$, by:

$$f(v) = \{i \in I : v \cup \{(a, i)\} \in V\}.$$

The function f tells us which values a can receive for given values of the B's. The *value dependence* $\text{VD}(a)$ or VD_a of a simpliciter is $\text{VD}(a, |a|)$. The function VD_a tells us which values a can receive for given values to its dependees.

In order for the possible A-model $\mathfrak{M}^+ = (I, \ldots, A, \prec, V)$ to be an *actual* A-model, it must be subject to further conditions (and similarly for A-structures and A-frames). These go as follows:

(v) (a) (Transitivity) $a \prec b \ \& \ b \prec c$ implies $a \prec c$;
    (b) (Foundation) The converse of the relation $\prec$ is well-founded, *i.e.* there is no infinite sequence of A-objects $a_1, a_2, a_3, \ldots$ for which $a_1 \prec a_2 \prec a_3 \prec \ldots$;

(vi) (Restriction). V is closed under restriction, i.e. $v \in V$ and $B \subseteq A$ implies that $v \upharpoonright B \in V$ (where $v \upharpoonright B$ is the restriction of v to B);

(vii) (Partial Extendibility). If $v \in V$, then there is a $v^+ \in V$ for which $v^+ \supseteq v$ and $\text{Dm}(v^+) \supseteq [\text{Dm}(v)]$;

(viii) (Piecing). Let $\{v_\xi : \xi \in \Omega\}$, for $\Omega \neq \Lambda$, be an indexed subset of V subject to the requirements that (a) each $\mathrm{Dm}(v_\xi)$ is closed and (b) the union $\bigcup v_\xi$ is a function. Then $v = \bigcup v_\xi$ is also a member of V.

Transitivity and Restriction are very reasonable under an appropriate construal of $\prec$ and V. If the value of a depends upon that of b, and the value of b upon that of c, then the value of a depends (if only indirectly) upon that of c. And suppose individuals $i_1, i_2, \ldots$ can be assigned to the A-objects $a_1, a_2, \ldots$ in the domain of v (i.e. $v(a_1) = i_1$, $v(a_2) = i_2, \ldots$), then we may agree that a selection of the individuals $i_1, i_2, \ldots$ can be assigned to the corresponding selection of the A-objects $a_1, a_2, \ldots$ (i.e. those in B).

Foundation is most reasonable when the dependency relation $a \prec b$ is specifically construed as meaning that the value of b can be *determined* on the basis of the value of a (and perhaps the values of other A-objects as well). Foundation then says that the attempt to determine the value of an A-object on the basis of the values of other A-objects will eventually lead to an end, that it will terminate in A-objects whose values are just given.

Given Foundation, each A-object $a \in A$ may be assigned an ordinal level $l(a)$. If a is independent, then $l(a) = 0$. If a is dependent, then $l(a) = \sup\{l(b) + 1 : a \prec b\}$. The level of an A-object represents the degree to which it is dependent upon other A-objects. So an A-object dependent only upon independent A-objects has level 1 (if it is not itself independent); an A-object dependent only upon A-objects of level 1 has level 2 (if it is not itself of level 1 or 0); and so on.

Condition (vii) (Partial Extension) says that a value assignment can at least be extended to the closure of its domain. To justify this condition, we should recall that the dependency relation is taken to indicate the dependency of the value of one A-object a upon that of another b. This relation of dependency is so understood that a cannot receive a value without the support of a value for b. But this then means that any assignment of values to the A-objects in B must be made on the basis of an assignment that it is at least possible to extend to the closure $[B]$ of B.

Condition (viii) (Piecing) says that value assignments with closed domains can be pieced together as long as they do not differ on common arguments. A simple instance of Piecing is provided by the arbitrary objects x, x^2 and $2x$. Since we can simultaneously assign 3 to

x and 9 to x^2 and simultaneously assign 3 to x and 6 to $2x$, we can 'piece' these assignments and simultaneously assign 3 to x, 9 to x^2 and 6 to $2x$. A more abstract instance is illustrated by the diagram below:

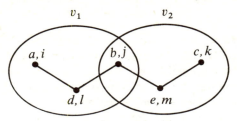

Here $d \prec a, b$ and $e \prec b, c$, and v_1 is the assignment $\{\langle a, i \rangle, \langle b, j \rangle, \langle d, l \rangle\}$ and v_2 the assignment $\{\langle b, j \rangle, \langle c, k \rangle, \langle e, m \rangle\}$ (with $\Omega = \{1, 2\}$). Since the requirements for the application of Piecing are satisfied, the assignment $v = v_1 \cup v_2 = \{\langle a_1, i \rangle, \langle b, j \rangle, \langle c, k \rangle, \langle d, l \rangle, \langle e, m \rangle\}$ is also admissible.

To justify this condition, let us suppose that $\langle v_\xi : \xi \in \Omega \rangle$ is an indexed set of value assignments that conforms to the requirements (a) and (b). Now the value assigned to an A-object depends only upon the values of the objects upon which it depends. Since requirement (b) is satisfied, the value assigned to an A-object by one v_ξ will not conflict with the value assigned to the same A-object by another v_ξ. Since also the domains are closed, the value assigned to an A-object by one v_ξ will not run into conflict with a value that another v_ξ assigns to one of its dependees. Therefore the different v_ξ's should be combinable into a single assignment v.

If requirement (a) were to fail, then there would be a manifest obstacle to combining the value assignments v_ξ; for that would require the simultaneous assignment of two values to the same A-object. If requirement (b) were to fail, then there might well be a hidden obstacle to combining the assignments. We can, for example, assign 4 to x^2 and assign 6 to $2x$. But we cannot simultaneously assign 4 to x^2 and 6 to $2x$; for the assignment of 4 to x^2 requires that x receive the value 2 (or -2), while the assignment of 6 to $2x$ requires that x receive the value 3. A more abstract example is provided by the previous diagram. It may well be that l can be assigned to d ($v_1 = \langle d, l \rangle$) and that n can be assigned to e ($v_2 = \langle e, n \rangle$). But we cannot then necessarily simultaneously assign l to d and n to e ($v = v_1 \cup v_2 = \{\langle d, l \rangle, \langle e, n \rangle\}$); for it may be that the assignment of l to d requires the assignment of j, let us say, to b, whereas the assignment of n to e

requires the assignment of another value to b. What Piecing says in effect is that, without these manifest or hidden obstacles, the combination of assignments is possible.

There are two simple but important methods for obtaining new A-models from a given A-model. The first is provided by restriction. Given an A-model $\mathfrak{M}^+ = (I, \ldots, A, \prec, V)$, call $\mathfrak{M}' = (I, \ldots, A', \prec', V')$ a *sub-model* of $\mathfrak{M}^+$ if (a) $A' \subseteq A$, (b) $\prec'$ is the restriction of $\prec$ to A', and (c) V' is the restriction of V to partial functions on A'. It is then readily checked that:

Lemma 1a
If $\mathfrak{M}^+$ is an A-model and $\mathfrak{M}'$ is a sub-model of $\mathfrak{M}^+$ whose A-domain A' is a closed subset of the A-domain A of $\mathfrak{M}^+$, then $\mathfrak{M}'$ is also an A-model, *i.e.* it conforms to the conditions (i)–(viii) above.

Proof
The only difficulty is provided by Piecing. But given that A' is closed in $\mathfrak{M}^+$, each closed subset of $\mathfrak{M}'$ will be a closed subset of $\mathfrak{M}^+$; and Piecing for $\mathfrak{M}'$ will then follow.

Use of this lemma will often be implicit.

The second method is provided by parametrization. Let $\mathfrak{M}^+ = (I, \ldots, A, \prec, V)$ be an A-model and let $v \in V$ be a value-assignment of $\mathfrak{M}^+$ with closed domain. Let $\mathfrak{M}^v$ be the structure $(I, \ldots, A', \prec', V')$, where (a) $A' = A - \text{Dm}(v)$, (b) $\prec'$ is the restriction of $\prec$ to A', and (c) $V' = \{v' : v'$ is a partial function from A' to I' for which $v' \cup v \in V\}$. In a parametrized A-model $\mathfrak{M}^v$, the values of the A-objects in $\text{Dm}(v)$ are 'fixed' by v. We now have:

Lemma 1b
If $\mathfrak{M}^+$ is an A-model and v is a value-assignment from $\mathfrak{M}^+$ with closed domain, then $\mathfrak{M}^v$ is also an A-model.

Proof
Again, the only real difficulty is provided by Piecing. But given that $\text{Dm}(v)$ is closed, $\text{Dm}(v \cup v'_\xi)$ will be closed in $\mathfrak{M}^*$ whenever $\text{Dm}(v'_\xi)$ is closed in $\mathfrak{M}'$; and so Piecing for $\mathfrak{M}^v$ will follow.

It should be noted that it is essential for the proof of this result that $\text{Dm}(v)$ be closed. Suppose that the dependencies among the A-objects a, b and c are as depicted below:

and that the value of a is fixed as i $(v=\{\langle a,i\rangle\})$. Then it may be that b can receive the value $j(v_1=\{\langle b,j\rangle\}\in V')$ and that c can receive the value k $(v_2=\{\langle c,k\rangle\}\in V')$, but that b and c cannot receive those values simultaneously $(v_1\cup v_2\notin V')$.

The conditions (i)–(iv) above form a very natural set. However, there is nothing sacrosanct about them and, for different purposes, various variants of them may be considered.

(1) It is not necessary that the underlying model $\mathfrak{M}$ be classical or first-order. The definition of the generic extension $\mathfrak{M}^+$ only depends upon the possibility of isolating a domain of individuals from $\mathfrak{M}$. Therefore a similar definition should be applicable to the forcing models of intuitionistic logic, let us say, or the possible world models of modal logic. However, it cannot be assumed that the most appropriate form of the extension is an exact replica of the one given here. For example, in the case of a possible worlds model, we may suppose that the assignment of individuals to the A-objects is relative to a possible world, so that, formally speaking, the set V of value-assignments is now indexed by the set of possible worlds.

(2) The Foundation condition splits into two parts. The first says that the dependence relation is irreflexive; the second says that there is no infinite sequence $a_1, a_2, a_3, \ldots$ of distinct A-objects such that $a_1 \prec a_2 \prec a_3 \ldots$. It is possible to retain the first part and drop the second. This would then allow cyclic dependencies, i.e. clusters of distinct A-objects that mutually depend upon one another. One might think of such cycles as being defined by clauses of the sort:

Let x and y be such that ....

(3) We have worked with a relation of mediate or indirect dependence. But it is possible to use a relation of immediate or direct dependence in its place. Such an account might result in a mere reformulation of the present account. But it might also serve to describe new possibilities. Consider the situation below:

where c immediately depends upon b, b upon a, c' upon b, and c' upon a (and that is all). To be more specific, it might be that a is the real variable x, $b=2x$, $c=\frac{3}{4}-2x$, and $c'=x+2x$. Then the dependency profiles of c' and c are clearly distinct, although this would not be so in a model that used only the notion of mediate dependence.

(4) The dependency relation might be dropped altogether. One then obtains what I call $\prec$-less models. An interesting question is to find an intrinsic characterization of those $\prec$-less models that can be obtained from regular models by dropping the relation $\prec$. However, this is not a question we shall pursue here.

(5) The extensions of the non-logical predicates of the language $\mathfrak{L}$ are drawn from the domain I of individuals. But, as we have already noted, the non-logical predicates (and, more generally, the non-logical constants) of our language may be divided into two classes, the generic and the classical, where a generic predicate applies to an A-object only as a representative of certain individuals and a classical predicate applies to an A-object as an object in its own right. If we effect such a division, then extensions drawn from the individual domain I will be assigned to the generic predicates whereas extensions drawn from the combined domain $I \cup A$ will be assigned to the classical predicates. If, for example, we had a predicate 'E' in the language with the meaning 'non-null', then we would assign to it the set of non-null A-objects; while if we had a predicate 'R' for dependence, then we would assign to it the set of ordered pairs (a, b) such that $a \prec b$. These are the simplest cases. In the more general case, we would need to consider predicates that were 'generic' in some of their argument-places and 'classical' in others; and we would also need to consider predicates whose classical extension was dependent upon the values of other A-objects. For example, we might want a predicate 'Val' with the meaning 'is the

value of', where the first argument-place was generic and the second classical; and again, we might want a predicate 'D' with the meaning of 'exists' or 'defined', where whether a dependent object was defined would depend upon the values of its dependees. In the general case, it becomes very cumbersome to indicate explicitly in the predicate which argument-places are susceptible of a classical or generic interpretation and it is better to adopt a notation in which the indication is given either in the argument-place itself or in the term that fills it.

(6) It has been required that the A-objects only take individuals as values, where these are distinct from the A-objects themselves. But it might be allowed that some of the A-objects can take other A-objects as values (or, alternatively, that some of the individuals might be A-objects). One would then obtain what I call a higher order theory of arbitrary objects. A natural 'typing' assumption on the higher order A-objects is that if one takes values of those A-objects, values of those values, and so on, then eventually one hits upon individuals alone.

The last two modifications have very important consequences for the subsequent development of the theory, especially when they are combined. But since they will not be of use in the more limited applications of the theory that are to follow, they will not be further considered here.

3
Conditions

We shall be interested in imposing additional conditions on an A-model. Four kinds of conditions will be considered. They concern the extendibility of value assignments, the existence of A-objects, their identity, and their multiplicity.

Extendibility

As the family of value-assignments has so far been determined, an assignment defined on certain A-objects may not be extendible to others. To take a simple intuitive example, if I is the set of individual reals, a is an arbitrary unrestricted real and b the square root of that real, then b will not be defined when a takes a negative value, *i.e.* a value-assignment v for which $v(a)$ is negative will not be extendible to b.

It is often convenient to suppose that the A-objects under consideration suffer from no such impediment to extendibility. Accordingly, we say that an A-model $\mathfrak{M}^+$ is *extendible over* a subset B of A if, for every subset B' of B and value assignment $v' \in V$ with domain B', there is a $v \in V$ that extends v' and is defined over B. We say that an A-model $\mathfrak{M}^+$ is *extendible* or satisfies *Extendibility* if it is extendible over its A-domain A.

A criterion for Extendibility may be developed in terms of the behaviour of value-dependencies. Say that a set-valued function is *total* if its values are always non-empty sets, and say that an A-object a in an A-model $\mathfrak{M}^+$ is *totally defined* if VD_a is a total function. This means, in case a is independent, that $VR(a)$ is non-empty and, in case

a is dependent, that, for any $v \in V_{|a|}$ there is an $i \in I$ for which $v \cup \{\langle a, i \rangle\} \in V$. We then have:

Theorem 2
The A-model $\mathfrak{M}^+$ is extendible over a closed subset B of A iff each $a \in B$ is totally defined.

Proof
⇒ Straightforward.
⇐ Let B' be a subset of B and v' a value assignment defined on B'. Then we need to know that v' can be extended to a value-assignment v defined over B. By Partial Extendibility and Restriction, v' can be extended to a value assignment v^* defined on the closure B^* of B'. So it suffices to extend v^* to B.

Given Foundation, it is possible to order the A-objects of $B - B^*$ by $\langle b_\xi : \xi < \alpha \rangle$, α an ordinal, in such a way that $C_\beta = B^* \cup \{b_\xi : \xi < \beta\}$, for each $\beta \leqslant \alpha$, is closed. We now prove, by transfinite induction on $\beta \leqslant \alpha$, that:

v^* can be extended to an assignment v^β defined on C_β.

$\beta = 0$. Let $v^0 = v^*$.

$\beta = \gamma + 1$. Since $C_{\gamma+1}$ is closed, $|b_\gamma| \subseteq C_\gamma$. By IH, there is a value assignment v^γ defined on c_γ. Let $u \in V$ be the restriction of v^γ to $|b_\gamma|$. Since b_γ is totally defined, there is an assignment $u^+ = u \cup \{\langle b_\gamma, i \rangle\} \in V$. But u^+ and v^γ satisfy the conditions of Piecing; and so we may let $v^{\gamma+1} = v^\gamma \cup \{\langle b_\gamma, i \rangle\}$.

$\beta = \lambda$. By IH, there is for each $\gamma < \lambda$ a value assignment v_γ defined on C_γ. Since the v_γ's form a chain, they satisfy the conditions of Piecing; and so we may let $v_\gamma = \bigcup_{\gamma < \lambda} v_\gamma$.

The result now follows upon setting $\beta = \alpha$.

This theorem shows that if the value-assignments can be extended locally, from $|b|$ for each $b \in B$, to $[b]$, then the value-assignments can be extended globally, from each $B' \subseteq [B]$ to $[B]$.

Existence

As far as the definition of A-models goes, it is compatible with their containing no A-objects. It therefore seems desirable to lay down conditions that require A-models to contain some of the A-objects we expect to exist.

Two types of existence condition may be distinguished, one for independent and the other for dependent A-objects. For independent A-objects, we want that, for each set of individuals, there is an A-object whose values are those individuals.

Existence (Ind)
For each $J \subseteq I$, there is an independent A-object $a \in A$ for which $VR(a) = J$.

For dependent A-objects, we want that, for any possible way in which one A-object may depend upon others, there is an A-object that depends upon those others in that way. The way in which an A-object depends upon others is given by our previous notion of value dependence. The condition therefore receives the following formulation:

Existence (Dep)
For each non-empty closed subset B of A and for each function f from V_B into $\mathfrak{P}(I)$, there is an $a \in A$ for which:
(a) $|a| = B$, and
(b) $VD_a = f$.

However, this condition can only be satisfied if A is a proper class and so, for many purposes, it is convenient to have a more circumscribed form of the condition.

d – Existence (Dep)
For each non-empty closed subset B of A of cardinality less than d and for each function f from V_B into $\mathfrak{P}(I)$, there is an $a \in A$ for which:
(a) $|a| = B$, and
(b) $VD_a = f$.

When $d \geq 1$, Existence (Ind) and d – Existence (Dep) may be combined into the single condition obtained by dropping the restriction that B be non-empty from d – Existence (Dep). This new condition might be called d – Existence.

There are various ways in which these existence conditions might be modified. First, as Existence (Ind) has been stated, there exists, for each individual i, an independent object a whose sole value is i. Given condition (ii) on a possible model, a is then distinct from i. However, one may wish to identify a and i. This would be somewhat like identifying a singleton set with its sole member.

Second, as Existence (Dep) has been stated, there exist A-objects, of level 1 let us say, that depend relevantly on only some or even none of their dependees; their values are the same regardless of the values of the other dependees. One may want to require that dependent A-objects *relevantly* depend upon other A-objects for their values, although it is somewhat hard to make this requirement reasonably precise.

Finally, one may want to give up the platonistic attitude that seems to underly the stronger forms of the existence condition. In many of the applications, all of the A-objects that are required may, in a certain sense, be defined within a previously specified language. For example, all of the A-objects required for the application to follow may be defined in an appropriate first-order language. One may therefore want to formulate the existence conditions in such a way that their satisfaction is compatible with the linguistic representation of all of the A-objects that are said to exist.

Identity

Our definition of A-models is also silent on the question of the identity conditions for A-objects. Again, two conditions may be given, one for independent and the other for dependent A-objects. In the first case, A-objects are the same when their values are the same:

Identity (Ind)
For any two independent A-objects a and b of A, $a=b$ if $VR(a) = VR(b)$.

In the other case, A-objects are the same when they depend upon the same A-objects in the same way:

Identity (Dep)
For any two dependent A-objects a and b of A, $a=b$ if (a) $|a|=|b|$ and (b) $VD_a = VD_b$.

The two conditions combine into the single condition obtained by dropping the requirement that a and b in Identity (Dep) be dependent. This new condition might be called *Identity*.

Multiplicity

As we have seen, there are certain philosophical reasons for supposing that A-objects conform to the identity conditions stated above. However, for certain technical purposes, a smoother theory is obtained by supposing that these conditions fail and that many different A-objects may conform to the same identity criterion. Accordingly, we arrive at the following alternative conditions:

c — *Multiplicity (Ind)*
For any independent A-object a there are at least c independent A-objects b for which $\text{VR}(b) = \text{VR}(a)$;

c — *Multiplicity (Dep)*
For any dependent A-object a there are at least c dependent A-objects for which $|b| = |a|$ and $\text{VD}_b = \text{VD}_a$.

Again, these two conditions may be combined into a single condition, c — *Multiplicity*, obtained by dropping the qualification that a and b be dependent in c — Multiplicity (Dep).

An A-model that satisfies d — Existence and c — Multiplicity is called c, d — *standard*. An A-model that is c, d — standard for $c, d \geq \omega$ is called *standard*, without qualification. For the most part, we shall suppose ourselves to be working within standard A-models.

Although the multiplicity conditions are incompatible with an extensional criterion for the identity of A-objects, they are compatible with an intensional criterion. We may suppose that the identity of an independent A-object is given by the concept that specifies its individual values and that the identity of a dependent A-object is given by the concept that specifies its value-dependence (and perhaps also by the concept that specifies the A-objects upon which it depends). Within the possible worlds framework, such concepts may be represented in the usual way.

4
Existence

We are here concerned to prove the existence of various sorts of A-model. The results are elementary but technical in character and may be omitted by the reader who is not too interested in formal detail.

The family V of value assignments contains a great deal of redundant information; many of the assignments in V may be thought of as deriving from others. Accordingly, call an assignment $v \in V$ *basic in* an A-model or A-structure if $\mathrm{Dm}(v) = [a]$ for some $a \in A$. In terms of our previous notation, the basic assignments are the members of $\bigcup_{a \in A} V_a$.

Call a subset U of V a *basis for* V if V is the closure U^+ of U under Restriction and Piecing, *i.e.* if V is the smallest superset of U to be closed under restriction and the union of compatible assignments with closed domains. We then have:

Theorem 3
The basic assignments form a basis U for any A-structure $\mathfrak{F} = (I, A, \prec, V)$.

Proof
Let U^+ be the closure of U under Piecing and Restriction. Since V is closed under Piecing and Restriction, $U^+ \subseteq V$. So it remains to show $V \subseteq U^+$. Suppose $v \in V$. By Partial Extendibility, there is a $v^+ \in V$ for which $v^+ \supseteq v$ and $\mathrm{Dm}(v^+)$ is closed. Let $v_a = v^+ \upharpoonright [a]$ for each $a \in \mathrm{Dm}(v^+)$. By Restriction, $v_a \in V$, and so $v_a \in U$. But then, by the closure of U^+ under Piecing, $v^+ = \bigcup_{a \in \mathrm{Dm}(v^+)} v_a \in U^+$, and, by the closure of U^+ under Restriction, $v = v^+ \upharpoonright \mathrm{Dm}(v) \in U^+$.

From this result it follows that any A-structure is uniquely determined by its basic assignments:

Corollary 4
Let $\mathfrak{F} = (I, A, \prec, V)$ and $\mathfrak{F}' = (I, A, \prec, V')$ be two A-structures whose basic assignments are the same. Then $\mathfrak{F} = \mathfrak{F}'$.

Proof
Let U by the set of basic assignments for $\mathfrak{F}$ and $\mathfrak{F}'$. Since U is a basis for $\mathfrak{F}$, $V = U^+$; and since U is a basis for $\mathfrak{F}'$, $V' = U^+$. But then $V = V'$.

Note that $\mathfrak{F}$ and $\mathfrak{F}'$ will share the same basic assignments when either of the following two conditions are satisfied:

(i) $V_a = V'_a$ for each $a \in A$;

(ii) $VD_a = VD'_a$ for each $a \in A$.

So an A-structure may also be uniquely determined from the sets V_a or the functions VD_a.

We may call the set of basic assignments the *canonical* basis for a structure. It may now be asked: When does a set of possible assignments supply a canonical basis for some A-structure? To answer this question, call a set U of possible assignments for an A-frame $(I, A, \prec)$ *regular* if:

(a) for each $u \in U$, $\text{Dm}(u) = [a]$ for some $a \in A$;
(b) if $u \in U$ and $a \in \text{Dm}(u)$, then $u \restriction [a] \in U$.

First note that, for regular sets U, their closure U^+ under Restriction and Piecing may be formed in an especially simple manner:

Lemma 5
Let U be a regular set of possible assignments for the A-frame $(I, A, \prec)$. Then, for each assignment u in the closure U^+ of U, there is an assignment u^+ satisfying the conditions:

(i) u^+ is a union of assignments in U,

(ii) $\text{Dm}(u^+) = [\text{Dm}(u)]$, and

(iii) $u^+ \supseteq u$.

Proof
By induction on the 'construction' of the members u of U^+.
  (1) $u \in U$. Set $u^+ = u$. Clearly (i) and (iii) are satisfied; and (ii) is

satisfied, since $\text{Dm}(u) = [a]$ for some $a \in A$ by clause (a) in the definition of regularity.

(2) u is the union of members u_ξ, $\xi \in \Omega$, of U^+. By IH, there is, for each u_ξ, a u_ξ^+ satisfying the conditions (i)–(iii) above. Let $u^+ = \bigcup u_\xi^+$. Clearly (i) and (iii) are satisfied; and (ii) is satisfied since $\text{Dm}(u^+) = \bigcup \text{Dm}(u_\xi^+) = \bigcup [\text{Dm}(u_\xi)] = [\bigcup \text{Dm}(u_\xi)] = [\text{Dm}(u)]$.

(3) u is the restriction of $v \in U^+$ to B. By IH, there is a v^+ satisfying conditions (i)–(iii) (with respect to v). By (i), v^+ is the union of assignments v_ξ, $\xi \in \Omega$, in U. Take any $a \in \text{Dm}(v^+)$. From clause (a) above, it follows that, for some $\xi \in \Omega$, $v_\xi \supseteq v^+1[a]$; and from clause (b) above, it then follows that $v^+1[a] \in U$. Let $u^+ = \bigcup_{a \in B \cap \text{Dm}(v)} v^+1[a]$.

Then u^+ is a union of assignments in U; $\text{Dm}(u^+) = \bigcup_{a \in B \cap \text{Dm}(v)} [a] = \left[\bigcup_{a \in B \cap \text{Dm}(b)} \{a\} \right] = [\text{Dm}(u)]$; and $u^+ \supseteq u$, since $v^+ \supseteq u^+$, u and $\text{Dm}(u^+) \supseteq \text{Dm}(u)$.

So we see that each assignment in U^+ is the restriction of the union of assignments in U. We now have:

Theorem 6
Each regular set U of assignments for the frame $(I, A, \prec)$ is the canonical basis for some structure $\mathfrak{F} = (I, A, \prec, V)$.

Proof
Let $V = U^+$. Then $\mathfrak{F}$ is indeed an A-structure; for Restriction and Piecing are trivially satisfied, and Partial Extendibility is satisfied by the previous lemma. Also, U constitutes a canonical basis for $\mathfrak{F}$. For each $v \in U$ is basic by clause (a) in the definition of regularity. But also, each basic assignment u of U^+ is in U. For by the above lemma, u is a union of assignments in U. Now $\text{Dm}(u)$ is $[a]$ for some a; and it is then clear that one of the assignments in the union must be u itself.

Theorem 6 allows us to specify the canonical basis for an A-structure in terms of a regular set of assignments. The well-foundedness of dependence allows us to specify an A-structure more directly in terms of the value dependencies of its A-objects:

Corollary 7
Let $(I, A, \prec)$ be an A-frame; and let f be a function on A that takes each A-object $a \in A$ into a function f_a from $I^{|a|}$ into $\mathfrak{P}(I)$. Then there is

a unique A-structure $\mathfrak{F} = (I, A, \prec, V)$ satisfying the condition:

(*) $\quad \mathrm{VD}_a = f_a \uparrow V_{|a|}$ for each $a \in A$.

Proof

First we establish existence. We define, by induction on the ordinal level $l(a)$, a collection U_a of value-assignments on $[a]$ for each $a \in A$. Suppose $l(a) = 0$, i.e. a is independent. Then we let $U_a = \{v : \mathrm{Dm}(v) = \{a\}$ and $v(a) \in f_a(\Lambda)\}$. Suppose now that $l(a) > 0$. Then each $b \in |a|$ has ordinal level less than a's and so is an A-object for which U_b is defined. Let $U_{|a|} = \{v : v \text{ is a function of the form } \bigcup_{b \in |a|} v_b,$ where each v_b is a member of $U_b\}$. Then we take U_a to be $\{v : v$ is of the form $u \cup \{\langle a, i \rangle\}$ for $u \in U_{|a|}$ and $i \in f_a(u)\}$.

Let $U = \bigcup_{a \in A} U_a$. It is readily checked from the definitions that U satisfies the clauses (a) and (b) for regularity. Therefore, by Theorem 6, U is the canonical basis for some A-structure $\mathfrak{F} = (I, A, \prec, V)$. Let VD_a be the function g. Then g and $f_a \uparrow V_{|a|}$ are the same. For $\mathrm{Dm}(g) = V_{|a|} = \mathrm{Dm}(f_a \uparrow V_{|a|})$; and for each $u \in V_{|a|}$, $g(u) = \{i : u \cup \{\langle a, i \rangle\} \in V_a\} = \{i : u \cup \{\langle a, i \rangle\} \in U_a\} = \{i : i \in f_a(u)\} = f_a(u)$. So $\mathfrak{F}$ satisfies the condition (*) on VD_a.

We now establish uniqueness. Suppose that the A-structures $\mathfrak{F} = (I, A, \prec, V)$ and $\mathfrak{F}' = (I, A, \prec, V')$ both conform to the condition on VD_a. Then we may show, by a transfinite induction on the level of a, that $V_a = V'_a$ for each $a \in A$. For

$$\begin{aligned} V(a) &= \{u \cup \{\langle a, i \rangle\} : i \in \mathrm{VD}_a^{\mathfrak{F}}(u), u \in V_{|a|}\} \\ &= \{u \cup \{\langle a, i \rangle\} : i \in f_a \uparrow V_{|a|}, u \in V_{|a|}\} \\ &= \{u \cup \{\langle a, i \rangle\} : i \in f_a \uparrow V'_{|a|}, u \in V'_{|a|}\} \quad \text{(by IH)} \\ &= \{u \cup \{\langle a, i \rangle\} : i \in \mathrm{VD}_a^{\mathfrak{F}'}(u), u \in V'_{|a|}\} \\ &= V'_a \end{aligned}$$

Since $V_a = V'_a$ for each $a \in A$, it follows from Corollary 4 that $V = V'$.

Two applications of the corollary are of particular interest. The first is to extendibility. Call a set-valued function *total* if its values are always non-empty sets. Then:

Corollary 8

Suppose, under the conditions of Corollary 7, that each of the functions f_a is total. Then the A-structure $(I, A, \prec, V)$ satisfies Extendibility.

Proof
Suppose each f_a is total. Then each restriction $f_a \upharpoonright V_a$ is total. Since $VD_a = f_a \upharpoonright V_a$, each VD_a is total; and the result follows from Theorem 2.

The second application is to the existence of standard A-models.

Corollary 9
Each I-model $\mathfrak{M} = (I, \ldots)$ underlies a c, d-standard model $\mathfrak{M}^+ = (I, \ldots, A, \prec, V)$.

Proof
Choose a regular cardinal $e \geq d$. Define the structures $(A_\beta, \prec_\beta)$ by transfinite induction on $\beta \leq e$ as follows:

$\beta = 0.\quad A_0 = \{(J, \zeta) : J \subseteq I \text{ and } \zeta < c\};$
$\quad\quad\quad \prec_0 = \Lambda$

$\beta = \gamma + 1.\quad A_{\gamma+1} = A_\gamma \cup \{(B, f, \zeta) : \zeta < c, B \text{ is a } \prec_\gamma\text{-closed subset}$ of A_γ of cardinality $< d$, and f is a function from I^B into $\mathfrak{P}(I)$;

$\quad\quad\quad \prec_{\gamma+1} = \prec_\gamma \cup \{(a, b) : a = (B, f, \zeta) \in A_{\gamma+1} - A_\gamma \text{ and } b \in B\};$

$\beta = \lambda.\quad A_\lambda = \bigcup_{\xi < \lambda} A_\xi;$

$\quad\quad\quad \alpha_\lambda = \bigcup_{\xi < \lambda} \alpha_\xi.$

For each $a \in A$, let:
$\quad f_a = \{\langle \Lambda, J \rangle\}$, for a independent and of the form (J, ζ);
$\quad f_a = f$, for a dependent and of the form (B, f, ζ).
The function f_a, as so specified, satisfies the requirements of Corollary 7. Therefore there is an A-model $\mathfrak{M}^+ = (I, \ldots, A, \prec, V)$ subject to the condition (*) on VD_a. It then follows that $VD_a = \{\langle \Lambda, J \rangle\}$ for independent $a = \langle J, \zeta \rangle$ and that $VD_a = f \upharpoonright V_{|a|}$ for dependent $a = \langle B, f, \zeta \rangle$; and from this, it readily follows that $\mathfrak{M}^+$ is c, d-standard.

This last corollary is of some philosophical interest, for it shows how a reduction of arbitrary object theory to set theory might be effected. It should be noted that there is no simple way of identifying a dependent A-object with a many-valued function. The dependee A-objects must also be made explicit and these must then be appropriately represented.

5
Truth

We have developed the theory of arbitrary objects in abstraction from its relation to language. We now show how a language may secure reference to A-objects and how the sentences of the language may be evaluated for truth and falsity. The basic principle is that a sentence concerning A-objects is true (false) just in case it is true (false) for all of their values.

Reference to A-objects is secured in our given first-order language $\mathfrak{L}$ through the addition of a new category of symbols. These might be called *A-names* or, less contentiously, *A-letters*. The resulting language will be called $\mathfrak{L}^*$. In the syntax of $\mathfrak{L}^*$, the A-letters will be treated in exactly the same way as individual names.

It is important to appreciate that in $\mathfrak{L}^*$ there are three kinds of symbol that can occur in subject position: the variables x, y, z, ...; the individual names m, n, p, ..., and the A-names a, b, c, ... The A- and I-names will be thought to play a properly designatory role, while the variables will merely serve as part of the apparatus of quantification. It is possible to give a semantics in which the so-called bound variables also play a designatory role; but this is not a possibility we shall consider.

Formulas from $\mathfrak{L}^*$ will be called *A-formulas*, formulas from $\mathfrak{L}$ alone *I-formulas*. We shall adopt the usual terminology of symbolic logic. However, it will be supposed that formulas contain no free occurrences of variables. Expressions that would be formulas, were it not for the presence of free variables, will instead be called *pseudo-formulas*.

The A-models for $\mathfrak{L}$ may now be extended to $\mathfrak{L}^*$. An A-model $\mathfrak{M}^*$ is of the form $(I, \ldots, A, \prec, V, d)$, where $(I, \ldots, A, \prec, V)$ is an A-model $\mathfrak{M}^+$ for the language $\mathfrak{L}$, as before, and d is a function from the set of A-names for $\mathfrak{L}^*$ into A. Intuitively, d provides each A-name with a designation. We shall often find it convenient to drop explicit mention of d and to use a for the designation $d(a)$ of a.

Two concepts of truth for generic statements may be distinguished, one *relative* and the other *absolute*. Let $\phi = \phi(a_1, \ldots, a_n)$ be a formula whose A-letters are as displayed. Then ϕ is true in the A-model $\mathfrak{M}^*$ *relative to* $v \in V$ – in symbols, $\mathfrak{M}^* \models_v \phi$ – if $a_1, \ldots, a_n \in \text{Dm}(v)$ and $\mathfrak{M} \models [v(a_1), \ldots, v(a_n)]$. Here, on the right-hand side of the definition, $\mathfrak{M}$ is the underlying classical model and $\models$ is the classical relation of truth. On the other hand, ϕ is (*absolutely*) *true in* $\mathfrak{M}^*$ – in symbols, $\mathfrak{M}^* \models \phi$ – if $\mathfrak{M}^* \models_v \phi$ for any $v \in V$ for which $a_1, \ldots, a_n \in \text{Dm}(v)$. In other words, a statement concerning A-objects is true just in case it is true for all of their values. This stipulation is what we have previously called the principle of generic attribution.

It will be helpful to introduce some notation. Let $\mathfrak{M}^*$ be an A-model for $\mathfrak{L}^*$. Let A_ϕ, the set of A-objects mentioned in ϕ, be $\{a : a$ is an A-letter of $\phi\}$. (This notation may be extended to sets of formulas or to items, like proofs, that are associated with sets of formulas.) Say that v is *defined on (over)* ϕ if v is defined on (over) A_ϕ. Let us suppose that the language $\mathfrak{L}$ contains each individual i of $\mathfrak{M}$ as a name of itself and that v is defined over ϕ. Then we use $v(\phi)$ for the result of substituting $v(a)$ for each occurrence of an A-letter a in ϕ. The principle of generic attribution now takes the following simple form:

$\mathfrak{M}^* \models \phi$ iff $\mathfrak{M} \models v(\phi)$ for each $v \in V$ defined over ϕ.

The principle may be extended to a set Δ of formulas in the obvious way. Say that $v \in V$ is *defined over* Δ if v is defined over A_Δ; and let $v(\Delta) = \{v(\phi) : \phi \in \Delta\}$. Then we stipulate that:

$\mathfrak{M}^* \models \Delta$ iff $\mathfrak{M} \models v(\Delta)$ for each $v \in V$ defined over Δ.

If $\Delta = \{\phi_1, \ldots, \phi_n\}$, then the truth of Δ (in $\mathfrak{M}^*$) is equivalent to the truth of $\phi_1 \wedge \ldots \wedge \phi_n$.

As one would want, the concept of generic truth agrees with the concept of classical truth over sentences that contain no reference to arbitrary objects:

Lemma 10
Let $\mathfrak{M}^*$ be an A-model and ϕ a sentence of $\mathfrak{L}$ *(not $\mathfrak{L}^*$)*. Then $\mathfrak{M} \models \phi$ iff $\mathfrak{M}^* \models \phi$.

Proof

⇒ Suppose $\mathfrak{M} \models \phi$. Take any $v \in V$. Now $v(\phi) = \phi$. So $\mathfrak{M} \models v(\phi)$ for each $v \in V$. But then $\mathfrak{M}^* \models \phi$.

⇐ Suppose $\mathfrak{M} \not\models \phi$. By condition (iv) in the definition of A-model, V is non-empty so we may choose a $v \in V$. Now $v(\phi) = \phi$. But then $\mathfrak{M} \not\models v(\phi)$ and $\mathfrak{M}^* \not\models \phi$.

Note that it is essential to the right-to-left direction of this result that V be non-empty. If V were allowed to be empty, then *every* sentence of $\mathfrak{L}$ would be vacuously true in $\mathfrak{M}^*$.

The notion of generic truth has been defined relative to a notion of classical satisfaction for a first-order language. We have said, in effect, that a sentence $\phi = \phi(a_1, \ldots, a_n)$ is true iff the pseudo-formula $\phi(x_1, \ldots, x_n)$ is satisfied by $v(a_1), \ldots, (a_n)$ for any suitable v. But this definition makes no essential use of the language being first-order or of the concept of satisfaction being classical. It is therefore possible to give a similar definition for any language for which a concept of satisfaction has been defined – to a classical infinitary language, for example, or to a first-order language with a suitable intuitionistic semantics.

For certain purposes, it is useful to drop the requirement that the generic truth of a statement concerning A-objects require its truth for all values to the A-objects. In analysis, for example, we may contemplate a proposal along the following lines. An infinitesimal is an A-object whose values are given by a sequence of reals that tend to 0. A statement $\phi(a_1, \ldots, a_n)$ concerning such objects $a_1, \ldots, a_n$ is then true, not if it is true for all of their values, but if it is true for all but finitely many of their values.

Again, we may perhaps think of kinds as A-objects. However, they cannot be subject to the usual principle of generic attribution for at least two reasons. First, a kind may possess a property not possessed by all of its instances. For example, the kind dog is four-legged even though abnormal dogs are not. Second, all instances of a kind may possess a property that is not possessed by the kind. For example, all dogs may accidentally have been loved by their owners even though this is not a characteristic of the kind. To take care of such difficulties, we may propose a principle along the following lines: a statement $\phi(a_1, \ldots, a_n)$ concerning kinds $a_1, \ldots, a_n$ is true iff it is necessarily true for all of their normal instances (or values).

If the language $\mathfrak{L}^*$ contained classical as well as generic predicates or if it embodied in some other way the distinction between classical and generic occurrences of A-letters, then the truth-definition would need to be modified. Suppose that $\phi(a_1, \ldots, a_m, b_1, \ldots, b_n)$ is a sentence of $\mathfrak{L}^*$ in which $a_1, \ldots, a_m$ are the A-letters that occur generically and $b_1, \ldots, b_n$ are the A-letters that occur classically (there may be some overlap). Then, in the simplest case, we may say:

$\mathfrak{M}^* \models \phi(a_1, \ldots, a_m, b_1, \ldots, b_n)$ iff $\mathfrak{M}^* \models (v(a_1), \ldots, v(a_m), b_1, \ldots, b_n)$ for all $v \in V$ defined over $\{a_1, \ldots, a_m\}$.

As long as there are suitable extensions for the classical predicates of $\mathfrak{L}^*$ in $\mathfrak{M}^*$, the right-hand side of this biconditional can then be evaluated in orthodox classical fashion.

If the generic model $\mathfrak{M}^*$ is allowed to contain higher-order A-objects, then there is the possibility of iteratively evaluating for truth. The sentence $\phi(a_1, \ldots, a_n)$ will be true if $\phi(v(a_1), \ldots, v(a_n))$ is true for all suitable v. But the $v(a_1), \ldots, v(a_n)$ may themselves be A-objects; so the truth of $\phi(v(a_1), \ldots, v(a_n))$, for given v, may consist in the truth of $\phi(u(v(a_1)), \ldots, u(v(a_n)))$ for all suitable u; and so on. Given our previous assumption that the process of successively taking values eventually terminates in individuals, the resulting iterative concept of truth will be well-defined.

The present theory on semantics for arbitrary objects has connections with other, more familiar, theories and semantics. A detailed treatment is out of place here, though we may mention some of the more salient points of contact.

(1) *Meinongian Theory*

Arbitrary objects may be regarded as a special kind of Meinongian object. (For a well-worked out contemporary version of the Meinongian theory, see Parsons' book [80].) My arbitrary man, for example, is the Meinongian incomplete man. In general, an arbitrary object with certain values is the Meinongian object with the properties common to those values. Three important differences between the two theories should be noted though. First, my arbitrary objects are specified 'from below', in terms of the values they take; Meinongian objects are specified 'from above', in terms of the properties they have. This makes a big difference both to the formulation and development of the respective theories. Second, the Berkeleyian problem of whether the incomplete or arbitrary triangle is isosceles or not is evaded on the Meinongian approach by denying the principle of abstraction, whereas on my approach it is evaded by denying the principle of bivalence. Third, there is no counterpart in the Meinongian theory to the relation of dependence, though to some extent the notion of correlates plays a similar role. (See Fine [82], pp. 123–9, or Fine [84] for an account of correlates.)

(2) Supervaluations
Generic truth may be regarded as an instance of supervaluational truth (see van Fraassen [66]). With each generic model $\mathfrak{M}^*$ and value assignment v may be associated a classical model that assigns the individual $v(a)$ to the A-letter a. Generic truth in $\mathfrak{M}^*$ then coincides with supervaluational truth over the resulting class of classical models. In one way, supervaluations would appear to provide a broader concept, since they allow for a variation in the extensions of the predicates. But we may also regard the predicates to be names of generic extensions or concepts, *i.e.* of A-objects whose values are ordinary extensions or concepts. We thereby obtain a similar flexibility. Indeed, one natural approach to the topic of implicit definition is to treat the implicitly defined predicates as names of generic extensions or concepts.

However, although our own theory can match the supervaluational theory in this way, there would appear to be no counterpart, within the supervaluational approach, to the relation of dependence.

(3) Boolean-valued Models
Let $\mathfrak{M}^*$ be a generic model and suppose that $\mathfrak{M}^*$ is extendible. With each formula ϕ we may associate the set of value assignments $|\phi| = \{v : v \text{ is defined on } A \text{ and } \mathfrak{M} \models v(\phi)\}$. Thinking of the sets of value assignments as elements of a Boolean algebra, we may then represent $\mathfrak{M}^*$ as a Boolean-valued model. (See Bell [77], Chapter 1, for an introduction to Boolean-valued models.)

This connection is not really new; since given the previous connection with supervaluation models, it follows from the natural correspondence between those models and Boolean-valued models. In the same way, given the natural correspondence between forcing and Boolean-valued models, we also obtain a connection with the forcing models. In this way, it is possible to see the generic sets of Cohen [66] as generic objects in our sense of the term.

In many ways, the theory of Boolean-valued models provides the most natural setting for the theory of arbitrary objects. Within this setting, we may provide a general account of the truth-conditions of statements concerning arbitrary objects. Where F is any filter, we may say that the statement ϕ from $\mathfrak{L}^*$ is true if the Boolean value $|\phi| \in F$. Such an account has a pleasing generality, since it both avoids any reference to an underlying set of individuals and abstracts from the specific versions of the principle of generic attribution.

(4) *Sheaf Models*
The definition of an A-structure is remarkably close to the definition of a sheaf. (See B.R. Tennison [75], Chapter 2.) This becomes even clearer if we take what I have called the 'closed' sets to be the open sets in the topology induced by the partial ordering $\prec$ and if we formulate the conditions on an A-structure in conformity with the idea that all value-assignments should be defined on open (*i.e.* what were before closed) sets. Piecing is then only subject to the requirement that the value-assignments to be pieced are compatible and Restriction is confined to the case in which the limiting set is open.

Sheaves have been used to provide a modelling for intuitionistic logic. It is therefore natural to suppose that there is a close connection between this modelling and the present semantics. But this is not so. On the sheaf-theoretic approach, the generic objects are taken to be what I call the value-assignments, and not the elements in the domains of the value assignments. Moreover, quantification is interpreted as being over the generic objects themselves and not as being over the underlying individuals. However, it may be that there is a useful synthesis of the two approaches.

(5) *Skolem Functions*
In certain ways, arbitrary objects behave like Skolem functions. Consider the sentence $\forall x \exists y Fxy$. It is true (relative to a model $\mathfrak{M}$) iff we can find an interpretation f for the function symbol f with respect to which the formula Fxf(x) is true for all values of x. Similarly, the sentence is true if, for a an unrestricted A-object, we can find a totally defined A-object b dependent upon a alone for which Fab is true.

There are, however, some important differences between A-objects and Skolem functions. First, A-objects, unlike functions, are treated, ontologically, on the same level as individuals, and A-names, unlike function symbols, are treated, syntactically, on the same level as individual names. Second, a dependent A-object may take *several* values for given values to its dependees, and not just a single value. In this respect, it is more like a multi-valued function. Finally, a dependent object of level >1, one that depends upon another dependent object, cannot properly be represented by a function at all. Consider A-objects *a, b* and *c* that enter into dependency relations indicated below:

We might have, for example, that $a=x$, $b=x^2$ and $c=2b$. Then *c* cannot be represented as a function with one argument, since that is to overlook the dependence on the other 'argument'. But nor can *c* be represented as a function of two arguments, since that is to overlook the dependence of one of the arguments upon the other.

6
Validity

We give an account of the conditions under which a statement or inference concerning A-objects can be deemed valid. We deal first with statements and then with inferences.

Given a sentence ϕ of $\mathfrak{L}^*$ and a collection X of A-models for $\mathfrak{L}^*$, we say that ϕ is *valid relative to* X – in symbols, $\models_X \phi$ – if, for each $\mathfrak{M}^* \in X$, $\mathfrak{M}^* \models \phi$. We say that ϕ is *generically valid* – in symbols, $\models_G \phi$ – if ϕ is valid relative to the class of all A-models for $\mathfrak{L}^*$. In this symbolism, 'G' might be thought to denote the classes of all A-models for $\mathfrak{L}^*$.

It should be noted that, in this definition, the A-letters a, b, c, ... are treated as denoting A-objects. It is perhaps not a logical matter that a given name denotes an arbitrary, as opposed to an individual, object; and so it is not clear to what extent our definition corresponds to the intuitive notion of logical truth. It might be better therefore to think of our definition as corresponding, not to the notion of logical truth simpliciter, but to that notion of logical truth which operates under the presupposition that the objects denoted by the A-letters are A-objects.

We say that a sentence ϕ of $\mathfrak{L}$ is *classically valid*, $\models_C \phi$, if ϕ is true in all classical models. This definition may be extended to sentences of $\mathfrak{L}^*$ by treating A-letters as names of individuals.

The notions of classical and generic validity are connected by the following results.

Lemma 11
Suppose the sentence ϕ of $\mathfrak{L}^*$ is classically valid. Then it is generically valid.

Proof
Suppose otherwise. Then for some A-model $\mathfrak{M}^* = (I, \ldots, A, \prec, V, d)$, not $\mathfrak{M}^* \models \phi$. So for some $v \in V$ defined over ϕ, not $\mathfrak{M} \models \phi(v(a_1), \ldots, v(a_n))$ for ϕ of the form $\phi(a_1, \ldots, a_n)$. But then ϕ is not classically valid.

Lemma 12
Let X be a collection of A-models for $\mathfrak{L}^*$ subject to the condition that, for each classical model $\mathfrak{M} = (I, \ldots)$ and each assignment of individuals $i_1, \ldots, i_n \in I$ to A-letters $a_1, \ldots, a_n$ in ϕ, there is an A-model $\mathfrak{M}^* = (I, \ldots, A, \prec, V, d)$ in X for which $v = \{(a_1, i_1), \ldots, (a_n, i_n)\} \in V$. Suppose that the sentence ϕ is valid relative to X. Then ϕ is classically valid.

Proof
Suppose otherwise. Then, for some classical model $\mathfrak{M}$ and some assignment of the individuals $i_1, \ldots, i_n$ to the A-letters $a_1, \ldots, a_n$ occurring in $\phi = \phi(a_1, \ldots, a_n)$, not $\mathfrak{M} \models \phi(i_1, \ldots, i_n)$. Choose $\mathfrak{M}^*$ and v as above. Then not $\mathfrak{M} \models v(\phi)$; so not $\mathfrak{M}^* \models \phi$; and hence not $\models_X \phi$.

Theorem 13
For any sentence ϕ of $\mathfrak{L}^*$, $\models_G \phi$ iff $\models_C \phi$.

Proof
$\Leftarrow$ From Lemma 11.
$\Rightarrow$ Since it follows, either by a direct construction or Corollary 9, that the class X of all A-models for $\mathfrak{L}^*$ satisfies the conditions of Lemma 12.

In contrast to the case for statements, there are basically two different concepts of generic validity for inferences: one, which we call truth-to-truth validity, corresponds to the absolute notion of truth; and the other, which we call case-to-case validity, corresponds to the relative notion of truth. Intuitively, an inference concerning A-objects is truth-to-truth valid if the truth of the premises logically guarantees the truth of the conclusion. To explain this notion more formally, take a *sequent* or *inference* to be an ordered pair (Δ, ϕ), where ϕ is a sentence and Δ a set of sentences from $\mathfrak{L}^*$. Where $\Delta = \{\phi_1, \ldots, \phi_n\}$, we may write (Δ, ϕ) as $\phi_1, \ldots, \phi_n/\phi$ or as: $\dfrac{\phi_1, \ldots, \phi_n}{\phi}$.

Let X be a collection of A-models for $\mathfrak{L}^*$. Then the inference (Δ, ϕ) is said to be *truth-to-truth valid in X* if, for any model $\mathfrak{M}^*$ of X, $\mathfrak{M}^* \models \phi$

whenever $\mathfrak{M}^* \models \Delta$. In case X is the class of all A-models for $\mathfrak{L}^*$, we say (Δ, ϕ) is *truth-to-truth valid simpliciter;* and in case X has a single member $\mathfrak{M}^*$, we say $\mathfrak{M}^*$ *truth-to-truth validates* (Δ, ϕ).

We say that an inference (Δ, ϕ) from $\mathfrak{L}$ is *classically valid,* if, for any classical model $\mathfrak{M}$, $\mathfrak{M} \models \phi$ whenever $\mathfrak{M} \models \Delta$. This notion is then extended to inferences from $\mathfrak{L}^*$ by treating A-letters as the names of individuals.

We have seen that all classically valid sentences hold for arbitrary objects. It would be desirable if all classically validly inferences also held for arbitrary objects. However, the extension of classical *inference* to A-objects is not completely straightforward. Consider the following classically valid inference:

$$\frac{Fa \wedge Gb}{Fa}$$

Is it generically valid? Suppose, for *reductio,* that Fa is not true in some A-model $\mathfrak{M}^*$. Then for some $v \in V$, $\mathfrak{M} \not\models Fv(a)$. We now wish to find a $v^+ \supseteq v$ in V defined over a and b; for then $\mathfrak{M} \not\models Fv^+(a) \wedge Gv^+(b)$; and so $\mathfrak{M}^* \not\models Fa \wedge Gb$. But we have, in general, no guarantee that such a v^+ can be found. For example, if b was a null A-object then, in the nature of the case, there could be no such v^+.

We overcome this difficulty by insisting upon extendibility.

Theorem 14
Suppose the inference (Δ, ϕ) from $\mathfrak{L}^*$ is classically valid. Let $\mathfrak{M}^*$ be an A-model that is extendible over the class of A-objects designated by the A-letters in Δ and ϕ. Then $\mathfrak{M}^*$ truth-to-truth validates (Δ, ϕ).

Proof
Suppose not $\mathfrak{M}^* \models \phi$. Then for some $v \in V$ defined over ϕ, $\mathfrak{M} \not\models v(\phi)$. By Restriction, we may suppose that v is exactly defined on the A-letters of ϕ. Given the extendibility requirement, there is a $v^+ \supseteq v$ in V that is also defined over Δ. Since (Δ, ϕ) is classically valid, $\mathfrak{M} \not\models v(\Delta)$. But then $\mathfrak{M}^* \not\models \Delta$, as required.

Though simple, the Theorems 13 and 14 are of great importance. For it will be essential to the applications to follow (and an intuitively acceptable requirement in itself) that the arbitrary objects should be subject to the classical principles of reasoning. In the case of the classically valid *laws,* this imposes no constraint on which arbitrary objects we may use. But in the case of classically valid *inferences*, we must be careful so to choose the arbitrary objects that the requirement of extendibility is satisfied.

We turn now to the second concept of validity for inferences. The intuitive idea behind this concept is that an inference is valid when every case in which the premisses are true is a case in which the conclusion is true. More formally, the inference (Δ, ϕ) is *case-to-case valid relative to* the class of A-models X for $\mathfrak{L}^*$ if, for any model $\mathfrak{M}^*$ of X and assignment v for $\mathfrak{M}^*$, $\mathfrak{M} \models v(\phi)$, whenever $\mathfrak{M} \models v(\Delta)$ and v is defined on both Δ and ϕ. We may then talk of case-to-case validity *simpliciter* or case-to-case validation by a model in the same way as before.

The difference between the two concepts of validity may be brought out by considering the inference from Fa to $\forall x Fx$. Suppose that, in each model of X, a is a value-unrestricted A-object. Then the inference Fa/$\forall x Fx$ is truth-to-truth valid; for the truth of Fa, given that a is value-unrestricted, will imply the truth of $\forall x Fx$. On the other hand, the inference Fa/$\forall x Fx$ will not be case-to-case valid (for reasonably diverse X); for Fa may be true upon the assignment of a certain individual i to a, even though $\forall x Fx$ is false.

For case-to-case validity there is no impediment to classical reasoning.

Theorem 15
Suppose the inference (Δ, ϕ) is classically valid. Then it is case-to-case valid.

Proof
Suppose otherwise. Then for some A-model $\mathfrak{M}^*$ and $v \in V$, $\mathfrak{M} \models_v \Delta$ and $\mathfrak{M} \not\models_v \phi$. But by letting the A-letters denote individuals in accord with v, it is then clear that there is a classical model in which ϕ is true and Δ is false.

However, for the concept of case-to-case validity, the transitivity of implication may fail. For suppose that ϕ implies ψ and that ψ implies χ (*i.e.* that the inferences ϕ/ψ and ψ/χ are valid relative to X). We wish to show that ϕ implies χ. So let v be an assignment defined on both ϕ and χ. If we could show that v was extendible to the A-objects denoted by the A-letters in χ, we would be done. But we have in general no guarantee that v can be so extended.

As in the previous case, the difficulty can be overcome by making the appropriate stipulation concerning extendibility:

Theorem 16 (Cut for Case-to-case Validity)
Suppose that the inferences Δ/ϕ and $\phi, \Gamma/\psi$ are case-to-case valid in X; and suppose that X is a class of models $\mathfrak{M}^*$ with the property that any $v \in V$ defined on $A_\Delta \cup A_\Gamma \cup A_\psi$ is extendible to a $v^+ \in V$ defined over A_ϕ. Then $\Delta, \Gamma/\psi$ is case-to-case valid in X.

Proof
Straightforward.

Later, in Part II, we shall provide a definition of validity that combines some of the features of truth-to-truth and of case-to-case validity.

7
Definitions

We come now to the topic of definition. The importance of this topic for the theory of A-objects can hardly be exaggerated. It is through definition that reference to particular A-objects is made; and it is in specifying the appropriate definitions that the application of the theory largely consists.

Any set Δ of pseudo-formulas in the single variable x can be regarded as a definition of the A-letter a. We accordingly take a *definition* to be a pair (a, Δ), where Δ is a set of pseudo-formulas in the single variable x and a is an A-letter. (We might also allow for the simultaneous definition of several A-terms; but this is not a topic we shall consider.) Given a definition (a, Δ), the letter a is called the *defined term* of the definition, the A-letters in Δ are called the *given terms,* and Δ itself is called the *defining condition*. We say that, in the definition (a, Δ), Δ defines a *from* each of the given terms, and *in terms of all* the given terms. We allow that Δ may be empty or even contain an occurrence of a. In case $\Delta = \{\phi\}$, we may write the definition (a, Δ) as (a, ϕ).

It is our view that definitions correspond to let-clauses in ordinary mathematical discourse. If, for example, we declare:
   Let $a = b^2$
then we may be taken to be fixing the A-object denoted by y in terms of the A-object denoted by x. Such a clause could be represented in our notation by the ordered pair $(a, x = b^2)$.

Given a definition (a, Δ) and a term t, let $\Delta(t)$ be the result of substituting t for the free variable x of Δ. Then we say that the A-model $\mathfrak{M}^*$ *realizes* the definition (a, Δ) if:

(i) $|a| = [A_\Delta]$, i.e. for any $c \in A$, $a \prec c$ iff $c = b$ or $b \prec c$ for some given term b of (a, Δ);

(ii) for any $u \in V_{|a|}$, $\mathrm{VD}_a(u) = \{i \in I : \mathfrak{M} \models u(\Delta(i))\}$, i.e. for any $u \in V_{|a|}$ and for any $v = u \cup \{\langle a, i \rangle\}$, $v \in V$ iff $\mathfrak{M} \models v(\Delta(a))$.

We also say that an A-model $\mathfrak{M}^+$ *realizes* a definition (a, Δ) if, for some denotation function d, the result $\mathfrak{M}^*$ of adding d to $\mathfrak{M}^+$ realizes the definition. When $\mathfrak{M}^*$ realizes the definition (a, Δ), we also say that (a, Δ) defines *a in $\mathfrak{M}^*$ from* each b, for b a given term, or *in terms of* the set of all b for which b is a given term.

The import of a definition is twofold. First, the object a denoted by the defined term a depends upon the objects $b_1, b_2, \ldots$ denoted by the given terms $b_1, b_2, \ldots$ and whatever else they depend upon. Second, the values of a, for given values of $b_1, b_2, \ldots$ and their dependees, consist of all those individuals that then satisfy $\Delta(a)$.

Our interest will be mainly in systems of definitions. A *definitional system* $\mathfrak{S}$ is simply a set of definitions. Its *defined terms* are the defined terms of the member definitions of $\mathfrak{S}$; and its *given terms* are those A-letters that are given terms of one of the definitions and yet not a defined term of another of the definitions. A model $\mathfrak{M}^*$ *realizes* the system of definitions $\mathfrak{S}$ if:

(i) $a \neq b$ for distinct defined terms a and b of $\mathfrak{S}$;

(ii) $\mathfrak{M}^*$ realizes each member definition of $\mathfrak{S}$.

The distinctness requirement (i) might be dropped; but its adoption makes the formulation of our results much easier.

The question now arises: when is a system of definitions realizable? To answer this question, it will be helpful to introduce some further characteristics of definitional systems. Say that a system $\mathfrak{S}$ is *unequivocal* if no A-letter a is the defined term of two distinct definitions (a, Δ) and (a, Γ) in $\mathfrak{S}$. In an unequivocal system, no term gets defined twice; its meaning, if determined at all by the definitions, is unequivocally determined. Given a system of definitions $\mathfrak{S}$ and A-letters a, b of $\mathfrak{S}$, say that a *immediately depends upon* b in $\mathfrak{S}$ – in symbols, $a \ll b$ – if, in some definition of $\mathfrak{S}$, a is the defined term and b a given term. We use $<$ (dependence) as the strict ancestral of $\ll$, so that $a < b$ if, for some sequence $a_1, \ldots, a_n$, with $n > 1$, $a = a_1$, $b = a_n$ and $a_i \ll a_{i+1}$ for $i = 1, 2, \ldots, n-1$. We say that the system $\mathfrak{S}$ is *well-*

founded if the converse of the relation of immediate dependence is well-founded. This condition may be seen as the combination of two other conditions. The first is that the system be non-circular in the sense that there be no sequence of terms $b_1, b_2, \ldots, b_n$ such that $b_1 = b_n$ and $b_i \ll b_{i+1}$ for $i = 1, 2, \ldots, n-1$. The other is that the system *embody no infinite regress* in the sense that there is no infinite sequence of distinct terms $b_1, b_2, b_3, \ldots$ such that $b_i \ll b_{i+1}$ for $i = 1, 2, 3, \ldots$. So in a well-founded system, the definition of a term ultimately terminates: there are no definitional circles, with one term ultimately being defined in terms of itself; and there are no infinite regresses, with the definition of one term always requiring the definition of a new term.

We now have the following sufficient condition for realizability:

Theorem 17
Suppose that the system $\mathfrak{S}$ of definitions is unequivocal and well-founded. Let $\mathfrak{M}$ be any classical model. Then there is an A-model $\mathfrak{M}^*$ that realizes $\mathfrak{S}$.

Proof
We specify an A-frame $(I, A, \prec)$ by letting A be the set of A-letters in $\mathfrak{S}$ and $\prec$ be the strict ancestral $<$ of the relation $\ll$ of immediate dependence for $\mathfrak{S}$. Since $<$ is transitive and its converse is well-founded, $(I, A, \prec)$ is indeed an A-frame.

We now define a function f_a with domain $V_{|a|}$ for each element a of A. If a is undefined in $\mathfrak{S}$, then $f_a(u) = I$ for $u \in V_{|a|} = \{\Lambda\}$. If a is defined in $\mathfrak{S}$, then $f_a(u) = \{i \in I : \mathfrak{M} \models u(\Delta(i))\}$ for each $u \in V_{|a|}$, where (a, Δ) is the definition of a in $\mathfrak{S}$. It then follows, by Corollary 7, that there is an A-structure $(I, A, \prec, V)$ subject to the condition that $VD_a = f_a \uparrow V_{|a|}$ for each $a \in A$.

Let $\mathfrak{M}^* = (I, \ldots, A, \prec, V, d)$ for d the identity function on A. It is then a simple matter to show that $\mathfrak{M}^*$ realizes $\mathfrak{S}$.

The above proof is somewhat devious, passing, as it does, through the proof of Corollary 7. A direct proof is given under Theorem 6 of Fine [85]. However, the present proof has the advantage of showing how the result is grounded in an abstract fact concerning A-frames.

The above requirements can be seen to be an instance of a more general requirement on systems of definitions. For it is a natural desideratum on any reasonable system of definitions that the same term not be defined twice and that there be no non-terminating sequence of definitions. The result itself can be seen as an instance of a more general principle concerning systems of definitions. For the requirements of unequivocality and well-foundation serve in general to guarantee the possibility of interpreting the defined terms in the manner prescribed by their definitions.

Although we shall not go into details, it may be shown that the model $\mathfrak{M}^*$ can always be taken to be standard. This means that, when we are dealing with definitions, we can always suppose ourselves to be working within a standard model.

A further question on definitional systems concerns not the existence of the defined objects but the extent to which they are uniquely determined. Say that two A-models $\mathfrak{M}^+ = (I, \ldots, A, \prec, V)$ and $\mathfrak{M}' = (I, \ldots, A', \prec', V')$ for the language $\mathfrak{L}^*$ are *generically equivalent* if there is a one–one map f from A onto A' such that:

(i) $a \prec b$ iff $f(a) \prec' f(b)$ for all $a, b \in A$;

(ii) $v \in V$ iff $\{\langle f(a), i \rangle : \langle a, i \rangle \in v\} \in V'$ for all possible assignments v for $\mathfrak{M}^+$.

Say that a system $\mathfrak{S}$ of definitions is *complete* if each A-letter of $\mathfrak{S}$ is a defined term of $\mathfrak{S}$. Then we have:

Theorem 18

Let $\mathfrak{S}$ be a complete, unequivocal and well-founded system of definitions. Suppose that the models $\mathfrak{M}^*$ and $\mathfrak{M}'$ for $\mathfrak{L}^*$ both realize $\mathfrak{S}$. Then the restrictions of $\mathfrak{M}^*$ and $\mathfrak{M}'$ to the respective denotations of the A-letters in $\mathfrak{S}$ are generically equivalent.

Proof

For any A-model $\mathfrak{M}^*$ that realizes $\mathfrak{S}$, it may be shown, by an easy induction on the level of a in $\mathfrak{S}$, that $[a] = \{b : a = b$ or a depends upon b in $\mathfrak{S}\}$. It therefore follows, for either $\mathfrak{M}^*$ or $\mathfrak{M}'$, that the denotations of the A-letters in $\mathfrak{S}$ form a closed class. So the required restrictions of $\mathfrak{M}^*$ and $\mathfrak{M}'$ are also A-models. Indeed, we may suppose that $\mathfrak{M}^*$ and $\mathfrak{M}'$ are already identical to these restrictions.

Since the denotation functions are one–one, we may suppose that they are the same and that $A = A'$. Since a depends upon b in either of the models iff a depends upon b in $\mathfrak{S}$, it follows that $\prec$ and $\prec'$ are the same. So it remains to show that $V = V'$.

Let a be any A-letter of $\mathfrak{S}$ and let (a, Δ) be its definition. Let f_a be the function with domain $I^{|a|}$ such that for each $u \in I^{|a|}$:

$$f_a(u) = \{i \in I : \mathfrak{M} \models u(\Delta(i))\}.$$

Since $\mathfrak{M}^*$ realizes $\mathfrak{S}$, $VD_a = f_a 1\ V_{|a|}$ for each $a \in A$; and similarly for $\mathfrak{M}'$. But then, by Corollary 7, $V = V'$.

Again, this result is very natural. For if all terms are defined, we would expect their denotations to be uniquely determined up to isomorphism.

A final question on definitional systems concerns the extent to which a system may be realized by an *extendible* A-model. Say that a definition (a, Δ) is *total* in the classical model $\mathfrak{M}$ if, for any function u from the set B of given terms of (a, Δ) into I, there is $i \in I$ for which $\mathfrak{M} \models u(\Delta(i))$. In a total definition, the defined object takes a value whenever the given objects take a value. A sufficient condition for extendible realization is given by:

Theorem 19
Let $\mathfrak{S}$ be a complete system of total definitions in the model $\mathfrak{M}$. Then any model $\mathfrak{M}^*$ that realizes $\mathfrak{S}$ is extendible over the class B of objects designated by the A-letters in $\mathfrak{S}$.

Proof
Suppose that $\mathfrak{S}$ is subject to the stated conditions and that $\mathfrak{M}^*$ realizes $\mathfrak{S}$. To show that $\mathfrak{M}^*$ is extendible over B, it suffices, by Theorem 2, to show that, for any $a \in B$, VD_a is totally defined. Given $a \in B$, let (a, Δ) be its definition in $\mathfrak{S}$. Pick any $u \in V_{|a|}$. Since (a, Δ) is total in $\mathfrak{M}$, there is an $i \in I$ for which $\mathfrak{M} \models u(\Delta(i))$. But since $\mathfrak{M}^*$ realizes (a, Δ), $v = u \cup \{\langle a, i \rangle\} \in V$. And so a is totally defined.

It is of interest that a relativized version of this theorem also holds. First, we need a result on the value assignments picked out by a system of definitions. Let $\mathfrak{S}$ be a system of definitions realized by the model $\mathfrak{M}^*$. We say that the possible assignment v *conforms* to $\mathfrak{S}$ if $\mathfrak{M} \models v(\Delta(a))$ whenever v is defined over every b for which b is a defined or given term of (a, Δ)$\in \mathfrak{S}$. We then have:

Lemma 20
Let $\mathfrak{S}$ be a complete system of definitions realized by $\mathfrak{M}^*$. Let v be a possible assignment from $\mathfrak{M}^*$ whose domain is closed and which is only defined on A-objects designated by A-letters in $\mathfrak{S}$. Then $v \in V$ if v conforms to $\mathfrak{S}$.

Proof
By a straightforward induction on the levels of the A-objects in the domain of v.

Note that it is trivial, if $v \in V$ and $\mathfrak{M}^*$ realizes $\mathfrak{S}$, that v conforms to $\mathfrak{S}$.

Given two systems of definitions $\mathfrak{S}$ and $\mathfrak{S}'$, call $\mathfrak{S}'$ a *refinement of* $\mathfrak{S}$ if the A-letters in $\mathfrak{S}$ and $\mathfrak{S}'$ are the same and, for each (a, Δ) in $\mathfrak{S}$, there is a (a, Δ') in $\mathfrak{S}'$ for which $\Delta \subseteq \Delta'$. Given a definition (a, Δ), say that it is *total relative to* the model $\mathfrak{M}^*$ for the language $\mathfrak{L}^*$ if, for any v from V defined on the A-objects designated by A-letters in Δ, there is an $i \in I$ for which $\mathfrak{M} \models v(\Delta(i))$. The relativized result is then given by:

Theorem 21
Let $\mathfrak{S}$ be a complete system of definitions realized by $\mathfrak{M}^*$. Let $\mathfrak{S}'$ be a refinement of $\mathfrak{S}$ in which each definition is total relative to $\mathfrak{M}^*$. Then any $\mathfrak{M}'$ that realizes $\mathfrak{S}'$ is extendible over the class B of objects designated by the A-letters in $\mathfrak{S}'$.

Proof
Since the A-letters in $\mathfrak{S}$ and $\mathfrak{S}'$ are the same, we may suppose without loss of generality that the designation a of any A-letter a of $\mathfrak{S}$ (or $\mathfrak{S}'$) is the same in both $\mathfrak{M}^*$ and $\mathfrak{M}'$. By Theorem 2 it suffices to show that, for any $a \in B$, VD_a (in $\mathfrak{M}'$) is totally defined. So take any u' from $V'_{|a|}$ (in $\mathfrak{M}'$). Since $\mathfrak{M}'$ realizes $\mathfrak{S}'$, u' conforms to $\mathfrak{S}'$. Since $\mathfrak{S}'$ is a refinement of $\mathfrak{S}$, u' also conforms to $\mathfrak{S}$. By hypothesis, $\mathfrak{S}$ is a complete set of definitions realized by $\mathfrak{M}^*$; and it is then readily seen that u' has a closed domain in $\mathfrak{M}^*$ and is only defined on A-objects designated by A-letters in $\mathfrak{S}$. It therefore follows from Lemma 20 that $u' \in V$ (in $\mathfrak{M}^*$). Let (a, Δ') be the definition of a in $\mathfrak{S}'$; and let u be the restriction of u' to the designation $\mathfrak{S}$ of the A-letters in Δ'. Then $u \in V$; and since (a, Δ') is total relative to $\mathfrak{M}^*$, there is an $i \in I$ for which $\mathfrak{M} \models u(\Delta'(i))$. So $\mathfrak{M} \models u'(\Delta'(i))$; and since $\mathfrak{M}'$ realizes (a, Δ'), $u' \cup \{\langle a, i \rangle\} \in V'$ as required.

The special case represented by Theorem 19 follows from Theorem 21 upon letting $\mathfrak{S}$ be a system of definitions of the form (a, Λ).

PART II

SOME STANDARD SYSTEMS

In this part, we apply the generic semantics to various standard systems of logic. The first three chapters deal, respectively, with the systems of Hilbert and Gentzen, of Quine, and of Copi. In the last two chapters, we deal with questions of a more informal nature: first, what advantages are to be gained from adopting the generic semantics?; second, is reference to arbitrary objects actually made in our ordinary quantificational reasoning?

8

Hilbert and Gentzen

We here consider the application of generic semantics to axiomatic systems of the sort proposed by Hilbert and to natural deduction systems of the sort proposed by Gentzen. We first give a semantics for a Hilbert system and then extend the account to a Gentzen system by treating suppositions as implicit antecedents. We go on to consider how a more plausible role might be assigned to suppositions. The application of the semantics in these cases is of a rather trivial nature. But it will serve to illustrate the concepts and methods that are of more use in the cases to follow.

In formulating the systems of this and later chapters, we shall use the language $\mathcal{L}^*$ in the case in which it is endowed with a countable infinity of A-letters. In such a language, the A-letters take the place of free variables. Our formulation is therefore closely allied to those in which a typographic distinction is made between free and bound variables (as in Hilbert and Bernays [34] or Lemmon [67]).

It is well known that the formulation of the restrictions on the axioms and rules in quantification theory become simpler when such a typographic distinction is made. For example: in the axiom of Specification $\forall x \phi(x) \supset \phi(t)$, it must normally be required that t be free for x in $\phi(x)$ whereas no such restriction is required with a typographic distinction between free and bound variables.

However, for us, the distinction is not merely one of syntactic convenience but is, at bottom, semantic. The letters a, b, c, ... are not variables, but are names, albeit of a strange sort of object; while the letters x, y, z, ... have no designatory role but merely serve, in Frege's phrase, as 'signs of generality'. To use an A-letter as a variable of quantification would be as bad, for us, as using an *individual* name as a variable of quantification.

Indeed, it is instructive in this regard to try to formulate a system of quantification theory in which it is the individual names that can double up as variables of quantification. One will then find oneself forced to impose the very same restrictions as are required when no typographic distinction is made between the so-called free and bound variables.

Let us now deal with each of the systems in turn.

The Hilbert System H

This has the following axioms and rules:

(1) All tautologous formulas
(2) $\forall x \phi(x) \supset \phi(t)$
(3) $\forall x(\phi \supset \psi) \supset (\forall x \phi \supset \forall x \psi)$
(4) $\phi \supset \forall x \phi$
MP $\phi, \phi \supset \psi / \psi$
Gen. $\phi(a)/\forall x \phi(x)$, for a not in $\phi(x)$

In (2), it is assumed that t is a term (containing no variables) and that $\phi(t)$ comes from $\phi(x)$ upon replacing all free occurrences of x with t. In Gen., it is assumed that a is an A-letter and that $\phi(a)$ comes from $\phi(x)$ upon replacing all free occurrences of x with a.

The notions of *proof* and *theorem* for such a system are defined in the usual way.

Under the generic semantics, the A-letters are conceived as designating suitable A-objects. What is required of these A-objects is given by the following definition. An A-model $\mathfrak{M}^*$ for $\mathfrak{L}^*$ is *suitable* if:

(i) $a \neq b$ for a and b distinct A-letters of $\mathfrak{L}^*$;

(ii) each *a*, for a an A-letter of $\mathfrak{L}^*$, is unrestricted.

It will be recalled that an A-object is unrestricted if it is both independent and value-unrestricted.

The requirement of suitability may be reformulated in terms of the realizability of a system of definitions. Let $\mathfrak{S}$ be the set of all definitions of the form (a, Λ) for a an A-letter of $\mathfrak{L}^*$. Then it is readily seen that an A-model $\mathfrak{M}^*$ is suitable iff it realizes the system of definitions $\mathfrak{S}$.

The important feature of unrestricted A-objects, in terms of the values they receive, is their value independence. We say that a set B of A-objects in a model $\mathfrak{M}^*$ is *value independent* if a function v from B into I belongs to V whenever $v(a) \in \mathrm{VR}(a)$ for each $a \in B$. We then have:

Lemma 1
In any suitable model $\mathfrak{M}^*$, the set B of designated A-objects is value-independent.

Proof
Let v be a function with domain B and with $v(a) \in \mathrm{VR}(a)$ for each $a \in \mathrm{Dm}(v)$. Pick an a in B. Since $v(a) \in \mathrm{VR}(a)$, there is a $u_a \in V$ for which $u_a(a) = v(a)$. By Restriction, the restriction t_a of u_a to $\{a\}$ also belongs to V. Since a is independent, $\mathrm{Dm}(t_a) = \{a\}$ is closed. But the domains of the different t_a's do not overlap. Therefore, by Piecing, $v = \bigcup t_a \in V$.

It will turn out that our proofs will only make use of the following three features of an A-model:

(i) $a \neq b$ for distinct a and b;

(ii) a is value-unrestricted for any A-letter a;

(iii) the set of designated A-objects is value-independent.

Given that these three conditions make no reference to an underlying relation of dependence, it may be wondered why our definition of suitability makes reference to such a relation. To some extent, the reasons will become clearer when we come to study the systems of Copi and Quine. But, for the moment, we may note that the structural independence of the A-objects actually serves to explain their value independence. The value independence is not simply assumed, but is seen to follow from an intrinsic structural characterization of the objects themselves.

We now wish to show that proofs within H are sound when suitably interpreted by means of A-objects. There are two standards of soundness that may be used. Under the first, which I call *Line Soundness*, it is required that each line of the proof be correct in an appropriate sense. Under the second, which I call *Rule* or *Line-to-line Soundness*, it is required that each application of a rule of inference preserve correctness. Under the first, it is the lines of the proof that are to be correct; under the second, it is the methods by which the lines are obtained.

It is clear that, in principle, a system may possess one kind of soundness and not the other. If validity is our standard of correctness, then the axioms may not be correct even though the rules of inference preserve correctness. On the other hand, if truth is our standard of correctness, then each theorem may be correct even though the rules of inference do not preserve correctness. This is the case, for example, with (suitably interpreted) modal systems that contain the rule of necessitation.

First we establish:

Theorem 2 (Line-to-line Soundness)
The inferences

$$\text{(a)} \quad \frac{\phi, \phi \supset \psi}{\psi} \qquad \text{(b)} \quad \frac{\phi(a)}{\forall x \phi(x)} \text{ (a not in } \phi(x))$$

are truth-to-truth valid in every suitable A-model $\mathfrak{M}^*$.

Proof
(a) The model $\mathfrak{M}^*$ is extendible over the set of designated A-objects. This follows from Theorem I.2 and the fact that each designated a is totally defined. Alternatively, it follows from the value independence of the designated A-objects and the fact that each of them has a non-null value-range. For let $u \in V$ be defined on a subset B of the designated A-objects. Let v be a function which agrees with u over B and which assigns to each designated A-object not in B a member of its value-range. Then v extends u and, by value independence, $v \in V$.

Since $\mathfrak{M}^*$ is extendible over the set of designated A-objects, it follows from Theorem I.14 that Modus Ponens is valid in $\mathfrak{M}^*$.

(b) Let the A-letters in $\phi(x)$ be $a_1, \ldots, a_n$, so that $\phi(x)$ may be written in the form $\phi(x, a_1, \ldots, a_n)$. Suppose, for *reductio*, that $\forall x \phi(x, a_1, \ldots, a_n)$ is not true in $\mathfrak{M}^*$. Then for some assignment $v \in V$ defined over $\{a_1, \ldots, a_n\}$, $\forall x \phi(x, v(a_1), \ldots, v(a_n))$ is not true in $\mathfrak{M}$. (Recall that we are using each individual $i \in I$ as a name of itself.) By Restriction, we may suppose that v is defined on $\{a_1, \ldots, a_n\}$. Given that v has the diagram:

$$v : \frac{a_1 a_2 \ldots a_n}{i_1 i_2 \ldots i_n}$$

we then have that $\forall x \phi(x, i_1, \ldots, i_n)$ is false in $\mathfrak{M}$.

By the classical truth-condition for $\forall$, there is an $i \in I$ for which $\phi(i, i_1, \ldots, i_n)$ if false in $\mathfrak{M}$. We wish to show that the assignment $v^+ = v \cup \{(a, i)\}$ with diagram:

$$v^+ : \frac{a \, a_1 \, a_2 \ldots a_n}{i \, i_1 \, i_2 \ldots i_n}$$

belongs to V.

Let u be the assignment $\{(a, i)\}$ with diagram:

$$u : \frac{a}{i}$$

We show that $v^+ \in V$ by showing that the assignments v and u can be pieced together.

First note that $u \in V$. For by a value-unrestricted, $i \in \text{VR}(a)$, i.e. $u^+(a) = i$ for some $u^+ \in V$; and so by Restriction, $u = u^+ \upharpoonright \{a\} \in V$.

Now note that the conditions for Piecing are satisfied. For since $a, a_1, \ldots, a_n$ are all independent, the domains of u and v are closed. But also u and v agree on common arguments, indeed have no common arguments: for by the syntactic restriction on the rule, a is distinct from each of $a_1, \ldots, a_n$; and so by clause (i) in the definition of suitability, the A-object a is distinct from each of $a_1, \ldots, a_n$.

We therefore have, by Piecing, that $v^+ = u \cup v \in V$. But $v^+(\phi(a)) = \phi(i, i_1, \ldots, i_n)$ is false in $\mathfrak{M}$; and so $\phi(a)$ is not true in $\mathfrak{M}^*$ – as required.

The proof for part (b) has been stated with some care in order to illustrate the rigorous use of the conditions on an A-model, the definition of suitability, and the restrictions on the rules. Note, in particular, how clauses (i) and (ii) in the definition of suitability are used and how it is significant both that a not occur in $\phi(x)$ and that distinct A-letters designate distinct A-objects. In future, we shall not bother to formulate our proofs with such care.

From Theorem 2 may be derived:

Theorem 3 (Line Soundness)
Each theorem of H is true in each suitable A-model $\mathfrak{M}^*$.

Proof
Given Theorem 2, it suffices to show that each axiom of H is true in $\mathfrak{M}^*$. But each axiom is classically valid and so, by Lemma I.11, is true in $\mathfrak{M}^*$.

A similar result may be proved for theories. We take a *theory* to be the result of adding a set Δ of non-logical axioms to H, with the rules of MP and Gen. allowed to apply without restriction in the resulting proofs. We then have in the same way as before:

Theorem 4
Let T be a theory with non-logical axioms Δ. For each theorem ϕ of T, (Δ, ϕ) is truth-to-truth validated in any suitable model.

These results on soundness lack interest unless it can be shown that each classical model $\mathfrak{M}$ underlies a suitable generic model $\mathfrak{M}^*$. We want to know, whatever the state of the real world (the model $\mathfrak{M}$), that suitable denotations for the A-letters can be found. This possibility is given by:

Theorem 5
Each classical model $\mathfrak{M}$ for $\mathfrak{L}$ underlies a suitable A-model $\mathfrak{M}^*$ for $\mathfrak{L}^*$.

Proof
Note that the system $\mathfrak{S}$ of definitions of the form (a, Λ), for a an A-letter of $\mathfrak{L}^*$, is unequivocal and well-founded. It therefore follows from Theorem I.17 that, for any classical model $\mathfrak{M}$, there is an A-model $\mathfrak{M}^*$ that realizes $\mathfrak{S}$ and hence is suitable.

A direct proof of this result may also be very simply given.

Call the system H *classically sound* if each theorem of H that lacks A-letters is classically valid. Note that this definition imposes no requirement on the theorems that contain A-letters. It may therefore be thought to reflect a perspective according to which theorems with A-letters have no interest in themselves but serve only to facilitate the derivation of theorems with A-letters.

Theorem 6
The system H is classically sound.

Proof
Let ϕ be a theorem of H without A-letters. From Theorem 5 it follows that the collection X of suitable models satisfies the condition of Theorem I.12 relative to ϕ. By Theorem 3, ϕ is generically valid relative to X; and so, by Theorem I.12, ϕ is classically valid.

It should be noted that, in this case, the restriction to theorems without A-letters can be dropped and, indeed, that the very same proof serves to establish the stronger result. Of course, the stronger result may also be established directly by classical methods. But the present proof serves to illustrate how, in the simplest case, classical soundness can be derived from generic soundness.

Call the system H *classically complete* if each classically valid formula without A-letters is a theorem of H. Like our previous definition, the present definition imposes no requirement on formulas containing A-letters. From the classical completeness result for H can now be established a generic completeness result:

Theorem 7
If ϕ is true in each suitable A-model, then ϕ is a theorem of H.

Proof
Suppose that ϕ is of the form $\phi(a_1,\ldots,a_n)$, with A-letters as displayed. Assume that $\phi(a_1,\ldots,a_n)$ is not a theorem of H. Then $\forall x_1 \ldots x_n \phi(x_1,\ldots,x_n)$ is also not a theorem of H. By classical completeness, there is a classical model $\mathfrak{M}$ for which $\forall x_1 \ldots x_n \phi(x_1,\ldots,x_n)$ is false. So for some individuals $i_1,\ldots,i_n \in I$, $\phi(i_1,\ldots,i_n)$ is false in $\mathfrak{M}$. By Theorem 5, $\mathfrak{M}$ underlies a suitable A-model $\mathfrak{M}^*$. Let $v = \{\langle a_1, i_1 \rangle, \ldots, \langle a_n, i_n \rangle\}$. Then $\mathfrak{M} \not\models \phi(v(a_1), \ldots, v(a_n))$. But since $\mathfrak{M}^*$ is suitable, $v \in V$; and therefore $\mathfrak{M}^* \not\models \phi(a_1,\ldots,a_n)$.

The Gentzen System G

We are interested in a system of the sort proposed by Gentzen [34]. Any reasonable formulation of the propositional rules will do; but it is important that the quantificational rules contain a principle of existential elimination rather than existential instantiation. To fix our ideas, we might suppose that we are working within the system of Lemmon's [67].

The quantificational rules, in schematic form, are as follows:

$$\forall E. \quad \frac{\forall x \phi(x)}{\phi(t)} \qquad \forall I. \quad \frac{\phi(a)}{\forall x \phi(x)}$$

$$\exists E. \quad \frac{\exists x \phi(x) \quad \begin{array}{c}[\phi(a)]\\ \vdots \\ \psi\end{array}}{\psi} \qquad \exists I. \quad \frac{\phi(t)}{\exists x \phi(x)}$$

In $\forall E$ and $\exists I$, it is supposed that t is a term (without free variables) and that $\phi(t)$ comes from $\phi(x)$ upon substituting t for the free occurrences of x; and in ∀I and ∃E, it is supposed that $\phi(a)$ comes from $\phi(x)$ upon substituting the A-letter a for the free occurrences of x. In ∀I, a must not occur in $\phi(x)$ or in the assumptions upon which $\phi(a)$ depends; and in ∃E, a must not occur in $\phi(x)$ or ψ or any assumptions, other than $\phi(a)$, upon which ψ depends.

The distinctive feature of the present system, as opposed to the ones we shall later consider, is that there is no rule for inferring an instance of an existential statement from the existential statement itself. Instead, we have the rule ∃E, which licenses the inference from the existential statement when we have the inference from an instance.

We wish to extend the generic treatment of H to G. This may be done most simply by treating each line of a derivation as equivalent to a conditional. Recall that a sequent (Δ, ϕ) is *derivable in* G if there is a derivation whose last line has the formula ϕ as a conclusion and has only formulas of Δ as suppositions. If $\phi_1 \ldots, \phi_n$ are the distinct members of Δ, let $\Delta \supset \phi$ be the formula $(\phi_1 \wedge \ldots \wedge \phi_n) \supset \phi$. (The order in which we take the members of ϕ will be immaterial.) We then have:

Theorem 8 (Line-to-line Soundness)
Let $(\Delta_1, \phi_1), \ldots, (\Delta_n, \phi_n)/(\Delta, \phi)$ be an argument pattern corresponding to one of the rules of inference of G. Then the inference $\Delta_1 \supset \phi_1, \ldots, \Delta_n \supset \phi_n / \Delta \supset \phi$ is truth-to-truth valid in the class of suitable models $\mathfrak{M}^*$.

Proof
All of the rules, other than ∀I and ∃E, correspond to classically valid inferences. Therefore their validation follows from the extendibility of $\mathfrak{M}^*$. The treatment of ∀I and ∃E follows that of the rule of generalization in the proof of Theorem 9, but with some slight adjustment to take care of the presence of suppositions.

We may now prove the other results – line soundness and classical soundness – in the same way as before.

The Role of Suppositions

The previous approach gives us the simplest way of unifying our treatment of the systems of Gentzen and Hilbert. But it is not based upon a very plausible view of the role of suppositions in the informal reasoning to which the derivations in systems of natural deduction are meant to correspond. Suppositions are treated, in effect, as the implicit antecedent to conditionals. So the supposition of ϕ itself is taken to be tantamount to the assertion of $\phi \supset \phi$, while the inference of $\phi \vee \psi$ from the supposition ϕ is taken to be tantamount to the inference of $\phi \supset (\phi \vee \psi)$ from $(\phi \supset \phi)$. A piece of reasoning, or a derivation, therefore becomes, in effect, the demonstration of a logical truth from logical axioms of the form $\phi \supset \phi$. Intuitively, however, we are inclined to think of the supposition of ϕ as not assertoric in force at all and we are inclined to think of the inference of $\phi \vee \psi$ from the supposition of ϕ as being, not an inference from conditional assertion to conditional assertion, but an inference in which the assertive element in premiss and conclusion is absent.

Can we give an account of validity that is more faithful to the role of suppositions in ordinary reasoning? If no suppositions are discharged, then there is no special difficulty in providing such an account. But once suppositions are allowed to be discharged, there are general difficulties, quite independent of the adoption of generic semantics.

In order to appreciate these difficulties, it is necessary to distinguish, at the informal level, between what Prawitz ([65], p. 23) has called proper and improper inference rules. A *proper inference* is one that is meant to be valid in the standard way; the conclusion is meant to follow straightforwardly from the premisses. As an example, we have the inference from a statement ϕ to its double negation. An *improper inference*, on the one hand, is one that is meant to be valid, but not in the standard way. As an example, we have the inference to $\phi \supset \psi$ in the case in which ψ has been inferred from ϕ. It is not possible to regard this inference as proper, since in the transition to $\phi \supset \psi$ the supposition ϕ has been discharged.

A *rule* of inference is called *proper* (or *improper*) if it is a rule for drawing proper (or improper) inferences.

Reasoning that contains improper inferences give rise to two problems. The first is: In what does the validity of improper inferences consist? The second is: How can two concepts of validity, one for the proper and the other for the improper inferences, legitimately operate in the same body of reasoning? Since inferences involving the discharge of suppositions must, by their very nature, be improper, reasoning containing such inferences will also give rise to these difficulties.

The first difficulty can be met by saying that in an improper inference we are inferring the validity of one inference from the validity of others. If you like, the premisses and conclusion of such an inference are themselves inferences. So in an application of conditional proof, for example, we are going from the claim that ψ can be inferred from the supposition ϕ to the conclusion that $\phi \supset \psi$ can be inferred without the benefit of the supposition.

No doubt the details of such an account need to be worked out. Is the improper inference to be stated in the meta-language or the object language? Is the validity of a higher-order inference to be a syntactic notion, a semantic notion, or what? But however the details are best worked out, it seems clear that an account along these lines can be given.

The second difficulty seems more problematic. On our account of improper inference, an improper inference 'feeds off' a proper inference; it requires a proper inference as premiss or 'input'. But how can it be legitimate both to make inferences and to use those inferences as the premisses for further inferences?

This difficulty can be met by supposing that the given body of reasoning simultaneously operates on the levels of object- and meta-inference. Let us be more exact. With each line or step of the reasoning we may associate two items: first, the statement made, which is either a supposition or the conclusion of an inference; second, the set of suppositions upon the basis of which the statement is made. In fact, it will be somewhat awkward to allow a dual status for the statements made, as either suppositions or conclusions; and so, for the purposes of the present discussion, we shall follow the convention whereby the suppositions are not taken to be included in the 'text' or main body of reasoning. We can then say that each statement made is a conclusion.

Suppositions enter into the reasoning by means of a rule that enables one to infer the statement of the supposition from the supposition itself. This rule corresponds to the rule of iteration in certain systems of natural deduction. In terms of such a rule, we might represent the inference of $\phi \vee \psi$ from the supposition ϕ in something like the following way:

	(1)	ϕ	supposition
1	(2)	ϕ	from 1
1	(3)	$\phi \vee \psi$	from 2.

Here, lines (2) and (3) constitute the main body of the reasoning. The numbers to the left indicate the suppositions on which the given lines are made. No number is given to the left of line (1), since at line (1) a supposition is *made*, not used.

With these understandings, we can now think of each line of a piece of reasoning as achieving two quite distinct logical goals. On the one hand, the statement made, call it ϕ, will have been *inferred* from the suppositions used, call them Δ. On the other hand, it will have been *demonstrated* that ϕ can be inferred from the supposition Δ.

Although the two goals are distinct, it should be noted that in achieving one I have, in effect, achieved the other. If I succeed in inferring ϕ from Δ, then that very inference can serve as a basis for demonstrating that ϕ is inferable from Δ; while if I succeed in demonstrating that ϕ is inferable from Δ, then that very demonstration can serve as a basis for inferring ϕ from Δ. How exactly the transition from inference to demonstration or demonstration to inference is to be made is problematic; but since it is clear that the transition *can* be made, let us not enquire too closely into *how* it is to be made.

It is now clear how proper and improper inferences can legitimately be combined into the same body of reasoning; since each line of the reasoning serves both to make an inference and demonstrate an inference, it can serve both as a basis for a proper inference and for an improper inference.

If a given piece of 'mixed' reasoning, as so conceived, is to be correct, then four requirements must be met. These are:

(i) the inference ϕ/ϕ is valid;

(ii) if $\phi_1,\ldots,\phi_n/\phi$ encodes a proper rule of inference, then the inference $\phi_1,\ldots,\phi_n/\phi$ is valid;

(iii) if the inferences Δ/ϕ and $\phi, \Gamma/\psi$ are valid, so is $\Delta, \Gamma/\psi$;

(iv) if $(\Delta_1,\phi_1),\ldots,(\Delta_n,\phi_n)/(\Delta,\phi)$ encodes an improper rule of inference, then the inference from the validity of each of $(\Delta_1,\phi_1),\ldots,(\Delta_n,\phi_n)$ to the validity of (Δ,ϕ) is 'valid'.

If, in condition (iv), we wanted to avoid the problematic application of validity to higher-order inferences, we might give the alternative formulation:

(iv)' if $(\Delta_1,\phi_1),\ldots,(\Delta_n,\phi_n)/(\Delta,\phi)$ encodes an improper rule of inference, then (Δ,ϕ) is valid whenever $(\Delta_1,\phi_1),\ldots,(\Delta_n,\phi_n)$ are valid.

Conditions (ii) and (iv) are immediate from the conceptions of validity for proper and improper inferences. Condition (i) derives from the requirement that a supposition ϕ should also serve to demonstrate the validity of the inference ϕ from ϕ. Condition (iii) (Cut) derives from the requirement that a proper inference should serve to demonstrate the validity of the conclusion from its premises. For suppose the proper inference is one in which ϕ has been inferred from the premises $\phi_1, \ldots, \phi_n$; and suppose $\phi_1, \ldots, \phi_n$ have been inferred from the respective suppositions $\Delta_1, \ldots, \Delta_n$. We will know that the inferences $\Delta_1/\phi_1, \ldots, \Delta_n/\phi_n$ are valid; and, from (ii), we will know that the inference $\phi_1, \ldots, \phi_n/\phi$ is valid. But then (iii) will be required to ensure that the inference of ϕ from its suppositions $\Delta = \Delta_1 \cup \ldots \cup \Delta_n$ is valid.

So far our discussion has been completely general. We must now apply it to the problem of providing an account of validity for the inferences embodied in the rules of natural deduction.

It is a requirement on the correctness of any such account that it should conform to the conditions (i)–(iv). However, if these conditions are to have any application, it must first be determined which of the inference rules are proper and which improper. Now, for the most part, there is no room for choice in this matter. Some of the rules require the discharge of suppositions and so have to be classified as improper. Others are so obviously proper that it seems absurd to classify them in any other way. The only real choice concerns universal generalisation ($\forall$I); this requires no discharge of suppositions and might, intuitively, be classified as either proper or improper. In considering any proposed account of validity therefore, it must be decided what status this rule is to have.

There would appear to be two main possible accounts. I shall state them in terms of the generic semantics, although they could equally well be stated in other terms. The first is to take validity in the truth-to-truth sense. The rule $\forall$I would then most naturally be classified as proper; since from the truth of $\phi(a)$, for a an unrestricted arbitrary object, the truth of $\forall x\phi(x)$ can be inferred.

But such a proposal runs into difficulties with the conditions (i)–(iv). Conditions (i) and (iii) are automatically satisfied. Condition (ii) is satisfied as long as the designated A-objects conform to Extendibility. But condition (iv) (or rather (iv)′) will not in general hold. The inference $\Delta, \phi/\psi$ may be valid, even though $\Delta/\phi \supset \psi$ is not valid. So Fa/$\forall$xFx is valid, even though /Fa$\supset\forall$xFx is not.

The proposal also runs into other difficulties. Given that $\forall x\phi(x)$ is inferable from the assertion $\phi(a)$, for a unrestricted, it should also be inferable from the supposition $\phi(a)$. But the inference from the supposition is not legitimate in standard systems of natural deduction, since the restriction on the presence of the term a in the suppositions will have been violated. Nor is the inference from the supposition legitimate in ordinary reasoning. If I argue as follows:

Let n be an arbitrary natural number. Suppose it is even....
Then I cannot go on to infer that every natural number is even.

The other proposal is to take validity in the case-to-case sense. The rule $\forall I$ must then be classified as improper; since the inference $\phi(a)/\forall x\phi(x)$ is not in general case-to-case valid. Such a proposal satisfies the conditions (i)–(iv). The satisfaction of conditions (i), (ii) and (iv) is automatic; while condition (iii) is satisfied as long as the designated A-objects conform to Extendibility (Theorem I.16). (It is interesting to note, in this regard, that the need for Extendibility now switches from condition (ii) to condition (iii).) In addition to satisfying the conditions (i)–(iv), the proposal appears to let in no unwanted inferences. It would therefore appear to suffer from none of the drawbacks of the previous proposal.

Despite its obvious strengths, the proposal still does not strike me as satisfactory as an account of our intuitions or ordinary practice. For can we not infer, from the fact that an arbitrary object of a certain kind ϕ's ($\phi(a)$), that every object of that kind ϕ's ($\forall x\phi(x)$)? In a given piece of elementary mathematics, for example, we may appeal to the identity $(x+y)^2 = x^2 + 2xy + y^2$. From this identity we can then infer any one of its instances, thereby indicating our commitment to its universal generalisation. But this inference to the instances is surely not a case of improper inference. It can hardly be a previous inference that warrants the given conclusion; for the identity may merely have been asserted, and so there may be no previous inference to refer to. It would therefore appear to be the identity claim itself that warrants the inference to the given conclusion.

We seem to have reached an impasse. Three accounts of the validity of the informal reasoning corresponding to the derivations in natural deduction have been proposed; and each has been found wanting.

The general difficulty is this. Any account of validity should, it seems, conform to three intuitive requirements:

(a) The (proper) inference from the *assertion* $\phi(a)$, for a unrestricted, to the conclusion $\forall x\phi(x)$ is valid.

The second is that:
(b) The (proper) inference from the *supposition* $\phi(a)$, for a unrestricted, to the conclusion $\forall x\phi(x)$ is not in general valid.

The third is that:
(c) A plausible role should be assigned to suppositions.

This seems to imply, in particular, that a *principle of suppositional indifference* should hold, according to which:
(c)' An inference is valid regardless of whether the premiss is a supposition or an assertion.

The three requirements, as they stand, are incompatible; and so a reasonable way of reconciling them must be found.

Our three accounts attempt to do this in three different ways. The first, which treats suppositions as the implicit antecedents to conditionals, respects (a) and (b) but gives up on (c)'. The second, which adopts a truth-to-truth conception of validity and treats suppositions as premisses in their own right, respects (a) and (c)' but gives up on (b). The third, which adopts a case-to-case conception of validity and also treats suppositions as premisses in their own right, respects (b) and (c)' but gives up on (a). But none of these three ways of reconciling the three requirements seems satisfactorily to explain the intuitions that originally underlay them.

What are we to do? When I first considered this problem, I was inclined to adopt the following solution. A supposition is not, properly speaking, a premiss at all but a delimiter of case. When I suppose ϕ, I am in effect defining the case in which ϕ holds; it is as if I had said 'Consider the case in which ϕ holds.' A supposition then has the effect of modifying the standards of truth for statements made within its scope; such a statement is to be considered true when it is true in the case defined by the supposition. When a supposition, such as $\phi(a)$, contains a reference to an arbitrary object, the case it defines is given by the restriction V' of the set of value-assignments V to those that make $\phi(a)$ true. A statement ψ within such a supposition will then be true if it is true relative to the restricted set of value-assignments V'.

Such a solution will be similar in its formal effects to our original solution, in which suppositions were treated as implicit antecedents; but it bases these effects on what is meant to be a more plausible account of the role of suppositions. However, such an account is still unsatisfactory. Whatever is the case for clauses of the form 'Consider the case in which...', it seems excessively paradoxical to suppose that suppositions do not really figure as premises at all. Moreover, in supposing that an arbitrary number n is even, I do not seem, intuitively, to be restricting its values to those numbers that are even. Rather I seem to be following through the fate of a particular arbitrary number, even one that 'might' be odd, and supposing that it is even.

I am now inclined to adopt the following solution. We suppose that, in any piece of reasoning, an arbitrary object has one of two states; either it is *vacant* or it is *occupied*. (Alternative terms are void/valued, free/fixed.) Intuitively speaking, the object is occupied if it has been assigned a value; and it is vacant otherwise. However, the status of being vacant or occupied is purely nominal. It is not that, when an A-object is occupied, it need actually have been assigned a value; it is sufficient if we treat it as if a value had been assigned.

We can, by extension, talk of A-names being vacant or occupied when their designata are vacant or occupied. This distribution between the names is very like the familiar distinction between the generality and conditional interpretations of free variables (see Kleene [52], pp. 149–50). For us, the distinction is, at bottom, at the level of the objects. But for those who are sceptical of the objects, a great deal of what we want to say could be re-interpreted at the level of language.

The distinction between the A-objects, or the variables, is very natural within the context of a programming language. A variable at a given point in a program is void if in any hypothetical running of the program up to that point the variable would not have been assigned a value; and otherwise it is valued. What I wish to do is to transfer this distinction, which is so natural within the context of a programming language, to the context of ordinary reasoning.

Consider now an inference from $\phi(a, b)$ to $\psi(a, b)$ in which a is vacant and b is occupied. We want to say that this inference is valid if $\psi(a, b)$ is true whenever $\phi(a, b)$ is true. Given that the value of b is (hypothetically) fixed and the value of a is free, $\phi(a, b)$ is true if, for the hypothetically fixed value j of b and for all values of a, $\phi(i, j)$ is true; and similarly for $\psi(a, b)$. So we may say that the inference $\phi(a, b)/\psi(a, b)$ is valid if, for any value j of b, $\psi(i, j)$ is true for all values i of a whenever $\phi(i, j)$ is true for all values i of a.

From this particular example, we may obtain the general account. Given a formula ϕ, an A-model $\mathfrak{M}^*$ and a $v \in V$ defined on a subset of A_ϕ, say that ϕ is true *at v in* $\mathfrak{M}^*$ – in symbols, $\mathfrak{M}^* \models_v \phi$ – if $\mathfrak{M}^* \models_{v^+} \phi$

for any $v^+ \supseteq v$ that is defined over A_ϕ. For Δ a set of formulas and v an assignment defined on a subset of A_Δ, the relation $\mathfrak{M}^* \models_v \Delta$ is similarly defined. Our two previous concepts of truth are special cases of this more general concept: absolute truth is obtained when v is null; and relative truth is obtained when v is defined on A_ϕ (or A_Δ).

Let an *occupancy* list L be a set of A-letters. Intuitively, we think of an occupancy list as a specification of the A-letters whose denotata are occupied. Given an occupancy list L and an A-model $\mathfrak{M}^*$, we let A_L, in the usual manner, be $\{a : a \in L\}$. We now say that an inference Δ/ϕ with occupancy list L is valid relative to the collection of A-models X if, for any model $\mathfrak{M}^* \in X$ and any $v \in V$ defined on A_L, $\mathfrak{M}^* \models_v \phi$ whenever $\mathfrak{M}^* \models_v \Delta$.

Our two previous concepts of validity are special cases of this more general concept: truth-to-truth validity is obtained when L is empty; and case-to-case validity is obtained when L contains all of the A-letters in Δ and ϕ. The other cases give something new. If, for example, only b is vacant and X is the collection of suitable models, then the inference Fab/∀yFay is valid while the inference Fab/∀xFab is not.

It should be noted that 'mixed' inferences are not allowed; if an A-letter is vacant in one formula or at one occurrence, then it is vacant in all formulas or at all occurrences. A definition of validity for mixed inferences could be given, but it would be of little use; for the identity between the vacant and the occupied occurrences of the same A-letter would be an accident and therefore of no significance.

The apparatus of vacancy may now be used to solve our previous puzzles over generalization. We wish first to explain why the assertion of $\phi(a)$, for a unrestricted, appears to validate the conclusion ∀xϕ(x) and why, in particular, it seems legitimate to appeal to an identity in a proof and infer from it all of its instances. The reason is that the A-object a in all such cases is vacant and that therefore the concept of validity operates, with regard to such an object, as if it were truth-to-truth. We next wish to explain why the inference from the supposition of $\phi(a)$, for a unrestricted, to the conclusion ∀xϕ(x) does not in general appear to be valid. The reason is that the A-object a in such cases is occupied and that therefore the concept of validity operates, with regard to such an object, as if it were case-to-case. We finally wish to reconcile the principle of suppositional indifference with our views on generalization. But here there is no difficulty. The similarity in the inferences from an assertion and from a supposition is apparent only; for the status of the A-objects and hence the A-names is not the same.

If we were to take a supposition in which the critical term were vacant, then we could generalize from it; while if we were to take an assertion in which the critical term were occupied, we could not generalize from it. In fact, I think there are actual cases of this sort. Suppose I begin a piece of reasoning with the declaration 'Let x and y be any two reals' and, at a later point in the argument, I appeal to the fact that $(x+y)^2 = x^2 + 2xy + y^2$. Then I cannot go on to infer that $(3+5)^2 = 3^2 + 2.3.5 + 5^2$: and this, intuitively, is because I am talking about two particular, but hypothetical, reals; and in terms of my theory, it is because the reals are occupied. Or suppose I wish to work out the consequences of the generalised continuum hypothesis. Then I may declare 'Suppose $2^{\aleph_\alpha} = \aleph_{\alpha+1}$.' I can then go on to infer $2^{\aleph_0} = \aleph_1$ etc.; and again, intuitively, this is because the value of α has not yet been fixed, it can be 'anything you like', while, in terms of my theory, it is because the arbitrary ordinal α is vacant.

What makes the data so misleading, and hence gave rise to our original puzzle, is that suppositions are naturally taken to concern occupied A-objects, while assertions, at least on their own, are naturally taken to concern vacant A-objects.

Although our ordinary practice would appear to embody a distinction between vacant and occupied A-objects, or vacant and occupied A-letters, none of the standard systems of natural deduction also embodies this distinction. It is, however, a fairly straightforward matter to modify them in this respect. Let the *vacancy-value* of an A-object or A-letter be its status as vacant or occupied. Then at each line of a derivation, it must be indicated what vacancy-values the A-letters have at that line. This may be done by marking 'a̸' to the right of the line when the letter 'a' is meant to be vacant and by marking 'a' to the right when the letter 'a' is meant to be occupied.

In practice, it is tedious to mark down the vacancy-value of each A-letter at each line, and so two conventions may be adopted for cutting down on the labour. The first is that an A-letter is assumed to be occupied unless there is an explicit indication to the contrary. The second is that an A-letter is assumed to have the same value that it was last given, again subject to the condition that there is no explicit indication to the contrary. In other words, the *presumption* is that an A-letter is occupied and that its vacancy-value does not alter from one line to the next.

It may further be supposed that at each line we indicate *exactly* the vacancy-values of the A-letters that occur in the statement of that line. However, if we were to extend the idea of distinguishing between vacant and occupied A-letters to the construction of free logics, it might be convenient to relax this supposition. We might allow, for example, that the theorem Fa ⊃ Fa could be derived, as long as a was occupied; and we might then allow that the theorem ∃x(Fx ⊃ Fx) be inferred, as long as a remained occupied. But we might disqualify the inference to ∃x(Fx ⊃ Fx) in the absence of any specification for the vacancy-value of a (*cf*. Jaskowski [34]).

It will be recalled that our extended concept of validity was only properly applicable to inferences in which there was a uniform assignment of vacancy-values to the different occurrences of the same A-letter. If therefore this concept of validity is to be applicable to the inference established at each line of a derivation, the inference must be one that permits a uniform assignment of vacancy-values. We are therefore led to the following requirement on derivations:

Coherence
The vacancy-values assigned at a given line and at all of the lines in which its suppositions are introduced must be compatible.

It will sometimes be difficult to ascertain whether a given line conforms to Coherence; and so it would be convenient to structure the derivations in such a way that conformity to the requirement is guaranteed. This is most naturally done within the presentations of natural deduction, such as those of Fitch [52] or Kalish and Montague [64], in which the derivations are explicitly built up from subderivations. Within each subderivation we may then require that the vacancy-values of the A-letters remain the same. This has the consequence that if a rule of inference changes the vacancy-value of an A-letter, it must move us from one subderivation to another.

There are various ways of formulating a complete set of rules for a system that assigns vacancy-values to its A-letters. But perhaps the most elegant and economical is as follows. The standard rules are to apply to all lines, but subject to the requirement that no supposition containing a vacant A-letter be discharged. Although this requirement may seem artificial, it can be seen to be the consequence of two other, quite natural, requirements. The first is that a distinction be made between suppositions and assumptions and that only suppositions be subject to discharge. The second is that vacant A-letters not be used in the formulation of suppositions. In other words, in so far as suppositional reasoning concerns A-objects at all, it concerns those A-objects that hypothetically have been assumed to receive a value. Since none of the other rules will require the discharge of suppositions containing vacant A-letters, this second requirement will impose no further, unwanted, limitation on our derivations.

There are to be two rules concerning vacant A-letters: one for inference *to* a vacancy, *i.e.* to a formula containing a vacant A-letter; the other for inference *from* a vacancy. According to the first, which we may call the *Rule of Liberation,* an occupied A-letter may be made vacant:

$$\frac{\phi(a)}{\phi(a)} \qquad \frac{a}{\not{a}}$$

Note that no restriction and, in particular, no restriction on the suppositions to the inference has been made. It will, however, be a consequence of the general requirement of Coherence that the A-letter a not occur in the suppositions (or assumptions). For if it did, a would be occupied in the suppositions, since it is occupied in the premiss; and so it could not be vacant in the conclusion.

The other rule is the familiar rule of universal generalization, but tied to a vacant instantial term:

$$\frac{\phi(a)}{\forall x \phi(x)} \qquad \not{a}$$

There is again no restriction, in this case either implicit or explicit, on the suppositions to the inference. So, in particular, we may go with this rule from the assumption Fa, for a vacant, to the conclusion $\forall x Fx$.

The Rule of Liberation is, of course, an improper rule. Indeed, our semantics does not even permit us to think of an inference with a switch of vacancy-value as a proper inference. On the other hand, the new rule of generalization is a proper rule: from the truth of $\phi(a)$, for *a* vacant and unrestricted, follows the truth of $\forall x \phi(x)$; and as a syntactic reflection of this fact, we have the indifference of the rule to any restriction on the suppositions.

The familiar rule of generalization may, in the present system, be regarded as a derived rule. Given that the A-letter a does not occur in the suppositions, we may perform the following two inferences:

$$\frac{\dfrac{\phi(a)}{\phi(a)}}{\forall x \phi(x)} \qquad \dfrac{a}{\cancel{a}}$$

The familiar rule may then simply be regarded as the result of omitting the middle line. However, in *stating* the derived rule, it is necessary to be explicit about the restrictions on the suppositions, since the general requirement of Coherence will not now automatically take care of them.

The standard rule of generalization is, of course, improper. But within the context of the present system, we may think of this impropriety as deriving from the impropriety of the Rule of Liberation. The basic, or strict, rule of generalization is itself proper.

It is interesting, in this regard, to note that there is evidence that the improper rule has a derived status in informal reasoning. Suppose we wish to establish that all triangles have interior angles summing to 180°. We start:

(1) Let ABC be an arbitrary triangle.

Next, we go through the body of the reasoning and reach the intermediate conclusion:

(2) ABC has interior angles summing to 180°.

We now feel uncomfortable in going straight to the desired conclusion:

(4) All triangles have interior angles summing to 180°.

Instead, we feel the need to interpolate some such remark as:

(3) But ABC can be any triangle we choose.

My analysis of the situation is this. At (1), we introduce an occupied A-object. At (2), we are reluctant to make the improper inference to (4). Instead, we first use (3) to vacate the A-object and then make a proper inference to (4).

Although other accounts of the role of the interpolant could be given, the present account is the one that strikes me as most in accord with our ordinary intuitions on the matter.

9

Quine

We now embark on a study of systems that contain a rule of existential instantiation. In this chapter we deal with the system proposed by Quine in *Methods of Logic* [52], and in the next chapter with the system Copi tried to formulate in *Symbolic Logic* [54] and that was successfully formulated by Kalish [67] and Prawitz [67]. Our plan in both chapters is more or less the same. We shall give a standard formulation of the systems and then one in terms of what I call dependency diagrams; we shall present soundness and completeness results in terms of the generic semantics; and finally we shall make critical remarks on the systems in the light of the semantics.

First Formulation

We may suppose that the system Q has the standard propositional rules for a system of natural deduction, although this is not in keeping with Quine's own presentation. The quantification rules may be schematically represented as follows:

$$\text{UI } \frac{\forall x \phi(x)}{\phi(t)} \qquad \text{UG } \frac{\phi(a)}{\forall x \phi(x)}$$

$$\text{EI } \frac{\exists x \phi(x)}{\phi(a)} \qquad \text{EG } \frac{\phi(t)}{\exists x \phi(x)}$$

Here, as before, $\phi(a)$ is the result of substituting a for all free occurrences of x in $\phi(x)$.

The rules come in pairs for each quantifier; one is a rule of instantiation (I), and the other a rule of generalisation (G). Note that UI is the same as ∀E and EG the same as ∃I. The difference in notation is used merely to indicate the difference in the kind of system from which the rule originates.

Without further restriction, the application of these rules quickly leads to the derivation of invalid sequents. For example, from $\exists x\phi(x)$ we may obtain $\phi(a)$ by EI; and from $\phi(a)$ we may then obtain $\forall x\phi(x)$ by UG. The system is therefore equipped with various restrictions designed to block the formation of these derivations.

One is the same as for the Gentzen system G:

LR (Local Restriction)
The A-letter a does not occur in $\phi(x)$ in any application of the rules UG and EI.

The other restrictions are peculiar to Quine's system. In contrast to LR, they are of a global rather than a local character; they concern not merely the immediate context in which the rule is applied but also its relation to the rest of the derivation.

To state the further restrictions, we shall need some terminology. Let $\phi(a)/\forall x\phi(x)$ or $\exists x\phi(x)/\phi(a)$ be an application of the rules UG or EI respectively. If a does not actually occur in $\phi(a)$, then the given application of the rule is said to be *vacuous*. In case the application is non-vacuous, a is said to be its *instantial term* and the A-letters of $\phi(x)$ its *given terms*. For example, in the application $\exists xFxbc/Fabc$ of EI, a is the instantial term and b, c are the given terms.

Let D be a *potential* derivation, *i.e.* one in accordance with the propositional and with the unrestricted version of the quantificational rules. Relative to such a derivation, we say that the A-letter a *immediately depends upon* b – in symbols, a ≪ b – if, in some non-vacuous application of UG or EI in D, a is the instantial term and b is a given term. Under the proposed semantics, a will actually denote an A-object that immediately depends upon the A-object denoted by b. But it should be noted that the present notion is purely syntactic.

The global restrictions on a potential derivation now take the following form:

(F) Flagging
No A-letter shall be an instantial term twice, *i.e.* to two applications of a rule;

Ordering

It should be possible to order the distinct instantial terms in such a way $a_1, a_2, \ldots, a_n$ that, for each i from 1 to n, none of $a_{i+1}, \ldots, a_n$ immediately depend upon a_i.

The derivations of Q are then those potential derivations that conform to the restrictions LR, Flagging and Ordering. It should be noted that, in contrast to G, no restriction is placed on the assumptions in any application of UG.

A Reformulation

Small differences aside, the above restrictions are the same as those in Quine's [52], p. 164. However, the ordering condition is not especially perspicuous and it is in fact possible to give it a much more perspicuous formulation.

First, we may note that Ordering is trivially equivalent to:

> It is possible to order the distinct instantial terms in such a way $a_1, a_2, \ldots, a_n$ that a_j does not immediately depend upon a_i for $1 \leqslant i \leqslant j \leqslant n$.

It would appear that Quine only chose the clumsier formulation because it stated most directly what was required for his Soundness proof.

By reversing the order of the terms $a_1, a_2, \ldots, a_n$, the new formulation may receive the form:

(O) It is possible to order the distinct instantial terms in such a way $a_1, a_2, \ldots, a_n$ that a_i does not immediately depend upon a_j for $1 \leqslant i < j \leqslant n$.

In future, we shall take this as our canonical formulation of Ordering.

To further simplify the condition, we need to extend the notion of immediate dependence. Say that the A-letter a *(syntactically) depends upon* b – in symbols, a ≺ b – if there is a sequence of A-letters $a_1, \ldots, a_n, n > 1$ such that $a = a_1$, $b = a_n$ and, for each $i = 1, \ldots, n-1$, a_i immediately depends upon a_{i+1}. So we see that the relation of dependence is the strict ancestral of the relation ≪ of immediate dependence. Under the generic semantics, the A-object denoted by a will depend upon the A-object denoted by b. We have called both the syntactic and the semantic relations dependence, but no confusion should arise as to which is intended in any given context.

Ordering may now take the form:

(AS) Anti-symmetry
The relation < of dependence is anti-symmetric, *i.e.* never a < b and b < a for distinct A-letters a and b.

Although the proof of equivalence is quite straightforward, it may be worthwhile to spell it out in some detail. It rests on two facts. The first is the equivalence of Ordering to:

(O^+) It is possible to order *all* of the distinct A-letters occurring in a derivation in such a way $a_1, a_2, \ldots, a_n$ that a_i does not immediately depend upon a_j for $1 \leq i < j \leq n$.

For given an ordering that satisfies (O^+), we may get an ordering that satisfies (O) by removing the A-letters that are not instantial terms; and given an ordering that satisfies (O), we may get an ordering that satisfies (O^+) by adding all the A-letters that are not instantial terms in any order at the beginning.

The second fact may be stated in general terms as follows:

Lemma 9
Let (X, R) and (X, R^*) be two finite relational structures with R^* the strict ancestral of R. Then (X, R) satisfies the condition (a) that there is an ordering $x_1, x_2 \ldots x_n$ of the distinct elements of X such that $x_i R x_j$ for $1 \leq i < j \leq n$ iff (X, R^*) satisfies the condition (b) that R^* is anti-symmetric.

Proof
First assume that (X, R) satisfies (a) with respect to the ordering $x_1, x_2, \ldots, x_n$. Then if $x_i R^* x_j$, for $i \neq j$, x_j must occur earlier in the ordering than x_i, *i.e.* $j < i$. (This may be proved by induction on the n for which $x_i R^n x_j$.) But then R^* must be anti-symmetric. For suppose $x_i R^* x_j$ and $x_j R^* x_i$, for $i \neq j$. Then $j < i$ and $i < j$, which is a contradiction.

Now assume that R^* is anti-symmetric. Call an element y of a relational structure (Y, S) *maximal* if for no z is $y S z$ and $z \neq y$. Then the ordering $x_1, x_2, \ldots, x_n$ satisfying (a) may be produced as follows. Let x_1 be a maximal element of (X, R^*). Since (X, R^*) is a finite partial ordering, there must be such an element. Suppose now that $x_1, x_2 \ldots x_i$ have been produced for $i < n$. Let x_{i+1} be a maximal element of the restriction (X_i, R_i^*) of (X, R^*) to $X - \{x_1 x_2, \ldots, x_i\}$. Again, there is such an element, since the restriction is also a finite partial ordering. It is then clear that the resulting ordering $x_1, x_2, \ldots, x_n$ satisfies (a); for if $x_i R x_j$, for $j > i$, then x_i was not maximal in the restriction (X_i, R_i^*) after all.

Given these facts, the equivalence between Ordering and Antisymmetry follows upon letting X be the set of A-letters occurring in a given derivation and letting R be the relation $\ll$ of immediate syntactic dependence.

The formulation of the rules can be simplified even further if we combine (LR) with the global restriction (O). Stated in terms of the relation of syntactic dependence, the local restriction amounts to:

(LR') No A-letter in a derivation should immediately depend upon itself, that is to say the relation $\ll$ is irreflexive.

But a quick check on the above proof immediately confirms the following result:

The finite relational structure (X, R) satisfies (a) and is irreflexive iff the structure (X, R^*) is irreflexive.

Therefore (LR) and (0) may be combined into the single condition

(I) Irreflexivity
The relation $<$ of syntactic dependence is irreflexive.

In the intended interpretation, the designated A-objects will stand in a relation of object dependence just in case their designators stand in the relation of syntactic dependence. Therefore (I) will amount to the condition that no designated object depend upon itself and (AS) to the condition that no two differently designated A-objects depend upon one another.

Dependency Diagrams

The advantage of the formulation (AS) over (O) or of (I) over (LR) & (O) is not merely one of perspicuity. The satisfaction of (O) is rather hard to determine, since it requires the discovery of an ordering and a verification that it conforms to the desired condition. The satisfaction of (AS) or of (I), on the other hand, is relatively easy to determine, since it requires only that we observe no cycles in the chains of immediate syntactic dependence.

Indeed, once the conditions are formulated in the form (F) & (I), it is rather easy to keep a running check on their satisfaction in terms of what I call *dependency diagrams*. The use of such diagrams is illustrated by the following derivation of $\exists y \forall v \exists u \exists x Fxyuv$ from $\exists x \exists y \forall u \forall v Fxyuv$:

(1) $\exists x \exists y \forall u \forall v\ Fxyuv$ Assumption
(2) $\exists y \forall u \forall v\ Fayuv$ 1, EI
(3) $\forall u \forall v\ Fabuv$ 2, EI
(4) $\forall v\ Fabdv$ 3, UI
(5) $Fabdc$ 4, UI
(6) $\exists x Fxbdc$ 5, EG
(7) $\forall u \exists x Fxbuc$ 6, UG
(8) $\forall v \forall u \exists x Fxbuv$ 7, UG
(9) $\exists y \forall v \forall u \exists x Fxyuv$ 8, EG

In this example, the successive partial diagrams:

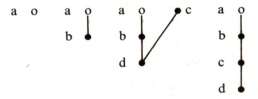

are drawn at the lines (2), (3), (7) and (8) respectively.

In general, a dependency diagram has the following form. It consists of a finite number of nodes scattered on the page. These nodes may be either points or circles. Each node is labelled with an A-letter, one node for each A-letter. One node may be connected to another node by an upward line that traverses no other nodes. In this case, the first node is said to be *linked directly below* the second node. No circular node is linked directly below another node; and no node linked directly below a node is also linked indirectly below that node, *i.e.* connected to it by a sequence of upward lines.

In a dependency diagram, the upward lines signify dependence; the circular nodes indicate that the A-object has been restricted (though without any ensuing dependence on other A-objects).

A dependency diagram is *appropriate for* a given derivation if the following conditions are met:

(i)   to each non-vacuous application of UG or EI there corresponds a single node labelled with its instantial term; and to each given term, in an application of UG to EI, there corresponds a node labelled with that term;

(ii) each label to a node is either an instantial or a given term to an application of UG or EI;

(iii) the node labelled a is linked below the node labelled b iff a depends upon b;

(iv) a top node is circular if its label is an instantial term; otherwise it is a point.

It is readily seen that if a potential derivation has an appropriate diagram then it conforms to the conditions (F) and (I). For no A-letter can be an instantial term to two applications of one of the rules EI or UG by (i) and the requirement that each A-letter label only one node. Further, by (i) and (ii) and that same requirement, the terms in the field of $<$ are in one–one correspondence with the nodes they label; and by (iii) this correspondence constitutes an isomorphism between the relation $<$ and the relation of being below. But the nature of the physical page is such that no node can be below itself. And so no term depends upon itself.

Conversely, we may show that each potential derivation conforming to the conditions (F) and (I) has an appropriate dependency diagram. For suppose $<$ is the relation of dependence for the derivation. Define 'a $<'$ b' by 'a $<$ b and for no c is a $<$ c $<$ b'. Draw the diagram for $<'$ in the obvious way, taking care to make the top-most nodes for instantial terms circular. Then it is readily shown that this diagram is appropriate for the derivation.

It is possible to construct the appropriate diagram in step with the derivation. At the start, the null diagram is 'drawn'. Now let us suppose we have reached a certain stage in the construction of the derivation and its associated diagram. If the next step of the derivation is not a non-vacuous application of UG or EI, then the diagram is left alone. If the next step consists of a non-vacuous application of either of these rules, then what happens depends upon the exact nature of the step and how the diagram has so far been constituted. Suppose that the instantial term is a and the given terms are $b_1, \ldots, b_n$. There are two cases:

Case 1

a does not yet occur in the diagram. If $n = 0$, *i.e.* if a has no immediate dependees, then a circular node with label a must be added to the diagram. If $n > 0$, *i.e.* if a has dependees, then point nodes for those of $b_1, b_2 \ldots b_n$ that do not already appear in the diagram must be added to the diagram, a point node for a must be positioned below the nodes for b_1 b_2 ... b_n, and lines should be drawn to link the node for a below the nodes for $b_1, \ldots, b_n$. (This means that the node for a will be directly linked below those of the nodes for $b_1, \ldots, b_n$ that are not linked above other nodes in the group.)

Case 2
a already appears in the diagram. a must then label a point that is not linked below any other node. If $n = 0$, the node for a should be converted into a circle. If $n > 0$, then none of the nodes for those of $b_1, b_2, \ldots, b_n$ that occur in the diagram may be linked below the node for a. If any of these nodes does not occur above the node for a, then the nodes in the diagram must be repositioned so that these nodes do occur above the node for a. New point nodes for those of $b_1, b_2, \ldots, b_n$ that do not already occur in the diagram must now be added above the node for a. Lines must then be drawn so as to link the node for a below the nodes for $b_1, \ldots, b_n$ (taking care not to add superfluous lines).

As the rules for constructing the accompanying diagram have been described, they also provide a running check on whether the derivation is correct. We see that the Flagging restriction must be satisfied: for if a does not already appear in the diagram, it cannot have been used as an instantial term; and if it appears in the diagram, but as a top-most point, then again it cannot have been used as an instantial term. We see that irreflexivity must be satisfied: for its violation would require that the same node be upwardly linked to itself, which is physically impossible.

The description of the actual procedure for constructing the diagrams may appear rather complicated. But the principle behind it is clear enough; one so modifies the diagram as to make it appropriate for the derivation. Once this principle is grasped, the exact nature of the procedure can be picked up from a few well-chosen examples.

The implementation of the procedure may also seem rather complicated. Lines can criss-cross; and when nodes are repositioned, whole parts of the diagram may need to be erased and duplicated elsewhere. These difficulties may be mitigated in actual practice: with few terms to deal with, lines will tend not to criss-cross; and by anticipating the course of the derivation, the need for subsequent re-alignment may to some extent be reduced. But it must be admitted that, when re-alignment occurs, its implementation can be clumsy.

However, these difficulties are nothing to the problems that arise when there is no diagram for checking correctness. Conformity to Flagging may be checked by Quine's device of flagging variables. But when it comes to Irreflexivity or Ordering, there would seem to be nothing better but to go through the whole derivation, isolate the applications of UG and EI, work out what the relationships of immediate dependence are, and then see whether its ancestral is irreflexive. Quine has suggested as a 'rule of thumb' ([52], p. 164) that you 'pick your letters so that each flagged variable is alphabetically later than all other free variables of the line it flags'. Conformity to Ordering is then assured. But the difficulty now takes another form. Variables (or A-letters) may be introduced into a derivation prior to their use as an instantial term. So one must so choose them that subsequent conformity to the alphabetic requirement can be maintained. For example, in the previous derivation, it is necessary that the A-letter introduced at line (4) be alphabetically later than the A-letter introduced at line (5). If one blunders, then the whole derivation must be re-written when it comes to the point at which conformity to the alphabetic condition is required. If, for example, one had (quite naturally) in the previous derivation introduced c at line (4) and d at line (5), then, when it came to line (7), the derivation would have had to be rewritten, with c interchanged with d.

It seems, then, that dependency diagrams constitute one of the most effective ways of checking the correctness of derivations. Indeed, we may think of the diagram as embodying just that information from the rest of the derivation as is required to check the correctness of the current line. So a complete survey of the whole derivation may, in this way, be replaced by a simple check on its diagram.

In the light of these advantages, the dependency diagrams would appear to have great pedagogic value as a way of presenting derivations within the system Q. They provide a simple, natural and unified method for checking the correctness of derivations, one that is readily mastered and relatively easily implemented. When combined with the semantics that is about to be given, they impose upon a derivation a structure that both motivates its development and gives it sense.

Semantics

We now wish to provide a generic interpretation for the system Q, one that will render each line of a derivation valid and each application of a rule sound.

Let us first provide an informal motivation for the semantics. The problematic rules are EI and UG; and so let us deal with each in turn. With EI, we pass from $\exists x\phi(x)$ to $\phi(a)$. Consider first the case in which we argue from the *supposition* $\exists x\phi(x)$ to $\phi(a)$, with no A-letters other than a occurring in $\phi(a)$. Since we want later to be able to conditionalize, we want so to interpret a that $\exists x\phi(x) \supset \phi(a)$ is true. So suppose that $\exists x\phi(x)$ is true. Then this means that the values of *a* must be confined to the individuals that satisfy $\phi(x)$. So, in general, *a* will be a restricted A-object. Now, in principle, *a* could take any set of individual ϕ-ers as its values. But there is no good reason to countenance one individual ϕ-er as a value rather than any other. Moreover, *a* must take some individuals as values; for otherwise *a* will be a null A-object and the Extendibility requirement will not be satisfied. Therefore the only natural choice for *a* is the A-object whose values are all of the individual ϕ-ers, what one might call the arbitrary ϕ-er.

Suppose now that $\exists x\phi(x)$ is false. Then it does not matter what *a* is, since there is no danger of the conditional failing to be true. There is no good reason for *a* to take one value rather than another; and, for the same reasons as before, a should take some value. So the only natural choice for *a* is an A-object which takes all individuals as values, what we have termed a universal or value-unrestricted A-object.

It is important to note that it is only in the case that $\exists x\phi(x)$ is true that *a* turns out to be the arbitrary ϕ-er. If we wanted to give a compendious description of *a*, one that covers both cases, we might call it the putative arbitrary ϕ-er. It is the A-object that ϕ's if anything does.

Consider now the case in which $\exists x\phi(x)$ contains other A-letters, say the A-letters b and c. $\phi(x)$ may then be written in the form $\phi(x, b, c)$. Since again we want to be able to conditionalize, we must so interpret the A-letter a that $\exists x\phi(a, b, c) \supset \phi(a, b, c)$ is true. In this case it is natural to treat *a* as an object dependent upon *b* and *c*; for what values *a* can take will be constrained by what values *b* and *c* take. It is also clear that, for given values of *b* and *c,* the values of *a* should be constrained in the same way as before. So we see that *a* is most naturally taken to be an A-object dependent upon *b* and *c* (and whatever *b* and *c* depend upon) and such that, for given values *j, k* of *b, c, a* will take all values *i* for which $\exists x\phi(x,j,k) \supset \phi(i,j,k)$ is true, i.e. all values *i* for which $\phi(i,j,k)$ is true should $\exists x\phi(x,j,k)$ be true and all values whatever should $\exists x\phi(x,j,k)$ be false.

Of course, in general, $\phi(a)$ will be derived, not from the *supposition* $\exists x\phi(x)$, but from a conclusion $\exists x\phi(x)$ that itself depends upon other suppositions. But it seems natural to suppose that the interpretation of a should not depend upon the status of the premiss $\exists x\phi(x)$ as supposition or conclusion. And so, in this case, the intepretation of *a* may be determined in the same way as before.

This brings us to applications of the rule UG. As before, first consider a case in which we argue from the supposition $\phi(a)$ to $\forall x\phi(x)$, with no A-letter other than a occurring in $\phi(a)$. One might suppose that one is here arguing from the truth of $\phi(a)$, for *a* an unrestricted A-object, to the truth of $\forall x\phi(x)$, in strict analogy to the Gentzen system G. But the principles of the present system give the lie to this interpretation. For in Q there is no requirement that, in generalizing, the instantial term not occur in the suppositions upon which the premisses depend. So we may pass to $\forall x\phi(x)$ from the *supposition* that $\phi(a)$; and so, by conditionalizing, we may then obtain $\phi(a) \supset \forall x\phi(x)$. But this formula is not in general true for *a* a value-unrestricted A-object.

So let us ask: What must *a* be for $\phi(a) \supset \forall x\phi(x)$ to be true? If $\forall x\phi(x)$ is false (in the underlying model), then $\phi(i)$ must be false for any value *i* of *a;* while if $\forall x\phi(x)$ is true, the value of *a* can be anything. It follows, by the same considerations as before, that the only natural choice for *a* is an A-object that has all non-ϕ-ers as its values in case $\forall x\phi(x)$ is false and that has all individuals whatever as its values in case $\forall x\phi(x)$ is true. So we see that far from being a universal A-object, *a* is best thought of as a arbitrary (putative) counterexample to the formula $\forall x\phi(x)$. The intuitive justification for the rule UG in Quine's system is not that everything must ϕ if the arbitrary individual ϕ's, but that everything must ϕ if even the arbitrary counterexample to the generalization $\forall x\phi(x)$ ϕ's.

The extension of the interpretation to the other cases proceeds in the same way as before. If $\phi(a)$ contains other A-letters, then *a* is still a putative counterexample to $\forall x\phi(x)$, but dependent upon the other A-objects mentioned in $\forall x\phi(x)$; and if $\phi(a)$ is not a supposition, then *a* must be interpreted in the same way as it would if $\phi(a)$ were a supposition.

After these informal remarks, let us now give a more rigorous formulation of the semantics for the system. An A-model $\mathfrak{M}^*$ is said to be *suitable for* a derivation D if:

(i) $a \neq b$ for a and b distinct A-letters of D;

(ii) if the inference $\exists x \phi(x, b_1, \ldots, b_n)/\phi(a, b_1, \ldots, b_n)$ occurs in D, then a is an A-object for which:
 (a) $|a| = [b_1, \ldots, b_n]$, i.e. $a < c$ iff $b_1 = c$ or $b_i < c$ for $i = 1, 2, \ldots, n$, and
 (b) for any v with domain $|a|$, $w = v \cup \{\langle a, i \rangle\} \in V$ iff $\mathfrak{M} \models w(\forall x \phi(x, b_1, \ldots, b_n) \supset \phi(a, b_1, \ldots, b_n))$;

(iii) if the inference $\phi(a, b_1, \ldots, b_n)/\forall x \phi(x, b_1, \ldots, b_n)$ occurs in D, then a is an A-object for which:
 (a) $|a| = [b_1, \ldots, b_n]$, and
 (b) for any v with domain $|a|$, $w = v \cup \{\langle a, i \rangle\} \in V$ iff $\mathfrak{M} \models w(\phi(a, b_1, \ldots, b_n) \supset \forall x \phi(x, b_1, \ldots, b_n))$;

(iv) a is unrestricted for each non-instantial letter a in D.

It should be noted that, in contrast to the semantics for G or H, the suitability of a model is relative to a derivation. So it is not as if we could fix the interpretation of the A-letters prior to the construction of any derivation. Rather, the interpretation of the A-letters gets determined in the course of the derivation.

The notion of suitability may also be explained in terms of definitional realizability. With each derivation D we may associate a system of definitions $\mathfrak{S}$. Its members are:

(i) all pairs $(a, \exists x \phi(x) \supset \phi(x))$, where $\exists x \phi(x)/\phi(a)$ is a non-vacuous application of EI in D;

(ii) all pairs $(a, \phi(x) \supset \forall x \phi(x))$, where $\phi(a)/\forall x \phi(x)$ is a non-vacuous application of UG in D;

(iii) all pairs (a, Λ), where a is an A-letter of D that is not an instantial term.

The derivation provides us, in effect, with a definition of each of the A-letters that it uses. It is now a trivial matter to show that an A-model $\mathfrak{M}^*$ is suitable for D iff it realizes the system of definitions $\mathfrak{S}$ associated with D.

It should also be noted that there is a close connection between the dependency relation for a suitable model $\mathfrak{M}^*$ and the dependency relation for its derivation D. The A-letter a will syntactically depend upon b in D just in case the A-object a objectually depends upon b in $\mathfrak{M}^*$. Thus the dependency diagram for a derivation will actually have semantic significance as a graph for the objectual dependence relation.

Soundness

We wish to establish results on both the line and the line-to-line Soundness of Q.

First, we need a result on the extendibility of suitable models.

Lemma 10
Let $\mathfrak{M}^*$ be a suitable model for the derivation D. Then $\mathfrak{M}^*$ is extendible over the class of A-objects designated by the A-letters in D.

Proof
By Theorem I.19 it suffices to show that each definition in the system of definitions associated with D is total in $\mathfrak{M}$. For definitions of the form (a, Λ), this is obvious; and for definitions of the form (a, $\exists x \phi(x) \supset \phi(x)$) and (a, $\phi(x) \supset \forall x \phi(x)$), it follows from the logical truth of $\exists y (\exists x \phi(x) \supset \phi(y))$ and $\exists y (\phi(y) \supset \forall x \phi(x))$.

We may now show:

Theorem 11 (Line-to-line Soundness for Q)
Let D be a derivation in Q and $(\Delta_1, \phi_1), \ldots, (\Delta_n, \phi_n)/(\Delta, \phi)$ an argument pattern corresponding to an application of one of the rules in D. Then the inference $\Delta_1 \supset \phi_1, \ldots, \Delta_n \supset \phi_n / \Delta \supset \phi$ is truth-to-truth valid relative to the class X of suitable models $\mathfrak{M}^*$ for D.

Proof
There are three cases:

(1) The inference rule is classical, *i.e.* not UG or EI. Then the inference $(\Delta_1, \phi_1), \ldots, (\Delta_n, \phi_n)/(\Delta, \phi)$ is classically valid. By Lemma 10, each suitable $\mathfrak{M}^*$ is extendible over the set of A-objects mentioned in the inference. So by Theorem I.14, the inference is truth-to-truth validated in X.

(2) The inference rule is UG. So it must be shown that $\Delta \supset \phi(a)/\Delta \supset \forall x \phi(x)$ is truth-to-truth valid relative to X. Now the

inference $\Delta \supset \phi(a), \phi(a) \supset \forall x\phi(x)/\Delta \supset \forall x\phi(x)$ is classically valid. So by Lemma 10 and Theorem I.14, the inference $\Delta \supset \phi(a), \phi(a) \supset \forall x\phi(x)/\Delta \supset \forall x\phi(x)$ is truth-to-truth valid relative to X. But by clause (iii) in the definition of 'suitable', $\phi(a) \supset \forall x\phi(x)$ is truth-to-truth valid relative to X. It therefore follows that $\Delta \supset \phi(a)/\Delta \supset \forall x\phi(x)$ is truth-to-truth valid in X.

(3) The inference rule is EI. Similar to case (2).

Just as in the case of G, we may give a proof of line-to-line soundness that accords with a more plausible view of the role of suppositions in ordinary reasoning. We take validity to be case-to-case and, with respect to a division of the rules into proper and improper, we show that the proper inferences are valid and the improper inferences preserve validity. However, in striking contrast to the case of G, there is now no difficulty in classifying UG as a proper rule: for it is immediate from the definition of 'suitable' that each application $\phi(a)/\forall x\phi(x)$ of UG is valid in the class of suitable models. So we may secure the propriety of the inference $\phi(a)/\forall x\phi(x)$, not by insisting upon a truth-to-truth concept of validity, but by appropriately modifying the interpretation of the instantial terms. For the same reason, there is little point in distinguishing between vacant and occupied A-letters, since all of the A-letters in a derivation can be assumed to be occupied compatibly with the propriety of the inferences falling under the rules UG and EI.

From Theorem 10, we may obtain:

Theorem 12 (Line Soundness for Q)
Let D be a derivation of the sequent (Δ, ϕ) in Q. Then $\Delta \supset \phi$ is generically valid in the class X of suitable models.

Proof
For each uninferred sequent (Γ, ψ) of D, $\Gamma \supset \psi$ is truth-to-truth valid relative to X since $\psi \in \Gamma$. The property of being truth-to-truth valid relative to X is preserved by the inferences of Theorem 10 that correspond to the applications of the rules in D. Therefore (Δ, ϕ) is truth-to-truth valid in X.

As before, the interest of our soundness results depends upon the existence of suitable models. But this may be established on the basis of our theory of definition.

Lemma 13

For any classical model $\mathfrak{M}$ and derivation D from Q, there is an A-model $\mathfrak{M}^*$ that is based upon $\mathfrak{M}$ and suitable for D.

Proof

Let $\mathfrak{S}$ be the system of definitions associated with the derivation D, and recall that a model $\mathfrak{M}^*$ is suitable for D just in case it realizes the system $\mathfrak{S}$. So, given a classical model $\mathfrak{M}$, there will be an A-model $\mathfrak{M}^*$ suitable for D just in case there is an A-model $\mathfrak{M}^*$ that realizes the system $\mathfrak{S}$. Now, by Theorem I.17, there will be an A-model $\mathfrak{M}^*$ that realizes the system as long as the system satisfies the joint requirements of unequivocality and well-foundedness. But it may immediately be checked that $\mathfrak{S}$ conforms to unequivocality just in case D conforms to Flagging and $\mathfrak{S}$ conforms to well-foundedness just in case D conforms to Irreflexivity. So since any derivation D of Q conforms to Flagging and Irreflexivity, there will be a suitable A-model $\mathfrak{M}^*$ for D.

The above proof enables us to see the restrictions on the rules in a new light. For suppose we think of a derivation as implicitly defining the A-letters that it uses. Then we may see Flagging as merely the requirement that the same term shall not be defined twice and Ordering (or Irreflexivity) as merely the requirement that there be no definitional circles. Thus the restrictions turn out to be the counterparts to general desiderata upon a system of definitions.

Given the above existence result, classical soundness may be proved in exactly the same way as for Theorem 6.

If we examine this proof of soundness and of the other results leading up to it, we see that only the following properties are required of a model $\mathfrak{M}^*$ that interprets a given derivation D:

(i) a is value-unrestricted for each non-instantial A-letter a of D;

(ii) $\mathfrak{M}^*$ is extendible over the set of A-objects designated by the A-letters in D;

(iii) if the inference $\exists x \phi(x, b_1, \ldots, b_n)/\phi(a, b_1, \ldots, b_n)$ occurs in D, then for any $v = \{\langle b_1, j_1 \rangle, \ldots, \langle b_n, j_n \rangle\} \in V$, $v \cup \{\langle a, i \rangle\} \in V$ iff $\mathfrak{M} \models \exists x \phi(x, j_1, \ldots, j_n) \supset \phi(i, j_1, \ldots, j_n)$;

(iv) if the inference $\phi(a, b_1, \ldots, b_n)/\forall x \phi(x, b_1, \ldots, b_n)$ occurs in D, then for any $v = \{\langle b_1, j_1 \rangle, \ldots, \langle b_n, j_n \rangle\} \in V$, $v \cup \{\langle a, i \rangle\} \in V$ iff $\mathfrak{M} \models \phi(i, j_1, \ldots, j_n) \supset \forall x \phi(x, j_1, \ldots, j_n)$.

In this stipulation, no reference is made to the relation of dependence; and so it may be wondered what role reference to this relation plays in our proofs.

The answer lies in the proofs of Lemmas 10 and 13, which together yield the result that, for any classical model $\mathfrak{M}$ and derivation D, there is an extendible A-model $\mathfrak{M}^*$ that satisfies the conditions (i)–(iv) above. This conclusion could have been obtained on the basis of a special *ad hoc* argument – an argument that, in any case, would have had to make appeal to a dependency-type ordering on the A-letters. But by going through the notion of suitability, with its explicit reference to dependence, we can see the given argument as an instance of a more general type of argument and thereby both illuminate the given argument and provide an extension to other cases.

It should also be noted that there are certain informal advantages to be obtained from making explicit reference to dependence. Under the interpretation by a suitable A-model, the referents of the A-letters in a derivation are uniquely determined up to isomorphism (Theorem I.18). But under an interpretation by an $\prec$-less A-model that is subject to the conditions (i)–(iv) above, the referents of the A-letters are not uniquely determined up to isomorphism. There could be a single value-assignment v in the set V of all value assignments from the model $\mathfrak{M}^*$ or very many such value-assignments. So under the former interpretation, but not the latter, we can suppose that in a derivation we are dealing with definite A-objects and that no real choice need be made as to their identity.

Again, when reference is made to dependence, we can think of the behaviour of A-objects (the values they receive) as being explained from their identity. It is, for example, because a, b and c are the A-objects defined by the definitions (a, Λ), $(b, \exists xRxa \supset Rxa)$, $(c, \exists xSxa \supset Sxa)$ that they can simultaneously receive the values i, j and k when the statements $\exists xRxi \supset Rji$ and $\exists xSxi \supset Ski$ are true. Without reference to dependence, no such explanation is possible.

Completeness

Classical completeness may be proved for Quine's system in the usual way. But the question of generic completeness also arises.

The meaning of 'generic completeness', in this case, offers some difficulty. For it is not as if we are presented with an interpretation of the A-letters that is prior to any derivation and so it is not as if we could simply say what the valid sequents are supposed to be. However, we can insist that, insofar as a derivation fixes the interpretation of the A-letters, there should be, for each sequent that thereby becomes valid, a continuation of the derivation in which the sequent is established. Accordingly, let us say that a sequent (Δ, ϕ) is *valid relative to* a derivation D if it is case-to-case valid in all suitable A-models for D. Generic completeness then means that, for any derivation D (including the null derivation) and any sequent (Δ, ϕ) case-to-case valid in all suitable A-models for D, there is a continuation of D that establishes (Δ, ϕ).

Rather surprisingly, it turns out that Quine's system is not complete in this sense. For let D be the following derivation:

(1) $P \wedge \exists xFx$ Ass.
(2) $\exists xFx$ 1, $\wedge$ E
(3) Fa 2, EI

Then $\exists xFx \supset Fa$ is valid relative to D. But no continuation of D establishes $\exists xFx \supset Fa$ as a theorem. For take a classical model $\mathfrak{M}$ in which P is false, $\exists xFx$ is true, and Fi_0 is false, for i_0 the name of an individual i_0. Let D^+ be any continuation of D and suppose, for reductio, that D^+ establishes the theorem $\exists xFx \supset Fa$. Let $\mathfrak{S}^*$ be the system of definitions associated with D^+, but with the definition for line (3) replaced by $(a, (P \wedge \exists xFx) \supset Fx)$. It is then a straightforward matter to show that there is a model $\mathfrak{M}^*$ that realizes $\mathfrak{S}^*$, that $\mathfrak{M}^*$ validates each line of D^+, but that $\mathfrak{M}^*$ does not validate $\exists xFx \supset Fa$.

Incompleteness is usually regarded as an undesirable trait in a system. But in the present case it is not such a defect. For our main interest is in establishing sequents without instantial terms; and we shall only be interested in establishing sequents *with* instantial terms in so far as they help us establish sequents without them. Therefore our concern will be with classical, and not generic, completeness.

However, it is still of interest to construct systems that are generically sound and complete and that may therefore be regarded as a complete codification, not just of a part of classical logic, but also of a part of the theory of arbitrary objects. In regard to the present incompleteness phenomenon, two questions arise. First, which system is sound and complete for the present semantics? Second, for which semantics is the present system sound and complete?

The first question may be answered by making a minor adjustment in the formulation of Flagging. As the restriction now stands, the same instantial term cannot be used in two different applications of EI (or UG), even though exactly the same inference is made in the two cases. Let us relax this aspect of the restriction. So we shall now require:

Weak Flagging
No A-letter shall be the instantial term to two inferences, unless those inferences are exactly the same.

Let the system resulting from this change in Flagging be called Q'. Then Line and Line-to-line Soundness for the new system may be established in the same way as for Q. But in contrast to the situation for Q, we now have:

Theorem 14
The system Q' is generically complete.

Proof
Let D be a derivation within Q' and assume that the sequent (Δ, ϕ) is valid relative to D. Let $\mathfrak{S}$ be the system of definitions associated with D, let $\mathfrak{S}^+ = \mathfrak{S} \cup \{(a, \Lambda): a$ is an A-letter that occurs in Δ or ϕ but is not a term of $\mathfrak{S}\}$, and let Γ consist of all formulas $\psi(a)$ for $(a, \psi(x))$ a definition of D. Given that (Δ, ϕ) is valid relative to D, it follows that the sequent $(\Delta, \Gamma \supset \phi)$ is classically valid. For suppose otherwise. Then for some classical model $\mathfrak{M}$ and function u from the A-letters of $\mathfrak{S}^+$ into I, $u(\Delta)$ and $u(\Gamma)$ are true in $\mathfrak{M}$ while $u(\phi)$ is false in $\mathfrak{M}$. It is clear that $\mathfrak{S}^+$, like $\mathfrak{S}$, conforms to unequivocality and well-foundedness; and so by Theorem I.17, there is an A-model $\mathfrak{M}^*$ that realizes $\mathfrak{S}^+$. Since $\mathfrak{S} \subseteq \mathfrak{S}^+$, $\mathfrak{M}^*$ is a suitable model for D. Now let v be a function defined, for each a in $\mathfrak{S}^+$, by $v(a) = u(a)$. Since $u(\Gamma)$ is true in $\mathfrak{M}$, v conforms to $\mathfrak{S}^+$. It is clear that $\mathfrak{S}^+$, like $\mathfrak{S}$, is a complete set of definitions; and since v is defined *exactly* on the A-objects designated by the A-letters in $\mathfrak{S}^+$, v satisfies the conditions of Lemma I.20. It therefore follows from that lemma that $v \in V$; and so is not true in $\mathfrak{M}^*$ after all.

Since $(\Delta, \Gamma \supset \phi)$ is classically valid, it follows from the classical completeness of Q, and hence of Q', that there exists a derivation E of the universal closure of $\Delta \supset (\Gamma \supset \phi)$. By rewriting the instantial terms used in E, we may ensure that none of them occurs in D. By continuing E in the obvious way, we obtain a derivation E' of $\Delta \supset (\Gamma \supset \phi)$. Let D^0 be the result of appending E' to D. Then it is clear that D^0 is still a derivation within Q'.

Each formula in Γ may now be derived. If the formula is $\exists x\phi(x) \supset \phi(a)$, its derivation is:

n	(n)	$\exists x\phi(x)$	Ass
n	$(n+1)$	$\phi(a)$	n, EI
	$(n+2)$	$\exists x\phi(x) \supset \phi(a)$	$n, n+1, \supset I$;

while if the formula is $\phi(a) \supset \forall x\phi(x)$, its derivation is:

n	(n)	$\phi(a)$	Ass
n	$(n+1)$	$\forall x\phi(x)$	n, UG
	$(n+2)$	$\phi(a) \supset \forall x\phi(x)$	$n, n+1, \supset I$.

Let D^1 be the result of appending to D^0 all of these derivations of the formulas in Γ. Given Weak Flagging, D^1 remains a derivation within Q'.

Finally, we may use propositional rules on the theorems of Γ and on the sequent $(\Delta, \Gamma \supset \phi)$ to obtain the desired derivation of (Δ, ϕ).

We come now to the second problem, of finding a semantics to fit the system Q. Here it does not seem possible to come up with such a simple or natural solution. Let D be a derivation within Q, a an instantial term from D, α the inference in which a is instantial, and Δ the set of suppositions to the inference α. We then let the *conditional* ϕ_a *for* a be the formula $\Delta \supset \phi(a)$ if the inference α is an application $\exists x\phi(x)/\phi(a)$ of EI and the formula $\Delta \supset \forall x\phi(x)$ if the inference α is an application $\phi(a)/\forall x\phi(x)$ of UG. Let $a_1, \ldots, a_n$ be all of the instantial terms of D in the order of their appearance; and let ϕ be the conjunction $\phi_{a_1} \wedge \ldots \wedge \phi_{a_n}$. We shall also write ϕ as $\phi(a_1, \ldots, a_n)$.

Let the system $\mathfrak{S}$ of definitions associated with D consist of:

(i) $(a_i, \exists x_{i+1} \ldots \exists x_n \phi(a_1, \ldots, a_{i-1}, x_i, x_{i+1}, \ldots, x_n))$ for $i = 1, \ldots, n$;

and

(ii) (a, Λ) for a a non-instantial term of D.

And call a model $\mathfrak{M}^*$ *suitable for* D if it realizes the associated system of definitions $\mathfrak{S}$. Then it may be shown, although we shall not go into details, that line soundness, line-to-line soundness, and generic completeness hold with respect to the given semantics.

Critical Remarks

Quine's system has peculiarities that make it appear unsatisfactory either as a system in its own right or as a good approximation to ordinary reasoning. The main source of these peculiarities is the rule UG. As we have already noted, this rule allows us to infer ∀xFx from the *supposition* Fa and then discharge the supposition to obtain Fa ⊃ ∀xFx. This corresponds to nothing in ordinary reasoning. We may say: let n be an arbitrary number and suppose that it is even. We cannot then go on to conclude that every number is even, let alone assert, unconditionally, that if n is even then every number is even.

This defect would not be so bad if every ordinary piece of reasoning could be represented in Quine's system; for then the extra inferences could be regarded as a 'rounding out' of ordinary practice. But there are, in fact, many ordinary cases of quantificational reasoning that cannot be represented in Quine's system. An example is the argument from ∀x(Fx ∧ Gx) to ∀xFx ∧ ∀xGx. This would ordinarily be represented as follows:

(1) ∀x(Fx ∧ Gx)   Assumption
(2) Fa ∧ Ga   1, UI
(3) Fa   2, ∧ E
(4) Ga   3, ∧ E
(5) ∀xFx   3, UG
(6) ∀xGx   4, UG
(7) ∀xFx ∧ ∀xGx   5, 6, ∧ I

However, such a derivation cannot go through in Quine's system since the Flagging restriction is violated; a is an instantial term to two applications of UG. Instead, the derivation is forced to take the following devious route:

(1) ∀x(Fx ∧ Gx)   Assumption
(2) Fa ∧ Ga   1, UI
(3) Fa   2, ∧ E
(4) Fb ∧ Gb   1, UI
(5) Gb   4, ∧ E
(6) ∀xFx   3, UG
(7) ∀xGx   5, UG
(8) ∀xFx ∧ ∀xGx   6, 7, ∧ I

So we see that Quine's system cannot be regarded as a rounding out of ordinary practice. Indeed, the two are strictly incomparable, with each containing inferences that correspond to nothing in the other.

This lack of deductive fit has an underlying semantical explanation. In ordinary reasoning, when we go from $\phi(a)$ to $\forall x \phi(x)$, a is meant to be an unrestricted A-object. We cannot therefore assert $\phi(a) \supset \forall x \phi(x)$, since that would have the force of the general claim $\forall x(\phi(x) \supset \forall x \phi(x))$. We can, on the other hand, generalise upon a as many times as we like. In Quine's system, when we go from $\phi(a)$ to $\forall x \phi(x)$, a is meant to be a putative counterexample to $\forall x \phi(x)$. We can therefore assert $\phi(a) \supset \forall x \phi(x)$, for if even the putative counterexample to $\forall x \phi(x)$ ϕ's then everything must ϕ. On the other hand, it is not permissible to generalise upon a more than once, since the interpretation of a is tied to the particular application of UG.

This unorthodox interpretation of the A-letters leads to peculiarities of its own. It is a natural requirement on a derivation containing A-names, or any other names, that we know what those names denote as soon as they are introduced; their interpretation should not depend upon what subsequently happens in the derivation. Now our ordinary practice, when construed in generic terms, seems to conform to this ban on retrospective interpretation. It is always clear, upon the introduction of an A-name, what A-object we are talking about. However, Quine's system, when construed generically, goes against the ban. Suppose that, at a given stage of a derivation, we have reached the conclusion $\phi(a)$, with a unflagged. We might then go on to infer $\forall x \phi(x)$; or we might go on to infer $\phi(a) \vee \psi(a)$ and, from that, $\forall x(\phi(x) \vee \psi(x))$. In the first case, a is interpreted as a putative counterexample to $\forall x \phi(x)$ and, in the second case, as a putative counterexample to $\forall x(\phi(x) \vee \psi(x))$. So what a means at a given stage of the derivation depends upon how the derivation is continued.

This semantical peculiarity is related to the difficulty in constructing dependency diagrams for derivations within Quine's system; and this, in its turn, is related to the more general difficulty in checking that derivations are correct. We have noted that the subsequent course of a derivation may require one not merely to extend the dependency diagram but to make bodily adjustments to it; new nodes are not merely added and suitably related to old nodes, but the old nodes may themselves be re-aligned. This is because the construction of a dependency diagram forces one to be explicit about the links among the different nodes and therefore about the dependency relations among the A-objects associated with them. Since we may not be sure, at a given stage of a derivation, exactly what A-objects we are talking about, the subsequent course of the derivation may compel us to revise our initial assay of the links.

It may be thought that such a problem can to a great extent be minimized. Although it lies in the nature of the case that the status of an instantial term to an application of UG will not be clear until after its introduction, it is possible to require that each such term be immediately followed upon its introduction by the relevant application of UG and also that each instantial term to an application of EI be immediately preceded, upon its introduction, by the relevant application of EI. For in place of a derivation that is not subject to this stricture, we may construct a new derivation in which we begin with a proof of all the conditionals $\phi(a) \supset \forall x \phi(x)$ and $\exists x \phi(x) \supset \phi(a)$ corresponding to the applications of UG and EI in the original derivation and in which we continue as in the original derivation but with applications of detachment replacing the applications of UG and EI. The derivations of the initial conditionals may be ordered in such a way as to be subject to the stricture, and, since there are no applications of UG or EI in the subsequent portion of the derivation, the whole derivation will also be subject to the stricture.

Such derivations do not put any great strains on the powers of semantical imagination. For when it comes to interpreting an instantial term, we either know what it means upon its introduction in the case of EI or immediately consequent upon its introduction in the case of UG.

However, such derivations are highly artificial. When it comes to derivations that we might actually construct, there will often be a great gap between the first appearance of an A-letter and the subsequent application of UG that fixes its interpretation. In the previous derivation, for example, it is only at line (6) that we know what the a at line (2) is, and it is only at line (7) that we know what the b at line (4) is.

What makes the derivations with the initial conditionals so artificial is that they are not well-motivated. It is not immediately clear, given the goal of deriving the final sequent, why the derivation should begin with the proofs of just those conditionals. In general, a well-motivated derivation is one that is structured according to an appropriate hierarchy of goals. For example, if our aim is to prove a conditional, we may follow the strategy of assuming the antecedent and inferring the consequent. Accordingly, we may place the assumption of the antecedent first and derivation of the consequent immediately prior to the inference of the final conditional. If now the consequent is a conjunction, we may follow the strategy of deriving each conjunct. Accordingly, we may put together derivations for each conjunct and place them immediately prior to the inference of the conjunction. Proceeding in this way, we can then structure the whole derivation according to an appropriate nesting of goals.

The notion of a well-motivated derivation would appear to be of general interest in the study of deductive systems and would appear to tie up with other, more familiar, notions, such as that of a normalised derivation. There are perhaps several different definitions of the notion that might be given. But whatever definition is finally settled on, it seems unlikely that a well-motivated derivation, within the context of Quine's system, would preserve the proximity between the first use of a term and its use as the instantial term in an application of UG.

10

Copi

In this chapter we shall deal with the system that Copi attempted to formulate in [54] and that was first correctly formulated by Kalish [67] and Prawitz [67]. (In [85], I omitted to mention Prawitz.) We shall present a standard formulation of the system and a reformulation in terms of dependency diagrams; we shall prove soundness with respect to the generic semantics; and finally we shall make a critical comparison between this system and Quine's.

The System

The system C has the usual propositional rules. The quantificational rules may be schematically represented in the same way as for Quine's system Q and with the same understanding concerning the relationship between the formulas $\phi(x)$, $\phi(t)$ and $\phi(a)$:

$$\text{UI} \ \dfrac{\forall x \phi(x)}{\phi(t)} \qquad\qquad \text{UG} \ \dfrac{\phi(a)}{\forall x \phi(x)}$$

$$\text{EI} \ \dfrac{\exists x \phi(x)}{\phi(a)} \qquad\qquad \text{EG} \ \dfrac{\phi(t)}{\exists x \phi(x)}$$

Insofar as it is separately stated, the local restriction on the rules is the same as for Quine's system. However, the global restrictions are different. For EI, there is one such restriction:

Novelty
In any application $\exists x \phi(x)/\phi(a)$ of EI, a is to be an A-letter that has not previously occurred in the derivation.

For UG, there are two global restrictions. Call an instantial term that comes from an application of EI an ∃-*instantial* term and one that comes from an application of UG an ∀-*instantial* term. Then the first restriction is:

Weak Flagging
No ∃-instantial term is also a ∀-instantial term.

Given Novelty, Weak Flagging can also be stated in the milder form:

No ∀-instantial term can previously have been used as an ∃-instantial term.

The second restriction is somewhat harder to state. Let us redefine the notion of immediate dependence for A-letters in a derivation by now saying that a *immediately depends* upon b – a ≪ b – if, in some application of EI, a is the instantial term and b is a given term. Note that the rule UG is no longer a source of dependency relations. We may call the present notion of dependence '∃-dependence' if it needs to be distinguished from the previous notion. As before, take *dependence* (<) to be the strict ancestral of immediate dependence. Then the second restriction on UG is:

Independence
In any application of UG, no A-letter occurring in either the conclusion or the suppositions to the inference can be identical to or depend upon the instantial term.

We may usefully think of this condition as consisting of three separate sub-conditions on an application of UG:

(i) the instantial term shall not occur in the conclusion or suppositions to the inference;

(ii) no given term shall ∃-depend upon the instantial term;

(iii) no A-letter in the suppositions shall ∃-depend upon the instantial term.

The two restrictions, Novelty and Independence, have been stated so as to incorporate the Local Restriction as a special case. They could have been stated so as to be independent of this further restriction; but this is not a formulation we shall adopt.

It will be instructive to consider a slightly more liberal version of the Novelty condition. This is:

∃-*Ordering*
The relation < of ∃-dependence is irreflexive.

The system that results from replacing Novelty with ∃-Ordering will be called C^+. Suppose Novelty is given. Then ∃-ordering must be satisfied. For if a ∃-depends upon b, b must occur earlier in the derivation than a. But then a term will not depend upon itself, since otherwise it would have to appear earlier in the derivation than itself. On the other hand, given ∃-ordering, Novelty may not be satisfied. So while every derivation of C is a derivation of C^+, not every derivation of C^+ is a derivation of C.

The Copi–Kalish systems C and C^+ are, in some ways, a cross between the Gentzen system G and the Quine system Q. Let the ∀-*derivations* of a system be those that contain no occurrences of ∃ (and hence use no applications of an ∃-rule), and let the ∃-*derivations* be those that contain no occurrences of ∀ (and hence use no applications of an ∀-rule). Then the ∀-derivations of C or C^+ and of G are the same (since the restrictions relating to dependency do no work); and the ∃-derivations of C^+ and of Q are the same (since the two notions of dependency then coincide). The ∃-derivations of C are not quite those of Q, since Novelty is a stricter requirement than Irreflexivity. However, parity between the two systems may be restored by adding Novelty as an additional constraint on Q. If the resulting system is called Q^-, then C and Q^- will have the same ∃-derivations.

The full systems, C and C^+, are not simply the result of putting together the fragments for ∀ and ∃. The restrictions themselves combine features of the restrictions for G and Q. As with G, there is no flagging restriction on the class of ∀-instantial terms; but, in line with Q, there is a weakened flagging restriction on the class of all instantial terms. As with G, we require that the instantial term in an application of UG not appear in the conclusion or suppositions to the inference (subcondition (i) above); but, in line with Q, we require that the given terms in an application of UG not depend upon the instantial term (subcondition (ii)). Subcondition (iii) may be seen as a sort of hybrid: as with G, it is imposed upon suppositions; but as with Q, it relates to dependence.

It might appear as if the restrictions on UG were stricter in C or C^+ than in Q. For if the given terms $b_1, \ldots, b_n$ in an application of UG do not depend upon the instantial term a, then adding the relationships $(a, b_1), \ldots, (a, b_n)$ to an otherwise irreflexive dependency relation will not make it irreflexive. So the Q-restriction will be satisfied as long as the C-restriction is; and yet the system C imposes further restrictions in the rule, that have no counterpart in Q. But this strengthening of the Q-restrictions is apparent only, for the dependency relation for the two systems is not the same. It may be that, for the first application of UG, the restrictions are tighter in C than in Q. But that application may have the effect of extending the dependency relation in Q, although it will have no such effect in C. Insofar as the dependency relation is extended, it will then be harder to satisfy the restrictions in the subsequent course of the derivation. So one might say, roughly, that the immediate impact of the restrictions is less in Q than in C, but that the subsequent impact is greater.

Dependency Diagrams

As with Quine's system, it is helpful to keep a running check on the correctness of derivations with the aid of dependency diagrams. The definition of a diagram is the same as before. We then say that a diagram is *appropriate for* a derivation D if:

(i) to each non-vacuous application of EI there corresponds a single node labelled with its instantial term; and to each given term, in an application of EI, there corresponds a node labelled with that term;

(ii) each label to a node is either an instantial or a given term to an application of EI;

(iii) the node labelled a is linked below the node labelled b iff a ∃-depends upon b;

(iv) a top node is circular if its label is an ∃-instantial term; and otherwise it is a point.

The intuitive significance of the lines and circles is the same as before: an upward line connecting an a-node to a b-node indicates that a depends upon b; a circular a-node indicates that a may be value-restricted.

The procedure for constructing an appropriate diagram for derivations within the system C is very simple. The diagram is left alone except at non-vacuous applications of the rule EI. So suppose there is such an application, with a the instantial term and $b_1, \ldots, b_n$ the given terms. We add to the diagram nodes for any of $b_1, \ldots, b_n$ that do not already appear, place an a-node beneath the resulting nodes, and draw lines to link it to the b_i-nodes (taking care not to add any superfluous lines). Since a is a new-comer to the derivation and hence to the diagram, there can be none of our previous problems over the realignment of nodes.

The procedure for C^+ is a little more complicated. Again, the diagram is only changed at non-vacuous applications of EI. If the instantial term a does not already occur in the diagram, then the modification to it is the same as before. However, if a does already occur in the diagram, then the position of nodes must be readjusted so that a can be linked up to nodes for the given terms $b_1, \ldots, b_n$.

In contrast to the situation for Quine's system, the existence of an appropriate dependency diagram does not guarantee the correctness of the derivation it accompanies. In the case of C, an appropriate diagram may exist even though the Novelty restriction is not satisfied; and in the case of both C and C^+, no account is taken of the restrictions on UG.

However, the diagram may still be used to keep a running check on the correctness of a derivation. Consider first the case of the system C. Suppose that, in the given derivation, we have reached an application of UG. Weak Flagging will continue to be satisfied as long as the instantial term either does not appear in the diagram or labels an upper-most point. Independence will continue to be satisfied as long as the instantial term does not occur in either the premises or suppositions to the inference (this information can be gathered entirely from the line in question) and as long as no A-letter in either premises or suppositions is the label for a node that is linked upwards to a node for a.

Suppose now that we have come to an application of EI. Then Novelty will be satisfied as long as the instantial term is new to the derivation. This is a simple matter to check, but it is not simply a matter of consulting the diagram and the line in question. If we want the diagram to encode all of the information from the rest of the derivation that is relevant to ascertaining the correctness of the current inference, then we may suppose that when an A-letter is introduced into a derivation, but not as an instantial or given term to an application of EI, then that A-letter is used to label a new node in the diagram that is not yet linked to any other node. The Novelty restriction will then be satisfied as long as the instantial term does not already occur in the diagram.

The case of the system C^+ is more complicated. The correctness of an application of UG may be checked in the same way as before. But when we come to an application of EI, there is a problem. For the dependency relation may change, and so previously correct applications of UG may not remain correct. One might recheck these applications, but this would violate our requirement that it be possible to check for the continued correctness of the derivation on the basis of the current line and the dependency diagram alone. An alternative is this. When we come to applications of UG, we draw mini-diagrams that link a node labelled by the instantial term up to nodes labelled by the A-letters occurring in the conclusion and suppositions to the inference. These mini-diagrams are kept separate from the main diagrams and are not meant to connect one to the other. The problem over preserving Independence can now be solved by insisting, at each application of EI, that in the main diagram a b-node never be linked up to an a-node when in a mini-diagram the a-node is linked up to a b-node.

Another alternative, if that is what it can be called, is not to let subsequent applications of EI impugn the correctness of previous applications of UG. This is, in effect, to change the definition of the system C^+. It turns out that the new system is, in fact, still sound; but this is not a matter we shall take up until we reach our general study of systems in Part III.

The construction of dependency diagrams and their use as a check on correctness may be illustrated by the following derivation of $\forall x \exists s \forall y \exists t Fxsyt$ from $\forall x \exists u \forall y \exists v Fxuyv$:

(1) $\forall x \exists u \forall y \exists v Fxuyv$ Assumption
(2) $\exists u \forall y \exists v Fauyv$ 1, UI
(3) $\forall y \exists v Facyv$ 2, EI
(4) $\exists v Facbv$ 3, UI
(5) $Facbd$ 4, EI
(6) $\exists t Facbt$ 5, EG
(7) $\forall y \exists t Facyt$ 6, UG
(8) $\exists s \forall y \exists t Fasyt$ 7, EG
(9) $\forall x \exists s \forall y \exists t Fxsyt$ 8, UG

In this example, the successive partial diagrams:

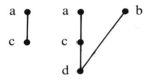

are drawn at lines (3) and (5). At line (7), we check that the a- and c-nodes are not linked upwards to the a-node.

The formulation of Copi's system may be further simplified by making a typographic distinction between ∀-instantial and ∃-instantial terms (*cf.* Borkowski–Słupecki [58], p. 88). Let us use a, b, c with variants for the former, and e, f, g with variants for the latter. This gives possibly *four* types of subject-term: variables of quantification; UG-terms; EI-terms; and individual terms. Intuitively, the letters a, b, c, ... are to be the names of unrestricted A-objects and e, f, g, ... the names of potentially restricted A-objects. Thus the distinction between UG- and EI-terms marks not a difference in semantic role or even in the category of objects denoted, but rather is used to signify whether there is the guarantee of a certain kind of denotation.

Armed with this typographic distinction, we may simplify the formulation of the rules and the construction of the dependency diagram. In the application $\phi(a)/\forall x \phi(x)$ of UG, we may require that a be a UG-term; and in the application $\exists x \phi(x)/\phi(e)$ of EI, we may require that e be an EI-term. The Weak Flagging restriction may then be dropped. Similarly, the distinction between point and circular nodes in the construction of dependency diagrams may also be dropped. What were formerly circular nodes will now be labelled by an EI-term and, by this fact alone, will be inadmissable as nodes for ∀-instantial terms. Furthermore, if it is required that no EI-term occur in a derivation until it has been introduced as an E-instantial term, then our previous difficulties over checking for Novelty disappear. For in the case of any occurrence of an EI-term at a step in a derivation, we may perform the following check: if the occurrence is non-instantial, then the term must already occur in the diagram; if the occurrence is instantial, then the term must not already occur in the diagram. This prevents both the violation of Novelty and the premature introduction of EI-terms.

The dependency diagrams, especially when used in connection with a typographic distinction between ∀- and ∃-instantial terms, provide a highly effective way of checking the correctness of derivations within C. It is certainly far superior to having no systematic method at all, *i.e.* to just surveying the derivation for dependencies at each application of UG. The only reasonably alternative I know of is to index the ∃-instantial terms with the ∀-instantial terms upon which they depend. This means, in effect, that the rule EI takes the form:

From $\exists x\phi(x)$ infer $\phi(a_{b_1,\ldots,b_n})$, where a is new and $b_1, \ldots, b_n$ are all of the ∀-instantial terms in $\exists x\phi(x)$.

The rule UG may then take the form:

From $\phi(a)$ infer $\forall x\phi(x)$, where a does not occur in $\forall x\phi(x)$ or any supposition.

We thus obtain a system of the sort proposed by Suppes [57] and Borkowski–Słupecki [58].

This formulation of the system has the advantage of reducing the rule UG to something familiar. But the method of letting the ∃-instantial terms carry the ∀-instantial terms upon which they depend as subscripts is very cumbersome. The same information is conveyed in a more structured and compact way by means of dependency diagrams.

In the light of these advantages and in the light of their semantic significance, we see that dependency diagrams should have great value as a method of presenting the derivations of C within the classroom.

Semantics

In view of the parallel treatment of Quine's system, we may be brief.

The basic idea behind the semantics is this: the ∀-instantial terms shall denote unrestricted A-objects; the ∃-instantial terms from inferences $\exists x\phi(x)/\phi(a)$ shall denote putative ϕ-ers, dependent upon the objects denoted by the given terms to the inference. Accordingly, let us say that an A-model $\mathfrak{M}^*$ is *suitable for* the derivation D in C or C^+ if:

(i) $a \neq b$ for distinct A-letters a and b of D;

(ii) a is unrestricted for each A-letter a of D not ∃-instantial in D;

(iii) if the non-vacuous inference $\exists x\phi(x)/\phi(a)$ occurs in D, then a realizes the definition $(a, \exists x\phi(x) \supset \phi(x))$ in $\mathfrak{M}^*$.

With each derivation D may be associated a system of definitions $\mathfrak{S}$ consisting of $(a, \exists x\phi(x) \supset \phi(x))$ for each non-vacuous application $\exists x\phi(x)/\phi(a)$ of EI in D and of (a, Λ) for each a in D that is not $\exists$-instantial. It is then readily shown that an A-model is suitable for a given derivation iff it realizes the associated system of definitions. If $\mathfrak{M}^*$ is suitable for D and a and b are A-letters of D then *a* will depend upon *b* in $\mathfrak{M}^+$ iff a syntactically depends upon b in D. As before, the dependency diagram for D will actually mirror the relevant portion of the dependency relation in $\mathfrak{M}^*$.

Soundness

We wish to establish line and line-to-line soundness for C and C^+.

First, we need a result on the extendibility of suitable models:

Lemma 16

Let $\mathfrak{M}^*$ be a suitable model for the derivation D. Then $\mathfrak{M}^*$ is extendible over the class of A-objects designated by the A-letters in D.

Proof

By Theorem I.19, it suffices to show that each definition in the system $\mathfrak{S}$ of definitions associated with D is total in $\mathfrak{M}$. For definitions of the form (a, Λ), this is obvious; and for definitions of the form $(a, \exists x\phi(x) \supset \phi(x))$, it follows from the logical truth of $\exists x(\exists x\phi(x) \supset \phi(x))$.

Theorem 17 (Line-to-line Soundness for C and C^+)

Let D be a derivation in C, and $(\Delta_1, \phi_1),\ldots,(\Delta_n, \phi_n)/(\Delta, \phi)$ an argument pattern corresponding to an application of one of the rules in D. Then the inference $\Delta_1 \supset \phi_1, \ldots, \Delta_n \supset \phi_n/\Delta \supset \phi$ is truth-to-truth validated relative to the class X of suitable models for D.

Proof

The extendibility property of suitable models takes care of the rules other than EI and UG. The rule EI is dealt with as before. This leaves UG.

So let $\phi(a, a_1, \ldots, a_n)/\forall x\phi(x, a_1, \ldots, a_n)$ be an application of UG in D with suppositions $\Delta(a_1, \ldots, a_n)$. Let $\mathfrak{M}^*$ be a suitable model for D; and suppose, for *reductio*, that $\Delta(a_1, \ldots, a_n) \supset \forall x\phi(x, a_1, \ldots, a_n)$ is not true in $\mathfrak{M}^*$. Then for some v' in V defined over $\{a_1, \ldots, a_n\}$,

$v'(\phi(a_1, \ldots, a_n) \supset \forall x(x, a_1, \ldots, a_n))$ is false in $\mathfrak{M}$. By Restriction we may suppose that v' is defined on $\{a_1, \ldots, a_n\}$. Given that v' has the diagram:

$$v': \frac{a_1 a_2 \ldots a_n}{i_1 i_2 \ldots i_n}$$

we then have that $\phi(i_1, \ldots, i_n) \supset \forall x \phi(x, i_1, \ldots, i_n)$ is false in $\mathfrak{M}$.

Let $a_1, a_2, \ldots, a_n, \ldots, a_p$, $p \geq n$, be the closure $[a_1, a_2, \ldots, a_n]$ of $\{a_1, a_2, \ldots, a_n\}$. By Partial Extendibility and Restriction, there is an assignment with diagram:

$$v: \frac{a_1 a_2 \ldots a_n \ldots a_p}{i_1 i_2 \ldots i_n \ldots i_p}$$

in V.

By the classical truth-condition for V, there is an $i \in I$ for which $\Delta(i_1, \ldots, i_n) \supset \phi(i, i_1, \ldots, i_n)$ is false in $\mathfrak{M}$. We wish to show that the assignment v^+ with diagram:

$$v^+: \frac{a\ a_1 \ldots a_p}{i\ i_1 \ldots i_p}$$

belongs to V.

Let u be the assignment with diagram:

$$u: \frac{a}{i}$$

We show that $v^+ \in V$ by showing that the assignments v and u can be pieced together.

Note first that $u \in V$. For by a value-unrestricted, $i \in VR(a)$; and so by Restriction, $u = \{\langle a, i \rangle\} \in V$.

Now note that the conditions for Piecing are satisfied. The domain $\{a\}$ of u is closed since a is independent; and the domain $\{a_1, \ldots, a_p\}$ of v is closed by stipulation. Also, u and v agree on common arguments, indeed have no common arguments: for by the syntactic restrictions, $a_i < a$ and $a_i = a$ fail for each $i = 1, 2, \ldots, n$; and so by the definition of suitability $a_i \prec a$ and $a_i = a$ fail for each $i = 1, 2, \ldots, n$.

We therefore have, by Piecing, that $v^+ = u \cup v \in V$; and the failure of the truth of $\Delta(a_1, \ldots, a_n) \supset \phi(a, a_1, \ldots, a_n)$ in $\mathfrak{M}^*$ follows.

The reader may find it instructive to compare the proofs of

Theorem 16 and Theorem II.2 for points of similarity and dissimilarity.

Again, we have:

Lemma 18

For any classical model $\mathfrak{M}$ and derivation D from C or C^+, there is an A-model $\mathfrak{M}^*$ that is based upon $\mathfrak{M}$ and suitable for D.

Proof

By Theorem I.17, it suffices to check that the system of definitions associated with D is unequivocal and well-founded. But unequivocally follows from Novelty (or Irreflexivity) and Weak Flagging; and well-foundedness follows from Novelty (or Irreflexivity) alone.

Note that, again, we may see some of the restrictions on the rules as having their origin in general desiderata upon a system of definitions.

From this theorem, classical soundness may be obtained in the usual way.

If we examine this proof of soundness and of the other results leading up to it, we see that only the following properties are required of a model $\mathfrak{M}^*$ that interprets a given derivation D:

(i) a is value-unrestricted for each A-letter a of D not ∃-instantial in D;

(ii) $\mathfrak{M}^*$ is extendible over the set of A-objects designated by the A-letters in D;

(iii)   if the inference $\exists x\phi(x, b_1, \ldots, b_n)/\phi(a, b_1, \ldots, b_n)$ occurs in D, then for any $v = \{(b_1, j_1), \ldots, (b_n, j_n)\} \in V$, $v \cup \{(a, i)\} \in V$ iff $\mathfrak{M} \models \exists x\phi(x, j_1, \ldots, j_n) \supset \phi(i, j_1, \ldots, j_n)$;

(iv)   if the inference $\phi(a, b_1, \ldots, b_n)/\forall x\phi(a, b_1, \ldots, b_n)$ occurs in D, then for any $v = \{(b_1, j_1), \ldots, (b_n, j_n)\} \in V$ and for any $i \in VR(a)$, $v \cup \{(a, i)\} \in V$.

In this stipulation, no reference is made to the relation of dependence; and so again, as in the case of Q, it may be wondered what role reference to such a relation plays in our proofs.

The answer, this time, lies in the proofs of Theorem 17 and Lemmas 16 and 18. Instead of deriving these results on the basis of special *ad hoc* arguments, they can be derived on the basis of very general considerations. The power of our methods reveals itself; for it is the same general considerations that serve to ground the results in this case as in the case of Q.

The same informal advantages also attach to using dependence: the identity of the A-objects is thereby determined; and the behaviour of the A-objects on the basis of that identity is thereby explained. It needs especially to be emphasized that the satisfaction of condition (iv) is explained in terms of the dependency status of the A-objects in question. For without such an explanation, the satisfaction of the condition would appear to be something of a mystery.

Vacancy Revisited

As in the case of the system G, we may give an account of validity that is more in accord with our ordinary view of suppositions. We may then see the special restrictions on the application of the rule UG as deriving from general restrictions on the construction of derivations.

As before, we effect a division of the A-letters into those that denote occupied A-objects and those that denote vacant A-objects. Accordingly, we let an *occupancy list* be a set of A-letters. Given an inference Δ/ϕ, an occupancy list L and a class of A-models X, we say that the inference Δ/ϕ is *valid under* L and *in* X if, for any model $\mathfrak{M}^* \in X$ and any $v \in V$ defined on the closure $[A_L]$ of A_L in $\mathfrak{M}^*$, $\mathfrak{M}^* \models_v \phi$ whenever $\mathfrak{M}^* \models \Delta$.

The important difference between the present and the previous definition is that it is now explicitly required that the domain of v be closed; if a is explicitly occupied (*i.e.* $a \in A_L$) and if a depends upon b, then b must be implicitly occupied (*i.e.* $b \in \text{Dm}(v)$). Of course, if, as was our original intention, the A-objects in A_L are to be independent, then the requirement will be automatically satisfied. So our old definition may simply be regarded as a special case of our new definition.

The additional requirement is intuitively plausible. We think of the A-objects as receiving their values in order: first the independent objects; then the objects that depend just upon the independent objects; and so on. Therefore a given A-object will not receive a value (be occupied) unless all of the A-objects upon which it depends also receive a value (are occupied).

There are compelling formal reasons for adopting the requirement. Given an occupancy list L, an A-model $\mathfrak{M}^*$ and a value-assignment $v \in V$ defined on A_L, there is a notion of truth which is given by the stipulation that $\mathfrak{M}^* \models_v \phi$. It is this notion of truth that is used in the above definition of validity. Now truth in this sense will reduce to truth in a suitably parametrized structure, *i.e.* the biconditional:

$$\mathfrak{M}^* \models_v \phi(a_1, \ldots, a_n) \text{ iff } \mathfrak{M}^v \models \phi(v(a_1), \ldots, v(a_n))$$

will hold for any formula $\phi(a_1, \ldots, a_n)$ in which $a_1, \ldots, a_n$ are all of the occupied A-letters.

As long as the resulting structure $\mathfrak{M}^v$ is also an A-model, the theory of truth under occupancy can be reduced to the ordinary theory of truth for parametrized models; and similarly for other concepts. But it is just the closure condition that is required for the structure $\mathfrak{M}^v$ to be an A-model (Lemma I.1b).

Let us now see how the system C might be modified so as to accommodate the distinction between vacant and occupied A-letters. We may, in the same manner as before, indicate the vacancy-values of the A-letters at each line of the derivation. Recall that vacancy values are only assigned to the A-letters that actually occur in the formula at the line in question.

Say that an A-letter is *vacant (occupied) at* a line if it is assigned the vacancy-value vacant (occupied) either at the line or at a supposition to the line. There are then two general requirements on derivations. The first is the previous requirement of coherence, which, in the present terminology, now reads:

Coherence
No A-letter is both vacant and occupied at a given line.

The second arises from our demand that no A-object be occupied unless the A-objects upon which it depends are also occupied:

Closure
If, at a given line of a derivation, the A-letter a is occupied and syntactically depends upon b, then, at that line, b is also occupied.

The formulation of the special rules is along the same lines as before. We must again require that no supposition (or assumption) containing a vacant term be discharged. There are also the same two rules for vacant terms:

$$\text{Liberation} \qquad \frac{\phi(a) \quad a}{\phi(a) \quad \cancel{a}}$$

$$\text{Generalisation} \qquad \frac{\phi(a) \quad \cancel{a}}{\forall x \phi(x)}$$

The only restriction on these rules is that a should not be an ∃-instantial term. The vacation of ∃-instantial terms could also be allowed, but then the formulation of some of the other rules would be more complicated.

Again, the standard rule of universal generalisation can be regarded as the result of juxtaposing these two other rules:

$$\frac{\phi(a)\quad a}{\frac{\phi(a)\quad \cancel{a}}{\forall x\phi(x)}}$$

There are no explicit restrictions on this inference, but the usual restrictions are a consequence of the general requirements on derivations. Given Coherence, the instantial term a cannot occur in any supposition. And given Closure, no A-letter in the suppositions or conclusion that depends upon a can be occupied. Since the other rules are such that no dependent A-letter is ever vacant, this means that no A-letter in the suppositions or conclusion can depend upon a.

The rule of existential instantiation takes the form:

$$\frac{\exists x\phi(x)}{\phi(a)\quad a}$$

It should be subject to the condition of Novelty, as before. Note that it is required that the instantial term a be occupied. This then has the consequence, given Closure, that all of the other A-letters in $\exists x\phi(x)$ be occupied.

Let us briefly indicate how the semantics and proof of soundness for such a system might go. We effect the natural division of rules into proper and improper. In particular, we take EI and the new rule of UG to be proper and we take Liberation to be improper.

The class of suitable models for a derivation is defined in the same way as before. Any proper inference that occurs in a derivation and any sequent established at a line will naturally be associated with an occupancy list. This list will only contain entries for A-letters that actually occur in a formula of the inference or sequent. So there will be no occupancy or fixing of values 'from the outside'.

We may take an inference or sequent to be *valid* if it is valid under its occupancy list in the class of all suitable models.

Under this conception of validity, we must then establish the analogues of the four requirements (i)–(iv) listed on p. 71 of Chapter

8. Condition (i), that ϕ/ϕ is valid, is trivial. In regard to condition (ii), first consider the case in which the inference $\phi_1, \ldots, \phi_n/\phi$ is classically valid. Then it is readily shown, by a direct argument, that any extendible A-model validates the inference $\phi_1, \ldots, \phi_n/\phi$ under any occupancy list. The same conclusion may also be reached by a reduction to parametrized models. Suppose that $\mathfrak{M}^*$ is an extendible A-model, $\phi_1, \ldots, \phi_n/\phi$ is a classically valid inference, and L is an occupancy list. Then it follows from the definitions that $\mathfrak{M}^*$ validates $\phi_1, \ldots, \phi_n/\phi$ with the list L iff, for any v defined on $[A_L]$, $\mathfrak{M}^v$ (truth-to-truth) validates $v(\phi_1), \ldots, v(\phi_n)/v(\phi)$. But we may readily check that $\mathfrak{M}^v$ is extendible when $\mathfrak{M}$ is; and so, by Theorem I.14, $\mathfrak{M}$ validates the latter inference. In this way, we may reduce the validity of an inference that contains both occupied and vacant terms to the validity of an inference that contains vacant terms alone.

The other two cases of proper inferences are given by the rules EI and UG. Again, we may establish validity through direct arguments or we may effect a reduction to previous arguments through parametrization. The reduction in the case of UG is especially interesting. We wish to show that the inference $\phi(a)/\forall x \phi(x)$ with occupancy list L (not containing a) is validated by the A-model $\mathfrak{M}^*$. It suffices to show, for any v defined on $[A_L]$, that the inference $v(\phi(a))/v(\forall x \phi(x))$ is validated by $\mathfrak{M}^v$. Now all of the A-letters occurring in the latter inference are independent; and so we would appear to have a reduction to the case of the rule $\forall$I in the system G. But for this to work, we must be assured both that a remains value-unrestricted in $\mathfrak{M}^v$ and that $\mathfrak{M}^v$ conforms to Piecing; and it is just the assumption that v is defined on a closed domain that entitles us to this assurance.

The verification of Cut (condition (ii)) raises problems of its own. We have that the inferences Δ/ϕ and $\phi, \Gamma/\psi$ are valid under the respective occupancy lists L_1 and L_2, and we wish to show that the inference $\Delta, \Gamma/\psi$ is valid under its own occupancy list L_3. Now if all of the lists were the same, there would be no difficulty; we could either establish the result by a direct argument or through parametrization. But in general the lists will not be the same. This therefore suggests that we should set $L = L_1 \cup L_2 \cup L_3$ and then show that the validity of Δ/ϕ and $\phi, \Gamma/\psi$ under L_1 and L_2, respectively, implies their validity under L and that the validity of $\Delta, \Gamma/\psi$ under L implies its validity under L_3.

Now the additional terms in L are all extraneous to the inference in question. We must therefore show that fixing the value of extraneous terms makes no difference to the validity of an inference. Let Δ/ϕ be *any* inference, L_1 a subset of A-letters from the inference, $\mathfrak{M}^*$ an A-model, and L a superset of L_1 with the property that $[A_L] \cap (A_\Delta \cup A_\phi) = [A_{L_1}] \cap (A_\Delta \cup A_\phi)$. Then for the one direction, we have:

(1) If $\mathfrak{M}^*$ validates Δ/ϕ under L and is extendible, then $\mathfrak{M}^*$ also validates Δ/ϕ under L_1.

And for the other direction, we have:

(2) If $\mathfrak{M}^*$ validates Δ/ϕ under L_1 and if never $a \prec b$ with a a vacant term from the inference ($a \notin L_1$) and b an occupied term from outside of the inference ($b \in L$), then $\mathfrak{M}^*$ also validates Δ/ϕ under L.

Since all of the suitable models are extendible, direction (1) is satisfied; and since dependent A-letters are never vacant, direction (2) is satisfied.

The verification of condition (iv) is unproblematic. It should be noted, however, that it is essential for the validation of the discharge rules that no suppositions containing vacant A-letters be discharged.

Critical Comparisons

Which of the two systems Q and C is to be preferred? There are various grounds for preference – naturalness, closeness to ordinary reasoning, ease of operation. But on all of them, it seems to me, the advantage lies with the system C.

First, the system Q embodies the restriction that no A-letter shall be generalised upon more than once. This is artificial and has no counterpart in ordinary reasoning. The system C, on the other hand, embodies no such restriction and, to that extent, is less artificial and closer to ordinary reasoning.

Secondly, the semantics of Quine's system requires that one interpret ∀-instantial terms in an artificial way as denoting some such thing as a putative counter-example to a generalisation. This is not in accord with our ordinary understanding and makes it hard to attach an intuitive significance to the derivations. On the other hand, the system C allows one to interpret ∀-instantial terms more naturally as denoting unrestricted A-objects. This is in accord with our ordinary understanding and makes it much easier to attach an intuitive significance to the derivations.

Moreover, the system Q cannot be interpreted in accord with the maxim that the designation of a term be fixed upon its introduction into the derivation; the interpretation of the ∀-instantial terms is retrospectively determined. In the system C the interpretation of all terms is fixed on introduction. Indeed, in this respect there appears to be a fundamental difference between the rule of existential instantiation and the rule of universal generalization. It is perfectly possible to interpret the a in $\exists x\phi(x)/\phi(a)$ in a way that depends upon ϕ and is in accord with the ban on retrospective interpretation. But this is not possible for inferences of the form $\phi(a)/\forall x\phi(x)$; for the term must be introduced before it is known with respect to which condition it is being interpreted.

Finally, checks on the correctness of derivations are clumsy for the system Q. If we think of the dependency diagram as embodying that information from the rest of the derivation that is required to check the current line for correctness, then this difficulty is reflected in the fact that the diagram is not merely extended from one line to the next but may need to be substantially overhauled. For the system C, on the other hand, no such difficulty arises.

In terms of this comparison, the system C^+ occupies an intermediate position. It is like C in providing a reasonable restriction on UG and permitting a natural interpretation for the ∀-instantial terms; and it is like Q in having a clumsy check on correctness and not conforming to the ban on retrospective interpretation. Given that C^+ permits more derivations than C and so, in a sense, may make the derivation of any given sequent easier, it may be wondered why C should seem intuitively preferable to C^+. But the answer may be sought in these further considerations. With the irreflexivity condition in place of Novelty, the correctness of derivations is harder to check and the ban on the retrospective interpretation of terms cannot be maintained.

What ultimately explains the artificiality of Q is its symmetry in the treatment of the rules for the universal and existential quantifier. The instantial terms for the universal or existential quantifier may be interpreted in two ways, either as designative of an unrestricted A-object or as designative of an appropriately restricted A-object. Our ordinary practice is to interpret ∀-instantial terms as designative of unrestricted A-objects and ∃-instantial terms as designative of restricted A-objects. However, in Quine's system, both ∀- and ∃-instantial terms are interpreted as designating restricted A-objects.

The universal quantifier is assimilated to the existential quantifier. At the syntactic level, it is as if the rules for the universal quantifier were derived from the usual rules for the existential quantifier on the basis of the definition $\forall x \phi(x) =_{df} -\exists x - \phi(x)$.

In this respect, Quine's system is like Gentzen's; for it too gives a symmetric treatment of the rules for the universal and existential quantifier. But, in contrast to Quine's system, it treats both kinds of instantial term alike as designating unrestricted objects. The existential quantifier is assimilated to the universal quantifier. At the syntactic level, it is as if the rules for the existential quantifier were derived from the usual rules for the universal quantifier on the basis of the definition $\exists x \phi(x) =_{df} -\forall x - \phi(x)$. (It might be mentioned that one possibility remains: we may interpret the $\forall$-instantial terms as designating restricted A-objects and the $\exists$-instantial terms as designating restricted A-objects. This gives a system in which a rule of existential elimination is combined with a rule of universal generalization of the sort prescribed by Quine. The system is asymmetric in its treatment of the universal and existential quantifiers, but in the wrong direction.)

Given the undeniable advantage of the Copi-style system over Quine's, it is unfortunate that not more use of it has been made in the classroom. Of the many logic textbooks that have appeared over the years, several have been devoted to Quine's system, but none to a system in the Copi-style. Copi himself had the chance in the third edition of *Symbolic Logic*; but at the last moment, he got cold feet and opted for a system along the lines of Gentzen. One can only hope that others will be more adventurous and that the system C will get the exposure at the introductory level that it deserves.

11
Why Go Generic?

We here enumerate some of the particular advantages to be gained from the adoption of the generic semantics for systems of natural deduction. It needs to be emphasized that the present application is a part of a much broader application of the theory and that therefore a large part of its interest lies in the connection and unification with those other applications. But this is not an aspect of the matter that we shall discuss here. The question of the relationship to ordinary language and to the schematic interpretation of names is taken up in the next chapter.

(1) A Method of Discovery

The generic semantics constitutes a powerful heuristic device for finding the proper restrictions on systems with a rule of existential instantiation. It is clear that some restrictions are called for; but it is not at all clear what they should be or how they are to be found.

One possibility is to proceed inductively. Restrictions are modified in the light of counter-examples and counter-examples are sought for in the light of the given restrictions until it seems likely that no further counter-examples are to be found. However, such a procedure is quite unsatisfactory. If the correct formulation of the restrictions is not at all obvious, it is not likely to be found; and even if found, it will not be clear that it is correct or has any intuitive significance beyond its origin in the particular counter-examples that were selected.

In regard to the system Q, it seems that Quine followed this method in the early formulation of his system ([50]). It is therefore interesting to note that the method led him to what was, in fact, an incorrect account of the rules.

In regard to the system C, the history of attempts in this direction is more disastrous. Copi tried first in his *Symbolic Logic* ([54]); but his formulations were soon seen to be defective. Various other attempts were made (Copi [56], Prawitz [65], Parry [65], Leblanc [65], Slater [66]), but with no better results. The only correct formulations that I know of are those of Kalish [67] and Prawitz [67].

Another, more satisfactory method, is to proceed proof-theoretically. One transforms derivations within the proposed system to derivations within a system antecedently known to be sound and then sees what restrictions on the rules in the original system are required for the transformation to go through. Such a method at least has the advantage of yielding a proof of correctness along with the formulation of the rules. But it is unlikely, given that the formulation is tied to the proof-theoretic strategy, that it will be the most perspicuous possible or that it will have any intuitive significance beyond the demands of the particular transformation that was adopted.

Quine may be supposed to have followed this method in [52]. He treats the applications of EI and UG as giving rise to implicit premisses and then works out what restrictions on the rules are necessary for those premisses to be eliminable from a line that contains no instantial terms. Again, it is interesting to note that the resulting restrictions on the rules are not especially perspicuous and presumably are shaped more by the demands of the proof than any intuitive consideration.

Prawitz [67] and Rosser [53] presumably also followed a similar strategy in devising their systems along the lines of C. Again, we find defects in formulation. Prawitz's is correct, but not at all transparent; Rosser's is more transparent, but unduly narrow.

There is, in fact, a proof-theoretic strategy that will lead to the required formulation of the restrictions for C. Quine proved the Soundness of *his* system in two steps: the first (which we may call *Addition*) was to show that if ϕ could be derived from Δ in his system then ϕ could be derived classically from Δ and all of the conditionals corresponding to applications of UG and EI; the second (which we may call *Elimination*) was to show that these conditionals could be dropped as long as neither Δ nor ϕ contained an instantial term and certain restrictions on the introduction of instantial terms were observed. Suppose now we modify the strategy by using only the conditionals from the application of EI. Then the elimination step may be established in much the same kind of way as before. But the addition step gives rise to a difficulty. For suppose that in the original derivation we go from $\phi(a)$ to $\forall x\phi(x)$ under the suppositions Δ. Then what justifies us in concluding that $\forall x\phi(x)$ can be derived from Δ and the set Γ of conditionals arising from applications of EI? It will not do merely to require that a not occur in Δ or $\forall x\phi(x)$, for a may also occur in Γ. What we would like to do is to eliminate from Γ all of those conditionals that contain a. But we may see the proposed restriction on UG as just what is required to carry out this partial elimination.

The required restrictions *might* have been discovered this way. But the strategy and proof are not too obvious; and it is not likely that the restrictions *would* have been discovered this way. Indeed, Kalish has informed me that he had, at the time of writing [67], a proof of Soundness for the system C^+ that was similar to but somewhat more elaborate than the one proposed above. However, the formulation of the restrictions came first, through trial and error; and the Soundness proof only served as a check on the correctness of the resulting system.

These difficulties in finding a correct formulation of the rules disappear once a generic approach is adopted. Instead of being guided by syntactic considerations, be they piecemeal or systematic, one is guided by the semantic consideration of what the A-letters in applications of EI and UG can denote. The required restrictions on the rules will then fall out as the necessary conditions for the correct application of the rules under the proposed interpretation.

We may see how this works, both in the case of Q and of C. First suppose that one interprets the term a in the inferences $\exists x\phi(x)/\phi(a)$ and $\phi(a)/\forall x\phi(x)$ as denoting the putative ϕ-er and the putative non-ϕ-er respectively. Under such an interpretation, one will naturally think of the A-object a as depending upon the other A-objects mentioned in ϕ. But then the required restrictions will be immediately forthcoming. Flagging will follow from the requirement that there should not be two different specifications of the same A-object; and Ordering or Irreflexivity will follow from the requirement that the dependency relation among the A-objects should be irreflexive.

Suppose now that one starts off with the idea that the instantial term a in applications $\exists x\phi(x)/\phi(a)$ of EI is to denote a putative ϕ-er, dependent upon the A-objects denoted by the given terms, and that the other A-letters are to denote unrestricted A-objects. Then the required restrictions on the rules in the system C will be almost immediately forthcoming. Weak Flagging will follow from the requirement that there should not be two different specifications of the same A-object; and Independence will follow from an informal version of the reasoning in the proof of Line-to-line Soundness. We do not quite get Novelty; but we do get the condition that the relation of ∃-dependence be irreflexive, since otherwise one of the designated A-objects would depend upon itself. In fact, the system with the irreflexivity condition in place of Novelty is classically sound; and the stronger condition of Novelty may be thought to result from the imposition of the additional requirement that A-letters be interpreted upon introduction.

(2) Semantic Significance

With the generic semantics, syntactic features or distinctions possess a significance that they would otherwise appear to lack.

We already have an example in the restrictions on the rules UG and EI. Considered on their own account, it is not clear why they take the particular form they do or what justifies them beyond the mere fact that 'they work'. With the generic semantics, the exact form of the restrictions is immediately explicable and their justification is immediately forthcoming.

The generic semantics also explains the syntactic discrepancies among systems. Why should the syntactic restrictions on the rule UG be so different for Quine's system than for Copi's? We see that there is an underlying semantical explanation in terms of the UG-instantial terms: in Quine's system, they denote putative counter-examples; in Copi's system, they denote unrestricted A-objects.

Finally, the generic semantics confers a meaning on the derivations themselves. We need no longer think of a derivation as taking us through a detour of meaningless steps in order to establish what we are interested in. Instead, each line of the derivation is endowed with a meaning and, through the relations of dependency, the overall structure of the derivation acquires a significance that it would otherwise lack.

(3) Proofs of Soundness

The generic semantics enables one to provide simple proofs of classical soundness for systems of natural deduction with a rule of existential instantiation.

Again, it needs to be emphasized that the question of establishing soundness is by no means trivial. In contrast to the case of the more orthodox systems, it is no longer possible to prove, by a straightforward induction on the construction of a derivation, that the sequent established at any line is classically valid; for with the introduction of instantial terms, not every sequent will be classically valid.

In the face of this difficulty, most authors have followed the devious strategy of first associating derivations in the given system with derivations in a more orthodox system, of proving (or presupposing) the soundness of the orthodox system, and of then showing how soundness for the orthodox system transfers to soundness for the given system. This is, in effect, the strategy of Quine ([52], pp. 163–4) and Prawitz ([67], p. 82). It is the strategy that goes with the proof-theoretic method for *discovering* the right restrictions on the rules.

With the aid of the generic semantics, these proofs become simpler and more direct. Indeed, they flow naturally from the adoption of a particular generic interpretation for the instantial terms and from the general results concerning such interpretations. True, the general results must first be established; and this requires as much work as any particular argument. But the general results provide a framework for dealing with particular cases. Once the framework is set up, the proofs in any particular case become routine.

The contrast between the two methods of proving soundness has a deeper philosophical significance. The classical ('non-inductive') method is suggestive of an instrumentalist conception of deduction. According to this conception, the justification of such rules as UG or EI depends not upon the validity of inferences that they sanction but upon the fact that their application never leads to any harm: they never take us from meaningful premises (ones without A-letters) to meaningful conclusions that are not classical consequences of them. Our own method, on the other hand, is suggestive of a more orthodox and, to my mind, more satisfactory conception of deduction. According to this conception, the justification of such rules as UG or EI rests upon the local character of the inferences that they sanction as valid and not upon the global character of the system of rules to which they belong.

12
Accord with Ordinary Reasoning

The rules of UG and EI correspond to procedures of ordinary reasoning. We may establish that all triangles have interior angles summing to 180° by showing of an arbitrary triangle that its interior angles sum to 180°; and having established that there exists a bisector to an angle, we feel entitled to give it a name and declare that it is a bisector to the angle.

Let us call the first of these procedures *informal* UG and the second *informal* EI. In using this terminology, however, I should not be taken to endorse any particular view as to how the procedures are to be formalized. Let us call the critical terms involved in the application of these procedures ∀-*instantial* and ∃-*instantial* terms respectively: and let us call the informal reasoning that employs such terms *instantial* reasoning.

Our question now is: what account should be given of instantial reasoning?

Two distinct sub-questions may be distinguished. The first is a descriptive one. It is the question of what we are *actually* doing when we reason instantially. The second is a normative one. It is the question of what *justifies* us in doing whatever it is we are doing when we reason instantially.

The two questions are, of course, connected. Any account of what we are actually doing must be capable of sustaining an account of what justifies us in doing it – unless (as is most unlikely) we decide that our actual practice is not justified. It is, however, possible that an account of the justification is based upon an erroneous account of our practice. Although our practice would be justified if *this* is what we were doing, this is not in fact what we are doing.

In the nature of the case, questions of descriptive adequacy will be harder to decide than questions of justification. They will turn on intuitions that seem to go far beyond the 'hard facts' of our inferential practice. I myself am inclined to put a great deal of stock in such intuitions and to think that what is dubious and apparently dispensable data at one stage of enquiry can become critical to a later stage of enquiry. But I am well aware that there are those who would regard such intuitions or data with a good deal more suspicion.

It will be helpful in discussing our questions to set up a certain framework, one that distinguishes between different stages of suppositional and of instantial involvement. At the first stage of suppositional involvement, it may be assumed that we merely make proper inferences from given assertions (or beliefs) to other assertions (or beliefs). This corresponds to the very simplest model of reasoning. At the second stage, it may be assumed that we are prepared to entertain suppositions (or hypotheses) and to make proper inferences from those suppositions (or hypotheses). At the third or final stage, it may be assumed that we make use of improper inferences by means of which suppositions (or hypotheses) may be discharged.

It should be clear that these three stages are all distinct: we can reason from assertions without having any idea what a supposition is; and we can reason from suppositions without having any idea that they might be discharged.

In the hierarchy of instantial involvement, the first stage is one in which no instantial terms are used. The second is one in which exclusive use is made of either $\forall$-instantial or $\exists$-instantial terms. The third and final stage is one in which both kinds of instantial terms are used.

Again, it should be clear that the three stages are all distinct. It should also be clear that the two hierarchies are independent of one another and that one position in one hierarchy is compatible with any position in the other hierarchy.

The hierarchies have a significance that extends far beyond our present use of them. They provide an analytical framework within which certain useful distinctions can be made. But they also provide a basis for various claims of priority. First, there is temporal priority. It might be held, as a developmental hypothesis, that one goes through the different stages in order: that, in regard to the suppositional hierarchy, one first learns to reason from assertions (or beliefs), then learns to make suppositions (or hypotheses) and reason from them, and finally learns to discharge the suppositions (or hypotheses); and that, in regard to the generic hierarchy, one first learns to reason without instantial terms, and then learns to reason with instantial terms, with perhaps the acquisition of ∀-instantial terms coming first.

Second, there is a conceptual priority. It seems that the concept of a supposition is derivative upon the concept of an assertion and that a supposition has to be understood as a kind of hypothetical assertion. ∃-instantial terms are not derivative in the same way upon ∀-instantial terms, but the mastery of their use does seem to require a greater conceptual sophistication.

Finally, there is epistemological priority. It seems plausible that reasoning which involves the discharge of suppositions is ultimately to be justified in terms of reasoning which involves proper inferences alone and that reasoning from suppositions is, in its turn, ultimately to be justified in terms of reasoning from assertions alone. It is likewise plausible that reasoning which involves instantial terms is ultimately to be justified in terms of reasoning which involves no such terms.

Bearing this framework in mind, let us return to the issue at hand. Any satisfactory view of instantial reasoning will have two essential components: first, an account of the logical form of the reasoning performed under the informal procedures of UG and EI; second, an account of the nature of the instantial terms involved in such reasoning. In regard to the first question, we may take it as unproblematic that informal UG is correctly formalised along the lines of formal UG. But for informal EI, the question is somewhat trickier.

Consider a typical application of informal EI:

There exists a bisector to the angle α.
Call it (let it be) B.

There then appear to be two standard views on how such a piece of reasoning is to be formalised. According to the first, the clause 'Call it B' either is itself or points to an *assumption* that B is a bisector to the angle. So what justifies us in subsequently declaring that B is a bisector to the angle is that we have already assumed that it is. According to the second view, the clause 'Call it B' corresponds not to an assumption but to a conclusion. In saying 'Call it B', we are inferring that B is a bisector to the angle or at least indicating that such an inference can be made.

The first view would have us represent the informal procedure of EI with the formal rule of ∃E: and the second view would have us represent the procedure with the formal rule of EI. Thinking of systems of natural deduction as an attempt to formalize our ordinary reasoning, it is these two views, we may suppose, that have given rise to the two different ways of setting up the rules for the existential quantifier.

In my opinion, both of the standard views are incorrect. The statement that B is a bisector to the angle is not assumed and nor is it inferred. Rather, the premiss that there is a bisector to the angle justifies us in introducing the term 'B' for the arbitrary bisector into the reasoning. Given what 'B' denotes, it then quite simply follows that B *is* a bisector to the angle. In a certain sense, the premiss does justify the claim that B is a bisector to the angle. But this is not a normal case of justification, in which the truth of one statement supports the truth of another. For what the premiss sustains is not the truth of the claim, but the means to formulate it.

Indeed, I would want to go even further and suggest that the premiss 'There is a bisector to the angle α', as it is used in English, cannot be understood along the lines of the logician's '∃x (x is a bisector to the angle α)'. For the premiss serves to introduce a certain arbitrary object into the discourse. The second clause then picks up reference to that object, gives it a name – just as the talk of 'calling' suggests.

However, this is already to adopt a very radical position on how quantifier phrases are used in ordinary discourse. Since, for dialectical purposes, I wish at this stage to be as conservative as possible, let us go along with the orthodox views by supposing that the premiss is a straightforward existential statement and that the claim concerning the bisector B is either separately assumed or inferred from the premiss. Putting the question in these terms, then, which of the two views is to be preferred?

It seems clear to me that it is the second. It is, in the first place, quite inappropriate to use the forms of words '*Let* it be B' or '*Call* it B', when an assumption is being made. But let us finesse the question of how such forms of words are to be interpreted by considering applications of EI in which they are not used. Consider the following piece of informal reasoning, in which it is argued from the density of the reals that there are two reals between any two other reals:

(1) Take any two reals a and b
(2) We may suppose $a < b$ (since the other case is similar)
(3) Since $a < b$, there is a real c with $a < c < b$.
(4) Since $c < b$, there is a real d with $c < d < b$.
(5) But $a < c < b$ (from (3)), $a < d < b$ (since $a < c < d < b$), and $c \neq d$ (since $c < d$)
(6) So between a and b there are two distinct reals (*viz.* c and d).

Allowing for obvious compression, the formalisation based upon EI can represent the reasoning pretty much as it stands. In step (3), we go from $a < b$ to $\exists c(a < c < b)$, and then to $a < c < b$. In step (4), we likewise go from $c < b$ to $\exists d(c < d < b)$, and thence to $c < d < b$.

However, the formalisation based upon $\exists$E calls for a radical modification in the structure of the reasoning. In the transition between (3) and (4), it must be supposed that the assumption $a < c < b$ is tacitly made. Likewise, in the transition between (4) and (5), it must be supposed that the assumption $c < d < b$ is also tacitly made. When it comes to the conclusion (6), it must be supposed that the two assumptions are then as quietly dropped as they were originally made.

But this is all most implausible. We have here a case of an appeal to 'intuition' or 'soft data'. In a sense, one is only 'given' the recorded inference; and whether an assumption is tacitly made or withdrawn is a matter for 'interpretation.' But surely, one wants to retort, if assumptions are being tacitly made or withdrawn then I should have some sense that they are; and yet, when I examine the reasoning, I have no sense that this is what I am doing.

Let us therefore take it as given that the informal procedure of EI is correctly formalized along the lines of the formal rule of EI. The question that remains is: what account is to be given of the instantial terms? What sort of term is the 'ABC' for the arbitrary triangle or the 'B' for the indefinite bisector to an angle?

Various answers to this question have been proposed. One is what may be called the *instrumentalist* proposal. It is very common and is often espoused in the absence of any satisfactory semantics for instantial reasoning. (See, *e.g.,* Gupta [68] and Suppes [57], pp. 84–85.)

According to this proposal, instantial terms are just meaningless marks used to facilitate the link between one meaningful statement and another. Since they are meaningless, there is no question of justifying the inferences that involve them in terms of the preservation of truth. Instead, we have a general justification for their use, one that shows that they never lead from given meaningful statements to other meaningful statements that they do not entail.

The trouble with this suggestion is that it does not do justice to our intuition that the inferences involving instantial terms have a purely local cogency, one that is intrinsic to the inferences themselves. In the case of inferences of a more orthodox kind, it is clear that they have a cogency that is intrinsic to the inferences themselves. When someone performs a step of *modus ponens*, let us say, it is not as if I have to say to myself 'whether I accept this particular inference depends upon what other inferences are made'. The cogency of the piece of reasoning, as a whole, depends upon the cogency of the particular inferences making it up, and not the other way round. But the situation does not essentially alter with the introduction of instantial terms. With the case of informal UG or EI, as with the case of *modus ponens*, it seems equally clear that the inference has a purely local cogency and it seems equally irrelevant to consider the context in which the inference appears.

Another proposal is to take the instantial term to be a variable. It is perhaps this view that is closest to standard logical practice; for it is normal to formulate the rules of UG and EI with a variable as the instantial term.

It is important that this proposal be properly understood. There is a way in which I too am prepared to hold that instantial terms are variables; for I take variables, as ordinarily used, to be the signs of variable objects. But it is essential to the present proposal that the variables be those of contemporary logical theory and that their use be inextricable from the apparatus of the quantifiers and other variable-binding operators.

There is an immediate difficulty with this view. Open sentences – that is to say, sentences containing variables in place of ordinary singular terms – are not susceptible of truth or falsehood and cannot therefore enter directly into inferential relationships. Since our understanding of variables is tied to their use with variable-binding operators, it must be presumed that the instantial terms are somehow implicitly bound and that the direct object of our reasoning is not the open sentences themselves but the closed sentences resulting from their bondage.

But how are the instantial terms to be bound? It will be illuminating to examine this question in relation to the various stages in our previous two hierarchies. Consider first the case in which we reason from assertions using only ∀-instantial terms. It may then be suggested that the instantial terms are implicitly bound by a universal quantifier at each step of the reasoning. The *point* of dropping the quantifier and having it implicit is the resulting ease of symbolic manipulation.

This suggestion suffers from a certain lack of psychological realism. When I reason about an 'arbitrary' triangle or an 'arbitrary' number, I do not seem to be making universal claims about all triangles or all numbers. I seem, in some sense, to be reasoning about a given object, to be following through its particular logical fate. The suggestion also seems to distort the logical structure of our actual reasoning. When I go from 'the arbitrary triangle ABC ϕ-s' to 'all triangles ϕ', it must be supposed that I am merely making explicit the universal quantifier that was already implicit; and when I go from 'ABC ϕ-s' and 'ABC ψ-s' to 'ABC ϕ-s and ψ-s', it must be supposed that I am, in reality, making a somewhat complex quantificational inference and not a relatively simple propositional inference.

But let us put these objections on one side as not at all decisive and consider the case in which we also reason from suppositions containing instantial terms. Then the previous suggestion breaks down. First, if I suppose that an 'arbitrary' number n is even, then I am not justified in concluding that every number is even, as the suggestion would have us believe. Second, I do seem to be justified in discharging suppositions containing instantial terms, though this would not be permitted if I was arguing from their universal closure.

These difficulties may be met by modifying the previous suggestion. It may be supposed that the scope of the universal quantifiers is not confined to any one line and that the reconstructed reasoning concerns not the universal closure of the sentences that actually appear in the reasoning, but the universal closures of the conditionals whose antecedent is the conjunction of the suppositions and whose consequent is the conclusion of a given line. The aberrant phenomena concerning generalization and the discharge of suppositions can then be explained; and in so far as proper inferences under UG are admitted, they can be explained in terms of the distinction between the conditional and generality interpretation for variables.

This new suggestion not only requires an implausible view on the logical structure of our ordinary reasoning; it also forces us into adopting an implausible position on the role of suppositions. As I have already remarked, in making a supposition α I am not asserting the trivial conditional $\phi \supset \phi$ and in making an inference (say $\phi \vee \psi$) from a supposition (say ϕ) I am not inferring one conditional assertion ($\phi \supset (\phi \vee \psi)$) from another ($\phi \supset \phi$). Inference from suppositions is like inference from assertions, but without the same unconditional commitment to each line of the reasoning. It therefore seems intolerable that our ordinary view of suppositions should have to be modified in order to accommodate the presence of instantial terms.

It is a desideratum on any satisfactory account of instantial reasoning, in general, and on reasoning from suppositions containing instantial terms, in particular, that it should be possible to see this account as a product of two other views: first, a view on reasoning from suppositions that pays no regard to the presence of instantial terms; second, a view on how instantial terms are used that pays no special regard to their occurrence in suppositional reasoning. The respective views on reasoning and on instantial terms should then conspire together to produce the desired account of instantial reasoning.

The present proposal, however, is unable to satisfy this desideratum. For if one insists, as part of one's general view on reasoning, that the suppositions must have a genuinely isolable role, and if one insists, as part of one's general view on instantial terms as variables, that they must be bound, then it will be impossible for the implicit quantifiers to have the requisitely wide scope.

This objection not withstanding, let us consider a further case of instantial involvement, the one in which we may reason from either assertions or suppositions using only ∃-instantial terms. If informal EI were merely an instance of ∃E, then this case would not introduce any essentially new considerations. But if informal EI is an instance of formal EI, then the case does raise essentially new considerations; and it is for this reason that it has been important to settle the status of the procedure.

Granted that informal EI is indeed an inference, it seems natural to treat it in analogy with informal UG. If ∀-instantial terms are to be implicitly bound by universal quantifiers, then ∃-instantial terms are to be implicitly bound by existential quantifiers. Just as we can 'tuck up' a universal quantifier for ease of symbolic manipulation, so we can tuck up an existential quantifier.

It should be noted that the present suggestion has the same lack of psychological realism about it as the original suggestion concerning ∀-instantial terms. When we reason with ∃-instantial terms, we seem to be reasoning about a particular object and not making existential claims. In going from an existential to an instance, we do not seem to be engaged in the process of making an explicit existential quantifier implicit; and in making apparently propositional inferences, we do not seem to be making somewhat indirect quantificational inferences.

But the suggestion has a more serious defect; it does not even deliver the correct inferences. Consider the following derivation (or rather, its informal counterpart):

1	(1)	∃xFx	Ass.
2	(2)	∀xGx	Ass.
1	(3)	Fa	1, EI
2	(4)	Ga	2, UI
1, 2	(5)	Fa ∧ Ga	3, 4, ∧I
1, 2	(6)	∃x(Fx ∧ Gx)	5, EG

If we imagine the ∃-instantial term a as bound by an existential quantifier at each step, then the inference from (3) and (4) to (5) is represented by the inference from ∃xFx and ∃xGx to ∃x(Fx ∧ Gx). But this latter inference is not valid and is, indeed, a well-known fallacy.

As in the case of suppositions with ∀-instantial terms, the present difficulties may be met by modifying the original proposal. It may be supposed that the scope of the implicit existential quantifiers is not confined to any one line and that the reconstructed reasoning concerns not the existential closure of the sentence from a given line but the existential closure of the conjunction of all of the sentences up to and including the sentence from the given line. So if the original reasoning is given by the sentences $\phi_1, \phi_2, \ldots, \phi_n$, the reconstructed reasoning will be given by the existential closures of the conjunctions $\phi_1, \phi_1 \wedge \phi_2, \ldots, \phi_1 \wedge \ldots \wedge \phi_n$ (where the sentences $\phi_1, \phi_2, \ldots, \phi_n$ must be taken to be conditionals in the case that suppositions are discharged in the original reasoning).

This modification results in an even greater distortion to the apparent logical structure of our ordinary reasoning. Before we were unable to give a separate role to the suppositions of a given line and had to wrap them all up with the conclusion of that line to form a single conditional. Now we are also unable to give a separate role to the conclusions of the different lines and must, at any point, wrap them all up to form a single conjunction. What appears to be a simple inference from one line to the next is, in reality, an extension to an ever-expanding existentially quantified conjunction.

When we reach the highest grade of instantial involvement, in which both ∀-instantial and ∃-instantial terms can be used, still greater complications arise. There is no obvious way of combining the separate accounts for ∀-instantial and ∃-instantial terms; for the implicit universal and existential quantifiers will compete for wide scope. We could agree to put the universal quantifiers first and the existential quantifiers second or to put them in the other order. But either account will lead to difficulties.

It seems clear, in general, that in restoring the quantifiers we must take account of the dependency relations among the different instantial terms. But even then, no simple-minded account will work. For example, one might follow a suggestion of Suppes ([57], p. 85) and restore the quantifiers in such a way that the existential quantifiers are given the widest scope compatibly with the requirement that when an ∃-instantial term a depends upon an ∀-instantial term b then the existential quantifier for a is within the scope of the universal quantifier for b. But although the resulting quantified conditionals will then all be valid, the reasoning cannot be taken to concern such conditionals.

It seems clear to me that, if one pursues this line of enquiry, one has very little alternative but to take the ∃-instantial terms to be not first-order variables at all but second-order variables for functions to which the ∀-instantial terms upon which they depend have been appended as arguments. One thereby obtains the Skolemite account, according to which there are existential quantifiers for functions on the outside and universal quantifiers for individuals on the inside. But although such an account 'works' – it delivers the right inferences, it embodies all of the informal inadequacies of the suggestions leading up to it.

A third proposal is to take the instantial terms to be the names of ordinary individuals. According to this view, when we reason about an 'arbitrary triangle ABC' or an 'indefinite bisector B', we are in fact reasoning about a particular triangle or a particular bisector, though which one we choose is immaterial. On this view, it is not the names themselves that are generic but the use we make of them; we so use the name that any other name from an appropriate range could be used in its stead.

This view may be traced, with rough historical accuracy, back to Berkeley ([1710]). It has also found its present-day advocates. An example is Mackie ([58]), p. 31), with his suggestion that in EI we are talking about a 'real individual'.

The present proposal gets round the basic defect of the previous proposal. Sentences containing instantial terms are already closed and consequently there is no need for an implausible reconstruction of the reasoning into sentences that become closed. The proposal has, however, grave defects of its own.

It is, in the first place, psychologically unrealistic. If we ask ourselves what we are doing in carrying out informal UG or EI, it is most implausible to suppose that we are reasoning about a particular individual. In this respect, the standard historical example of a triangle is misleading. For in geometric demonstrations of a traditional sort, it is usual to draw a diagram of the figures that one is reasoning about; and so there is some room for the hypothesis that one is actually reasoning about those figures. But change the example and the implausibility of the hypothesis becomes immediately clear. Suppose I wish to establish that all natural numbers have a prime factorization. I take an arbitrary natural number n, establish that it has a prime factorization, and then conclude that all natural numbers have a prime factorization. But in this case one is under no temptation to suppose that the reasoning is about a particular number. For which one is it? 3? 15? $10^{10}+6$?

Indeed, one should have been wary of supposing, in the original geometric case, that the reasoning was about a particular triangle. For again, we may ask: which triangle? All one has before one is a *diagram* of a triangle. But even if one takes all triangles to be the same 'up to congruence', no diagram is sufficiently accurate to constitute a triangle for the purposes of abstract geometry.

The fact is that our visual imagination has certain peculiar powers in regard to geometric reasoning. From even the roughest drawing, we are capable of 'reading off' general features of the geometric figures that we take it to represent. It is for this reason that diagrams are such a valuable aid in the proof of geometric truths. But these peculiarities in the geometric case should not blind us to the general nature of instantial reasoning.

But, putting aside the question of psychological realism, I am not even sure that the present proposal can be taken to provide a *possible* account of how we reason with instantial terms. What if the domain of quantification is empty? Although standard classical logic deals only with non-empty domains, ordinary reasoning countenances the empty domain. We may reason about all Fermat numbers (counter-examples to Fermat's theorem) even though, under the supposition that Fermat's Theorem is true, there are no Fermat numbers. In such a case, it is legitimate to declare 'Take an arbitrary Fermat number n' and to go on and reason with 'n', even though there is no object in the domain which one's reasoning can be taken to be about.

In the case of $\exists$-instantial terms, the corresponding difficulty turns not on the domain being empty but on the existential premiss being false. At a given stage in a piece of reasoning, I may have established that there is a Fermat number (perhaps on the basis of certain additional suppositions) and I may then go on to 'call' that Fermat number 'n'. Given that there are no Fermat numbers, there is then no question of 'n' denoting an object of the required sort.

Let it be granted that the domain is non-empty and that the existential premiss is true. Still, difficulties can arise; for I may be in no position to name an object from the domain or an object satisfying the condition of the existential premiss. I may want to reason about all unnamed dogs (I assume there are some) or I may want to instantiate the claim that there exists a non-principal ultrafilter. But I am in no position either to name an unnamed dog or a non-principal ultrafilter. In case a nominalist proposal for $\exists$-instantial terms is combined with a variabilist proposal for $\forall$-instantial terms, an additional difficulty arises. For in going from $\exists x \phi(x, b)$, for b an $\forall$-instantial variable, to $\phi(a, b)$, there may be no constant object to foot the bill; a may be a 'dependent' variable.

Let it even be granted that suitable names can be found. Yet further difficulties arise from the status of the inference. If the $\forall$-instantial term a is an individual name, then it would appear in contrast to either the variabilist or generic approach, that the inference from $\phi(a)$ to $\forall x \phi(x)$ must be improper. But we seem to have an intuition that there is a proper inference in these cases. The claim that an arbitrary triangle ϕ-s is just what we appear to need in order to establish that all triangles ϕ.

The problem is more acute still in the case of $\exists$-instantial terms. For the transition from $\exists x \phi(x)$ to $\phi(a)$, in case a is an individual name, is not valid either as a proper or as an improper inference. It is therefore hard to see in what the justification of the transition could consist.

A fourth proposal is to take the instantial terms to be schematic or ambiguous names. On this view, when I talk of an 'arbitrary' triangle ABC or an 'indefinite' bisector B, the expressions 'ABC' and 'B' are being used as schematic or ambiguous names. Under a more careful account, I would want to sort out the different ways in which a name could be taken to be schematic or ambiguous. At the most basic level, one would make a distinction, somewhat analogous to the distinction between the objectual and substitutional interpretations of the quantifiers, between names that indifferently denote certain objects and names that indifferently stand in for certain expressions. But the main contrast, for present purposes, is with the variabilist proposal. On the latter proposal, sentences containing instantial terms have to be understood in terms of the closed sentences in which they are embedded; on the present proposal, the use of instantial terms is not linked to the apparatus of variable binding and, consequently, sentences containing such terms can be understood in some other way.

Once the distinction between variables and schematic letters was established, this view became quite popular as an alternative to the variabilist view. It may be traced back to Frege [1893] with his corresponding distinction between variable signs and indicators.

As an account of reasoning with ∀-instantial terms, the present proposal fares well by comparison with the two previous proposals. Since the use of the terms is not tied to their part in variable-binding, it is able to assign a separate role to suppositions; and since the use of the terms is schematic, it is able to do this without making an implausible assumption about the object of reasoning.

The proposal is also able to satisfy the desideratum, mentioned in connection with the variabilist account, that it should be possible to see the account of instantial reasoning as a product of separate accounts of reasoning and of instantial terms. For let us take the general explanation of the use of schematic or ambiguous names to be that any particular usage of such names is correct just in case all 'instances' of that usage are correct (where this means either that we substitute different unambiguous names for the given ambiguous names or that, keeping the unambiguous names fixed, we let them unambiguously denote different individuals). Applying this general explanation to the use of ambiguous names in derivations, we see that a derivation containing such names can be considered correct, just as it stands, when all of its 'instances' are correct and that therefore the separate role of the suppositions can be preserved.

It should be remarked, however, that the usual account of the status of and justification of the procedure UG under such a proposal is incorrect. Consider a case $\phi(a)/\forall x\phi(x)$ of UG. Then it is usually claimed that in establishing $\phi(a)$ from suppositions that do not contain a, I have, in effect, established $\phi(a_1)$, $\phi(a_2)$, ... for names $a_1, a_2, \ldots$ that run through all of the individuals and that from all of $\phi(a_1)$, $\phi(a_2)$, ..., the conclusion $\forall x\phi(x)$ may be inferred. Thus the status and justification of the procedure is similar to that for $\wedge$ I.

But to this account it may be objected that the inference from $\phi(a_1)$, $\phi(a_2)$, ..., where $a_1, a_2, \ldots$ name all of the individuals, to $\forall x\phi(x)$ is simply not valid. One also needs as an additional premiss that $a_1, a_2, \ldots$ *are* all of the individuals. From the fact that Tom, Dick and Harry are mortal, it does not follow that every man is mortal, even should Tom, Dick and Harry be all of the men.

This is not, however, an objection to the schematist approach as such; for there are other, more satisfactory, accounts of UG. One might regard it as an *internal* improper rule. Applying the general explanation of the use of schematic names to this case, the inference $\phi(a)/\forall x\phi(x)$ would be valid because every instance of the inference was valid; and an instance would be valid because of an appropriate improper rule for unambiguous names. Or one might, more plausibly, regard UG as an *external* improper rule. Its justification would then be to the effect that since the inference from the given suppositions to $\phi(a)$ is valid (under the appropriate construal of validity for schematic inferences), so too is the inference from the same suppositions to $\forall x\phi(x)$.

The schematist proposal also fares well in the extension to $\exists$-instantial terms. It must now be supposed, though, that the values of the $\exists$-instantial terms (be they denotata or substituends) are systematically correlated with the values of the $\forall$-instantial terms. It might even be assumed that the ambiguous names are given some structure from which the systematic correlation can be determined. To this end, we might appropriate the symbolism of the ε-calculus. So in the inference $\exists x\phi(x)/\phi(a)$, the term a would be taken to be of the form $\varepsilon x\phi(x)$ (as in Routley [69]) and the denotative values of the resulting terms would be correlated in such a way that the particular terms $s = \varepsilon xPx$ and $t = \varepsilon yRys$, for example, would take all values i and j for which $\exists xPx \supset Pi$ and $\exists yRyi \supset Rji$ (or Pi and Rji) were true.

On this proposal, however, there is a difficulty in satisfying the desideratum we previously imposed on accounts of instantial reasoning. For on the general explanation of the use of schematic names, the inference from $\exists x \phi(x)$ to $\phi(x)$ cannot be regarded as proper, since it is not valid as a proper inference when a is regarded as an unambiguous name. Nor can it be regarded as an internal improper inference, since it is not valid as an improper inference when a is taken to be an unambiguous name. And nor can it be regarded as an external improper inference, since the inference from certain suppositions to $\phi(a)$ will not in general be valid when the inference from those same suppositions to $\exists x \phi(x)$ is valid.

But this difficulty does not strike me as intrinsic to the schematic approach. It also besets our own generic approach and has its source, it seems to me, in an over-simple view on the inferential relationship between the existential premiss and its instance. If we take a more radical view of this relationship, of the sort outlined before, then it seems likely that the difficulty could be removed.

Given that the schematic approach delivers the right inferences without unduly distorting the apparent logical structure of our ordinary reasoning, it may be wondered why it should not be preferred to our own generic approach. After all, does not the generic approach merely interpose a superfluous ontological layer between the generic names and the individuals that are their values? Why not drop this intermediate level altogether?

One reason has to do with our lingering intuition that, in instantial reasoning, we are reasoning about a distinctive object. The generic approach respects this intuition; the schematic approach does not.

But even if it were decided that there were no arbitrary objects in ordinary instantial reasoning, it would still be useful, for the purposes of conceptual clarity, to introduce them. For our approach, through its definition of an A-model and the attendant conditions of Partial Extendibility, Piecing etc. provides an analysis of that abstract structure which is required to secure the suitable assignment of values to other items. The structure may be realized linguistically; A-objects may be taken to be A-names and objectual dependency to be syntactic dependency. But, for the purposes of the analysis, this is entirely incidental.

In this respect, the distinction between our approach and the schematic approach is somewhat akin to the distinction between Kripke's treatment of possible worlds as unstructured elements and Carnap's treatment of them as state-descriptions. Even if one believes that possible worlds *are* state-descriptions, it will still be helpful to provide an account of those properties of possible worlds required to secure a semantics of modal discourse, quite independently of any considerations of their identity. It is in somewhat the same spirit that we may set up our own generic semantics.

But these reasons are, at best, marginal. The decisive reason lies not in instantial reasoning itself but in its relation to the general use of variables in mathematics or of pronouns in ordinary language. Instantial reasoning constitutes but part of this general use. When one looks at the other uses, it becomes clear that variables and pronouns alike are used to signify arbitrary objects. Considerations of uniformity then force one to adopt the same view of instantial terms.

This broader thesis is not one I can defend here; it is a vast topic in its own right. But I can indicate two pieces of evidence from mathematical discourse that seem to favour the thesis. The first is a standard application of the chain rule:

Let $y = x^2$

and $z = 2y$.

Then $\frac{dy}{dx} = 2x$

and $\frac{dz}{dy} = 2$.

But $\frac{dz}{dx} = \frac{dz}{dy} \cdot \frac{dy}{dx}$

So $\frac{dz}{dx} = 2.2x$

$= 4x$

The second is a fragment of reasoning that relates directly to the application of informal EI (*Cf.* Hardy [14], top line of p. 205):

Let $y = f(x)$ be a continuous function. Take any real h. Then for some k, $f(x+h) = y+k$. Now since f is continuous, $k \to 0$ as $h \to 0$. So ...

On the schematic approach, it is hard, if not impossible, to make sense of these two pieces of reasoning, since the statements concerning the derivative or the arrow are not simply schematic in the different variables. On the generic approach, however, these pieces of reasoning present no special difficulties.

PART III

SYSTEMS IN GENERAL

I shall embark on a general study of systems containing a rule of existential instantiation. It needs to be emphasized that a great deal more work needs to be done in this area and that here I make only a beginning. It should be possible, in particular, to prove further results of the sort proved here and to extend those results to a broader range of systems, ones in which the derivations need not be in linear format and in which the quantifier rules may assume somewhat different forms.

I first give a general characterization of a system of natural deduction in terms of what restrictions on the quantifier rules are permitted. I then give a full account of which systems, as so characterized, are sound and a partial account of which systems, as so characterized, are complete. I consider some further results of this sort that may be established and conclude with a sketch of a general semantical framework for generic interpretations.

13

The General Notion of a System

We are concerned to give a general characterization of systems that contain a rule of existential instantion. We may take it that any such system will contain the usual propositional rules and that it will contain quantificational rules which may schematically be represented as follows (with the usual understanding concerning $\phi(x)$, $\phi(t)$ and $\phi(a)$):

$$\text{UI } \frac{\forall x \phi(x)}{\phi(t)} \qquad \text{UG } \frac{\phi(a)}{\forall x \phi(x)}$$

$$\text{EI } \frac{\exists x \phi(x)}{\phi(a)} \qquad \text{EG } \frac{\phi(t)}{\exists x \phi(x)}$$

A system will then be defined by a set of restrictions on UG and EI. But what counts as an admissible restriction? It does not seem reasonable that we should require, say, that the premiss $\exists x \phi(x)$ in EI be obtained by an application of *modus ponens* or that the premiss to an application of UG contain exactly 23 symbols. But then what information from the derivation may properly be made use of in formulating the restrictions?

It seems reasonable to suppose that all of the relevant information can be gained by running through the derivation and noting, at each application of UG or EI, which rule it is an application of, which A-letter is the instantial term, which A-letters are side terms in the premiss and which in the suppositions, and which other A-letters may have been used in the derivation. Thus we can take no cognizance of what kinds of formulas may have been used or which rules, outside UG or EI, may have been applied.

We are therefore led to give the following definitions. A *line-type* is a quintuple $\langle q, t, R, S, T \rangle$, where q is a quantifier $\forall$ or $\exists$, t is an A-letter, and R, S, T are sets of A-letters subject only to the condition that $T \supseteq R \cup S \cup \{t\}$. Given a line of a derivation obtained by a non-vacuous application $\exists x\phi(x)/\phi(a)$ of EI, *its* line-type is $\langle a, t, R, S, T \rangle$, where q is $\exists$, t is a, R is the set of A-letters in $\exists x\phi(x)$, S is the set of A-letters in the suppositions to the inference, and T is the set of A-letters that occur in the derivation up to and including the line in question.

Given a line of a derivation obtained by a non-vacuous application $\phi(a)/\forall x\phi(x)$ of UG, *its* line-type is $\langle q, t, R, S, T \rangle$, where q is $\forall$, t is a, R is the set of A-letters in $\forall x\phi(x)$, S is the set of A-letters in the suppositions to the inference, and T is the set of A-letters that occur in the derivation up to and including the line in question. So a line-type encodes the information to be extracted from the line in question.

A *derivation-type* is a finite sequence $\tau_1 \ldots \tau_n$, $n \geqslant 0$ of line-types subject to the condition that, if T_i is the last term of τ_i and T_j the last term of τ_j, for $j > i$, then $T_j \supseteq T_i$. A putative derivation D is said to be *of* derivation-type $\tau = \tau_1 \ldots \tau_n$ (and the type τ is said to *permit* the derivation D) if the applications of EI and UG in D (in that order) are $\alpha_1, \ldots, \alpha_n$ and, for each $i = 1, \ldots, n$, τ_i is the line type of α_i. So a derivation-type encodes the information that can be extracted from a derivation as a whole.

We now take a *system* to be a set of derivation types or what we shall also call a *restriction class*. A system is said to *permit* a derivation if its type belongs to the system.

Say that two derivations are *type equivalent* if they are of the same type. Then any system, intuitively understood, that does not discriminate between type equivalent derivations, *i.e.* that does not render one of them correct and the other incorrect, can be characterized as a restriction class. For example, an explicit definition of the restriction class for the system Q may be formulated as follows. Given a derivation-type τ, say $a \ll_\tau b$ if one of the terms of τ is of the form $\langle q, t, R, S, T \rangle$ with $a = t$ and $b \in R$. Let $<_\tau$ be the ancestral of $\ll_\tau$. Then the system Q may be defined as the set of derivation-types τ for which $<_\tau$ is irreflexive and for which distinct terms of τ always have distinct second components.

Often we shall treat systems, such as C or CQ, as restriction classes without giving an explicit definition of which restriction classes they are. But it will always be clear, for the particular cases at hand, how the definition is to go.

It is important to observe that we have not here attempted to give a full account of what a reasonable restriction on the rules should be. There are many further conditions that might properly be imposed on the restrictions, and some of these will be considered later. We have only been concerned to specify the general form that a restriction on the rules should take.

Conversely, our definition of the form of a restriction could have been made to depend upon a more fine-grained analysis of derivations. Perhaps the major omission from our definition is that no mention is made of the structure of a derivation as revealed by its presentation in tree form. We cannot make use of the fact, for example, that two A-letters or two occurrences of the same A-letter are not 'connected' within a derivation. In the case of all of the systems we have considered, such extra information is not rquired. But in the case of certain systems, such as that set out in the remark on page 28 of Prawitz [65], it might quite legitimately be used.

I suspect that, to a large extent, our results on soundness will not be sensitive to any reasonable refinement on the notion of a restriction. However, some of our other results may be, and it would therefore be of interest to determine to what extent they are.

14
Soundness

One very natural condition to impose on a system is that it should be classically sound; any derivable sequent free of A-letters should be classically valid. Indeed, part of the point in setting up a system is that this condition should obtain.

We may now ask: which systems are classically sound, *i.e.* which restrictions on the rules will guarantee that no invalid sequent (free of A-letters) can be derived?

If the systems $S_1, S_2, \ldots$ are classically sound, then so is their union $S_1 \cup S_2 \cup \ldots$, *i.e.* the system that permits any derivation permitted by one of $S_1, S_2, \ldots$. So, in place of our original question, we may ask: what is the maximal system that is classically sound, *i.e.* what are the weakest restrictions on the rules UG and EI that will not impugn the soundness of the system?

To answer this question, we need to define a new system CQ that is a sort of hybrid of the systems of Copi–Kalish and Quine. These latter two systems are strictly incomparable with respect to derivations; each permits derivations not permitted by the other. For example: in Q we can go from the *supposition* Fa to ∀xFx; and in C, we can generalize twice upon the same A-letter a. The new system CQ is not exactly the union of C and Q, but it is obtained from the rules for C and Q by attempting to blend them in the most obvious fashion.

We first need to redefine the notion of immediate syntactic dependence. This is done by an induction on the length n of the derivation under consideration. If $n=0$, then the relation is null. Suppose now that D is a derivation of length n and that D^+ is obtained from D by adding a new line. If that line is not a non-vacuous application of either UG or EI, then the relation of immediate dependence is the same for D^+ as for D. So suppose the new line is an application $\exists x\phi(x)/\phi(a)$ of EI. Then the relation of immediate dependence for D^+ is that for D plus all the pairs (a, b) for b an A-letter of $\exists x\phi(x)$. Finally, suppose the new line is an application $\phi(a)/\forall x\phi(x)$ of UG under the suppositions Δ. There are two cases. (1) Either a or an A-letter dependent upon a (relative to D) occurs in Δ or $\forall x\phi(x)$. Then the relation of immediate dependence for D^+ is that for D plus all the pairs (a, b) for b an A-letter of $\forall x\phi(x)$. (2) Neither a nor an A-letter dependent upon a (relative to D) occurs in Δ or $\forall x\phi(x)$. Then the relation of immediate dependence is the same for D^+ as for D.

Say that an A-letter in a derivation D is *restricted* if it is either an instantial term to an application of EI or an instantial term to an application of UG of the kind under case (2) above. Then a putative derivation D is *correct in* CQ in case it conforms to the following conditions:

(i)   (a) no term is restricted twice, *i.e.* by two applications of a rule;
     (b) no A-letter occurs as both an unrestricted instantial term to an application of UG and as a restricted term in the sub-derivation leading up to that application;

(ii) the relation of dependence is irreflexive.

The above characterization of the system CQ has been given directly in terms of the derivations it permits. But it is clear that two derivations of the same type are either both correct or incorrect, and so the characterization could equally well have been given in terms of a restriction class.

It is important to note that these restrictions make essential reference to sub-derivations. An application $\phi(a)/\forall x\phi(x)$ of UG, with a unrestricted, may well be correct, even though *subsequently* in the derivation a becomes restricted or a side term becomes dependent upon a. For example, the following sequence of steps may occur in a correct derivation of CQ:

```
Λ     (n)      φ(a)
Λ     (n+1)    ∀xφ(x)
...   (n+2)    ∃xψ(x)
...   (n+3)    ψ(a)        n+2, EI;
```

though if the pairs of lines (n), $(n+1)$ and $(n+2)$, $(n+3)$ were interchanged the derivation could not be correct.

Each derivation permitted by either C^+ or Q is permitted by CQ. However, some derivations permitted by CQ are not permitted by either C^+ or Q. An example is provided by a derivation embodying the steps above. Another example may be obtained as follows. Let D_1 be a derivation in C^+ but not Q, and D_2 a derivation in Q but not C^+. Then, upon rewriting the A-letters in D_1 so as not to overlap with those in D_2, the derivation consisting of D_1 succeeded by D_2 will be in CQ but in neither C^+ nor Q. So the derivations in CQ are not simply the union of the derivations in C^+ and Q. We may put the matter this way: an application of UG is treated as an instance of the C^+ rule if it possibly can; otherwise it is treated as an instance of the Q rule.

We now proceed to show that CQ is the maximal sound system. One direction is relatively straightforward.

Theorem 1
The system CQ is classically sound.

Proof
We may avoid a heavy proof-theoretic argument by exploiting the generic semantics. Interpret the ∃-instantial terms in the way common to the systems C and Q; interpret the restricted ∀-instantial terms in the way peculiar to Q; and interpret the unrestricted ∀-instantial terms in the way peculiar to C. To be more exact, let the system $\mathfrak{S}$ of definitions associated with derivation D from CQ consist of:

(a) (a, Λ), for a not restricted in D;
(b) $(a, \exists x\phi(x) \supset \phi(x))$, for $\exists x\phi(x)/\phi(a)$ a non-vacuous application of EI in D;
(c) $(a, \phi(x) \supset \forall x\phi(x))$, for $\phi(a)/\forall x\phi(x)$ a non-vacuous application of UG in D in which the term a is restricted.

We then call a model $\mathfrak{M}^*$ *suitable for* D if it realizes the system $\mathfrak{S}$ of definitions associated with D.

From the previous restrictions (i) (a) and (ii) it follows that the system of definitions associated with a derivation from CQ is always unequivocal and well-founded. So from Theorem I.17 it follows that for any classical model $\mathfrak{M}$ there always exists a suitable A-model $\mathfrak{M}^*$ for D; and, given the form of the definitions under (b) and (c) above, it follows from Theorem I.19 that any suitable model for a derivation is extendible over the A-objects designated in the derivation.

It remains to show that if D is a derivation of CQ and $\mathfrak{M}^*$ a suitable model for D then $\mathfrak{M}^*$ (case-to-case) validates the sequents established at each line of D. This we show by induction on the length of D. The basis case is trivial; and so assume that D′ is a one-line continuation of D and that $\mathfrak{M}'$ is suitable for D′. There is then an essential difficulty; for given that a term restricted in D′ may be unrestricted in D, the model $\mathfrak{M}'$ may not be suitable for D and so it will not be possible to apply the IH to obtain the result that $\mathfrak{M}'$ validates the sequents established at each line of D.

This difficulty may be got round in the following way. Let $\mathfrak{S}$ and $\mathfrak{S}'$ be the systems of definitions for D and D′ respectively; and let $\mathfrak{M}^*$ and $\mathfrak{M}'$ be A-models suitable for D and D′ respectively. Clearly, we may suppose $\mathfrak{M}^*$ and $\mathfrak{M}'$ assign the same denotations to the A-letters occurring in $\mathfrak{S}$. Take now a sequent (Δ, ϕ) established at a given line of D. We wish to show that $\mathfrak{M}' \models \Delta \supset \phi$. So take any $v' \in V'$ defined on the closure of $A_\Delta \cup A_\phi$ in $\mathfrak{M}'$. Since $\mathfrak{M}'$ realizes $\mathfrak{S}'$, v' conforms to $\mathfrak{S}'$; and since $\mathfrak{S}'$ is a refinement of $\mathfrak{S}$, v' conforms to $\mathfrak{S}$. Let v be the restriction of v' to the closure of $A_\Delta \cup A_\phi$ in $\mathfrak{M}^*$. Then v also conforms to $\mathfrak{S}$ and so, by Lemma I.20, $v \in V$. Since $\mathfrak{M}^*$ is suitable for D, it follows by the IH that $\mathfrak{M} \models v(\Delta \supset \phi)$. But then $\mathfrak{M} \models v'(\Delta \supset \phi)$ – as required.

Given this result, the inductive step of the proof may be completed. There are four cases. (1) The last line of D′ is justified by the rule of supposition. Trivial. (2) The last line of D′ is justified by a classical inference. By extendibility. (3) The last line is justified by an application of UG in which the instantial term is restricted. By the argument familiar from the study of the system C. (4) The last line is justified by an application of EI or by an application of UG in which the instantial term is restricted. By the argument familiar from the study of the system Q.

Classical soundness now follows in the usual manner.

We must now show that CQ is maximally sound. For the purposes of the present argument, we shall assume that the language contains a name-letter, a monadic predicate F, and a predicate for identity, and that the system is equipped with the usual rules for identity:

$$=I \quad \frac{}{t=t} \qquad =E \quad \frac{s=t \quad \phi(s)}{\phi(t)}$$

Once the argument is through, it will be clear how these assumptions can be dropped.

Say that a derivation is *unsound* if its final sequent is free of A-letters and classically invalid. Call a derivation type *unsound* if there is an unsound derivation of that type. Then we must show:

(1)   Each derivation-type τ excluded by CQ is unsound.

Our strategy will be to produce a series of lemmas that successively simplify (1).

We may first exclude from consideration derivations that contain an application of UG with restricted instantial term.

Lemma 2
Suppose τ is a derivation type. Let $\tau_k = (\forall, a, R, S, T)$ be a term of τ for which a is restricted in $\tau_1 \ldots \tau_k$; and let τ' be the result of replacing τ_k in τ with $(\exists, a, R, S, T)$. Then
(i) τ is permitted by CQ iff τ' is, and
(ii) τ is sound iff τ' is.

Proof
(i)   a is restricted by the occurrences of both $(\forall, a, R, S, T)$ and $(\exists, a, R, S, T)$ in τ and τ' respectively. Moreover, the dependence relation is the same for both τ and τ'. Therefore it is clear that τ will satisfy the conditions (i)-(ii) for a permitted derivation of CQ iff τ' does.

(ii)   Suppose τ is unsound. Let D be a derivation of type τ of a sequent that is free of A-letters but classically invalid. Suppose it is line (n) that manifests the type $(\forall, a, R, S, T)$. So the relevant part of the derivation looks as follows (with ... indicating the assumptions of a line):

$\quad \ldots \quad (m) \quad \phi(a)$
$\quad \quad \vdots$
$\quad \ldots \quad (n) \quad \forall x \phi(x) \quad m, \text{UG}$

We now replace line (n) with the following lines (the gaps are filled out in an obvious way and $\forall \psi$ is used to abbreviate the universal closure of an arbitrary formula ψ):

$\quad n \quad \quad \quad (n) \quad \quad \exists x - \phi(x) \quad \quad \quad \quad \text{Ass.}$
$\quad \quad \quad \quad \quad \quad \vdots$
$\quad \ldots, n \quad \quad (p) \quad \quad \exists x - \phi(x)$
$\quad \ldots, n \quad \quad (p+1) \quad -\phi(a) \quad \quad \quad \quad \quad n+k, \text{EI}$
$\quad \ldots \quad \quad \quad (p+2) \quad -\exists x - \phi(x) \quad \quad \quad p, m, p+1, -\text{I}$

$p+3$	$(p+3)$	$\forall[-\exists x - \phi(x) \supset \forall x \phi(x)]$	Ass
		$\vdots$	
$p+3$	$(q-1)$	$-\exists x - \phi(x) \supset \forall x \phi(x)$	
$\ldots, p+3$	(q)	$\forall x \phi(x)$	$p+2, q-1, \supset$E

The numbering of the subsequent lines is adjusted accordingly, and lines that evolve from (n) in the original derivation must now be made to depend upon the assumption $(p+3)$. The resulting derivation is clearly of type τ' and, since the formula at line $(p+3)$ is free of A-letters and classically valid, the final sequent will be free of A-letters and yet remain classically invalid.

The other direction of the equivalence is established in a similar way.

This lemma means that to establish (1) it suffices to establish:

(2) A derivation type is unsound if it is excluded by CQ and lacks a term of the form $(\forall, a, R, S, T)$ for which a is restricted in the corresponding sub-type.

For take any derivation-type τ excluded by CQ. Successively replace each term $(\forall, a, R, S, T)$ in τ, with a appropriately restricted, by $(\exists, a, R, S, T)$; and let the resulting type be τ'. By repeated applications of part (i) of the lemma, τ' is excluded from CQ; by (2) above, τ' is unsound; and so by repeated applications of part (ii) of the lemma, τ is unsound.

We may now reduce the length and complexity of the derivation-types that need to be considered. Say that one *line*-type (q', a', R', S', T') *reduces* another (q, a, R, S, T) if $q' = q$, $a' = a$, $R' \subseteq R$, $S' \subseteq S$ and $T' \subseteq T$. Say that one *derivation*-type $\tau' = \tau'_1 \ldots \tau'_m$ *reduces* another $\tau = \tau_1 \ldots \tau_n$ if there are $i_1, \ldots, i_m$, with $1 \leq i_1 < i_2 < \ldots < i_m \leq n$, for which τ'_j reduces τ_{i_j} for each $j = 1, \ldots, m$.

Lemma 3

Suppose τ' reduces τ. Then τ' permits an unsound derivation only if τ does.

Proof

Since τ' reduces τ, we may select terms $\tau_{i_1}, \ldots, \tau_{i_m}$ of τ as above. Suppose τ' is the type of the unsound derivation D'. Then we go through the terms of τ in order, successively modifying D' so as eventually to obtain an unsound derivation D of type τ.

We may suppose that the term τ_k under consideration is of the form

156 SYSTEMS IN GENERAL

(q, a, R, S, T), where $R = \{b_1, \ldots, b_r\}$, $S = \{c_1, \ldots, c_s\}$, and $T = \{d_1, \ldots, d_t\}$. We shall consider only the case in which $q = \exists$, since the other case is similar.

Suppose first that the term τ_k is not one of the terms τ_{i_j}. Then pick out a name-letter n and at the appropriate juncture in the derivation D' (or what has already been obtained from D'), interpolate the following lines:

	(1)	$d_1 = d_1$	$= I$
	$\vdots$		
	(t)	$d_t = d_t$	$= I$
$t+1$	$(t+1)$	$c_1 = c_1$	Ass
	$\vdots$		
$t+s$	$(t+s)$	$c_s = c_s$	Ass
	$\vdots$		
	(p)	$n = n \wedge \bigwedge_{i=1}^{r} b_i = b_i$	
	$(p+1)$	$\exists x(x = x \wedge \bigwedge_{i=1}^{r} b_i = b_i)$	p, EG
	$\vdots$		
$t+1, \ldots, t+s$	(q)	$\exists x(x = x \wedge \bigwedge_{i=1}^{r} b_i = b_i)$	
$t+1, \ldots, t+s$	$(q+1)$	$a = a \wedge \bigwedge_{i=1}^{r} b_i = b_i$	q, EI

The gaps are filled out in an obvious way and, in inserting these lines, the numbering must be appropriately adjusted.

Now suppose that τ_k is a term τ_{i_j}, for $j = 1, \ldots, m$. Then, at the appropriate juncture in the derivation D', there is a line (p) of type $\tau'_j = (\exists, a, R', S', T')$, where τ'_j reduces τ_{i_j}. Suppose this line is displayed as follows:

$\ldots$	(p)	$\exists x \phi(x)$	
	$\vdots$		
$\ldots$	(q)	$\phi(a)$	p, EI

We then replace line (q) in D' or its sequel with the following lines (filling in the gaps in the obvious way):

	(q)	$d_1 = d_1$	$= I$
	$\vdots$		
	$(q+t-1)$	$d_t = d_t$	$= I$
$q+t$	$(q+t)$	$\bigwedge_{j=1}^{s} c_j = c_j$	Ass
$q+t+1$	$(q+t+1)$	$\forall y_1 \ldots y_r(\exists x \phi(x) \supset$	
	$\vdots$	$\exists x(\phi(x) \wedge \bigwedge_{i=1}^{r} y_i = y_i))$	Ass

SOUNDNESS

$q+t+1$ *(o)* $\exists x\phi(x) \supset \exists x(\phi(\phi(x) \wedge \bigwedge_{i=1}^{r} b_i = b_i))$

$\ldots, q+t+1$ *(o+1)* $\exists x(\phi(x) \wedge \bigwedge_{i=1}^{r} b_i = b_i)$ $p, o, \supset E$

⋮

$\ldots, q+t, q+t+1$ *(u)* $\exists x(\phi(x) \wedge \bigwedge_{i=1}^{r} b_i = b_i)$

$\ldots, q+t, q+t+1$ *(u+1)* $\phi(a) \wedge \bigwedge_{i+1}^{r} b_i = b_i$ u, EI

$\ldots, q+t, q+t+1$ *(u+2)* $\phi(a)$ $u+1, \wedge E$

⋮

$\ldots, q+t+1$ *(v)* $\phi(a)$

In the resulting derivation, lines that originally evolved from line (q) must now be made to rest upon the new assumption $(q+t+1)$.

Working through the terms of τ in this way, we obtain a derivation D that is of type τ. Its final sequent differs from that of D' only in containing certain additional formulas as assumptions. But all of these formulas are classically valid and free of A-letters. Therefore the new derivation D will also be unsound.

This lemma is useful in establishing (2); for to show that τ is unsound, it suffices to show that an appropriate reduced type is unsound.

Let us now consider the various cases in which a type τ is excluded by CQ and show that, in each of these cases, τ is unsound. By Lemma 2 we may stipulate that τ contains no restricted ∀-instantial A-letters. We may think of the reasoning in this part as a generalisation of the *ad hoc* reasoning that was used by various logicians to expose the faults in certain of the earlier formulations of systems with a rule of existential instantiation.

Case 1

The term (q, a, R, S, T) belongs to τ with a∈R. This is a violation of what I have called Local Restriction. Let τ' be the reduced type whose sole term is (q, a, {a}, {a}, {a}). Since a is restricted in τ', we need only consider the case in which q is ∃. It must be shown that τ is unsound. But this is a consequence of the following derivation:

  1   (1) $\exists x \, x \neq a$ Ass
  1   (2) $a \neq a$ 1, EI
        (3) $a = a$ $=I$
        (4) $-\exists x \, x \neq a$ 1, 2, 3, $-I$
        (5) $\exists y - \exists x \, x \neq y$ 4, EG.

Case 2
An A-letter a is restricted in the term (q, a, R, S, T) and in a subsequent term (q', a, R', S', T') of τ. This is a violation of what has previously been called Flagging. Let τ' be the reduced derivation-type whose two terms are (q, a, Λ, Λ, {a}) and (q', a, Λ, Λ, {a}) (in that order). There are four possible sub-cases in all, according as to whether the pair (q, q') is ($\exists$, $\exists$), ($\exists$, $\forall$), ($\forall$, $\exists$) or ($\forall$, $\forall$). But the last three are ruled out by the stipulation arising from Lemma 2. So that leaves only the first case.

We wish to show that the type whose terms are ($\exists$, a, Λ, Λ, {a}) and ($\exists$, a, Λ, Λ, {a}) is unsound. But this is shown by the following derivation:

1	(1)	$\exists x Fx$	Ass
1	(2)	Fa	1, EI
3	(3)	$\exists x - Fx$	Ass
3	(4)	$-Fa$	3, EI
3	(5)	$-\exists x Fx$	1, 2, 4, $-$I
	(6)	$\exists x - Fx \supset -\exists x Fx$	3, 5 $\supset$ I

Case 3
An A-letter a is restricted in the term (q, a, R, S, T) and unrestricted in the subsequent term ($\forall$, a, R', S', T'). By our stipulation, we may suppose that q is the quantifier $\exists$. Let τ' be the reduced derivation-type whose terms are ($\exists$, a, Λ, Λ, {a}) and ($\forall$, a, Λ, Λ, {a}). Then this type is shown to be unsound by the following derivation:

1	(1)	$\exists x Fx$	Ass
1	(2)	Fa	1, EI
	(3)	$\exists x Fx \supset Fa$	1, 2, $\supset$I
	(4)	$\forall x(\exists x Fx \supset Fx)$	3, UG

Case 4
The relation of dependence (as determined by τ) is not irreflexive. There is therefore a sequence of A-letters $a_1, a_2, \ldots, a_m, a_{m+1}, m \geq 1$, for which $a_{m+1} = a_1$, and, for $i = 1, \ldots, m$, a_i is immediately dependent upon a_{i+1}. We may suppose that Case 1 fails to obtain. It then follows that a_i is distinct from a_{i+1}; and so we may suppose that the $a_1, \ldots, a_m$ are all distinct.

There will be for each a_i, $i = 1, \ldots, m$, a term τ_{k_i} of τ of the form ($\exists$, a_i, R, S, T), where $a_{i+1} \in R$. By initiating the sequence $a_1, \ldots, a_{m+1}$ at a different point, we may suppose that τ_{k_m} is the last of such terms to occur in τ. Let τ' be the result of dropping the terms not belonging to the sequence from τ and replacing each term τ_{k_i} of the form $(\exists, a_i, R, S, T)$ by $\tau'_{k_i} = (\exists, a_i, \{a_{i+1}\}, \Lambda, T'_i)$, where T'_i is chosen so as to be minimal. Then τ' reduces τ; and so it suffices, by Lemma 3, to produce an unsound derivation of type τ'.

With each term $(\exists, a_i, \{a_{i+1}\}, \Lambda, T'_i)$, $i = 1, \ldots, m-1$, we may associate the derivation:

(1) $a_{i+1} = a_{i+1}$ = I
(2) $\exists x (x = a_{i+1})$ 1, EG
(3) $a_i = a_{i+1}$ 2, EI

We may then string these derivations together in the same order as their corresponding terms. This gives a derivation of the type of τ', but without its last term. By using the transitivity of $=$, this derivation may be continued (without change of type) into a proof of $a_1 = a_m$. To this derivation, (which we may suppose ends at line $(n-1)$), append the lines:

n (n) $\forall y \exists x (y \neq x)$ Ass
n $(n+1)$ $\exists x (a_1 \neq x)$ n, UI
n $(n+2)$ $a_1 \neq a_m$ $n+1$, EI
     $(n+3)$ $-\forall y \exists x (x \neq y)$ $n-1, m, n+2, -I$

The resulting derivation is of type τ' and provides a proof of a formula $-\forall y \exists x (x \neq y)$ that is free of A-letters and yet classically invalid.

This completes our survey of the cases, and so we have:

Theorem 4
The system CQ contains every sound system, *i.e.* any derivation-type not permitted by CQ is the type of an unsound derivation.

Putting together Theorems 1 and 4 then gives:

Theorem 5
The system CQ is maximally sound.

This result can be strengthened in various directions. First, a more refined notion of restriction might be used. In our actual definition of line- and derivation-type, the A-letters of the suppositions were listed under a single head S. But it is clear that we could have listed them separately, under the different heads $S_1, \ldots, S_m$, to indicate that there are m suppositions to the inference whose respective A-letters are specified by $S_1, \ldots, S_m$. If it had been allowed that the restrictions take account of the tree structure of derivations, then the system CQ would not quite do as it stands. But it is fairly clear what further modifications to the system would need to be made in order to obtain one that was maximally sound.

It will be recalled that we had presupposed that the underlying language contained (a) the predicate of identity, (b) a monadic predicate F, and (c) a name-letter n. These requirements can, to some extent, be relaxed. The identity and monadic predicate can be dropped in favour of a single binary predicate R. The role of the rules for identity can then be played by appropriate assumptions on R and the role of F by an appropriate monadic predicate defined from R, say $\exists y\, xRy$. The role of the name-letter n in the proof is somewhat peculiar. Consider the line type $(\exists, a, \Lambda, \Lambda, \Lambda)$. Then no line of a derivation can be of this type unless the language contains a term other than an A-letter. So any derivation-type that contains this particular line-type will be vacuously sound should the language contain no name-letters. If we wish to determine the sound derivation types with regard to languages that contain no name-letters, then we should insert the line type $(\exists, a, \Lambda, \Lambda, \Lambda)$ at any appropriate point in the derivation-types that were previously characterized as sound. However, if our interest is solely in the sound derivations, not the sound derivation-types, then we may stick to our original characterization, for the new derivation types will not permit any further derivations.

With this qualification, we see that the result will go through for any language that contains a binary predicate. However, it does seem essential to the proof that the language contain a binary predicate and not just monadic predicates. It would therefore be of interest to work out a corresponding result for monadic languages.

The above result gives us a general method for showing systems with a rule of existential instantiation to be classically sound or unsound. For as long as the restrictions on the rules conform to our general requirements, we may simply determine whether or not they are weaker than the restrictions for CQ. In this way, for example, it could easily be verified that the system of Hendry [75] is classically sound.

15

Completeness

It will be recalled that a system of natural deduction is *classically complete* if every valid sequent that is free of A-letters is derivable. Just as we may attempt to determine the most liberal restrictions that are compatible with classical soundness, so we may attempt to determine the most confined restrictions that are compatible with classical completeness.

In contrast to the result for soundness, we have:

Theorem 6
There is no minimal system that is classically complete.

Proof
Take the system C, which is clasically complete. Let C^0 be the system in which the A-letters appearing in derivations must have even subscripts and let C^1 be the system in which the A-letters must have odd subscripts. Then it is readily seen that C^0 and C^1 are also classically complete. But the intersection of the two systems contains no derivations and so clearly is not classically complete.

Say that a system S is *closed under re-lettering* if any re-lettering of a derivation permitted by S is also permitted by S or, more exactly, if for any derivation type τ in S and any permutation ρ of the A-letters, $\rho[\tau]$ is in S. Then the systems C^0 and C^1 in the proof above are not closed under re-lettering. But even with this condition, we will have:

Theorem 7
There is no minimal system that is classically complete and closed under re-lettering.

Proof

Let Q′ be the system that differs from Q in the single respect that, in the non-vacuous inference $\phi(a)/\forall x\phi(x)$, a must actually occur in some supposition. Then Q′ and C are both closed under re-lettering. But their intersection will contain no proof of $\forall x(Fx \supset Fx)$. For in the derivations permitted by the intersection, no non-vacuous applications of UG will be used. But then non-vacuous generalizations $\forall x\phi(x)$ may everywhere be replaced by $\bot$ in a derivation and correctness be preserved. But under such a transformation, $\forall x(Fx \supset Fx)$ becomes $\bot$ and is therefore not provable.

It would be of interest to know whether there are general and reasonable conditions which are such that there *is* a minimal system that is classically complete and conforms to those conditions.

Even though minimality is problematic, it is possible to establish some very strong necessary conditions for classical completeness. In order to state these conditions, it will be convenient to suppose that derivations are presented in the form of trees as described by Prawitz ([65], §1-2 and §1-3). To any derivation in linear form there will correspond, in an obvious way, a derivation in tree form. This tree form derivation will be unique up to placing of nodes to either the left or the right. We may then say that a system S permits a derivation D in tree form if it permits a linear derivation to which D corresponds. The variations in the tree form derivations corresponding to the given linear derivation will turn out to be of no significance.

To any derivation in tree form may be associated a dependency diagram. We wish, however, to give a more sophisticated account of the identity of instantial terms. Consider the following derivation:

$$\frac{\dfrac{\dfrac{\forall x(Fx \wedge Gx)}{Fa \wedge Ga}}{\dfrac{Fa}{\forall xFx}} \quad \dfrac{\dfrac{\forall x(Fx \wedge Gx)}{Fa \wedge Ga}}{\dfrac{Ga}{\forall xGx}}}{\forall xFx \wedge \forall xGx}$$

We wish to treat the a on the left and the a on the right as essentially different instantial terms.

Let us define a connection in essentially the same way as Prawitz ([65], p. 28). Suppose, for the sake of definiteness, that the propositional rules are $\wedge I$, $\wedge E$, $\supset I$, $\supset E$, and $\wedge_c$. Then a *connection in* a derivation D is a sequence of formula occurrences $\phi_1, \ldots, \phi_n$, $n \geq 1$, of D such that one of the following holds for each $i = 1, 2, \ldots, n-1$:

(i) ϕ_{i+1} stands immediately below ϕ_i or *vice versa*;

(ii) ϕ_i is a premiss of $\supset$E and side connected with ϕ_{i+1};

(iii) ϕ_i is a consequence of an application of the $\supset$I or the $\wedge_\mathrm{C}$ rule and ϕ_{i+1} is an assumption discharged by the application or *vice versa*.

Now let us say that two occurrences o_1 and o_2 of A-letters in D are *related* if (i) they are occurrences of the same A-letter a, and (ii) there is a connection $\phi_1, \ldots, \phi_n$ in D such that o_1 is part of ϕ_1, o_2 is part of ϕ_n, and a occurs in each formula occurrence of the connection. In Prawitz's terminology, the formula occurrences ϕ_1 and ϕ_n would then be said to be linked.

It is clear that the relation of being related is an equivalence relation. Therefore let a *quasi-letter* in a derivation D be an equivalence class of an occurrence of an A-letter under this relation. In the previous example, we see that the occurrences of a to the left belong to one equivalence class and the occurrences of a to the right to another. We may say that a quasi-letter α *occurs* in a formula occurrence when more strictly we should say that a member of α is part of the formula occurrence.

We now wish to label the nodes of a dependency diagram with quasi-letters rather than with the A-letters themselves. Given two quasi-letters α and β of a derivation D, we say that α *immediately depends upon* β if there is a non-vacuous application $\exists x \phi(x)/\phi(a)$ of EI or $\phi(a)/\forall x \phi(x)$ of UG, the occurrences of a in $\phi(a)$ are members of α, and β occurs in the occurrence of $\phi(x)$. Note that this is the definition appropriate to the Quinean system. Let a *dependency structure* simply be a finite relational system $\langle X, R \rangle$, with X a non-empty set and R a transitive relation on X. We then let the dependency structure *for* a derivation D be the pair $\langle L, < \rangle$, where L is the set of quasi-letters that occur as instantial or side terms in D and $<$ is the relation of dependence on L.

Call a relational structure $\langle L, < \rangle$ *regular* if $<$ is irreflexive and if $<$ is upwardly linear, *i.e.* if a$<$b and a$<$c implies b$<$c or b$=$c or c$<$b. The significance of upward linearity is this. Suppose that the members of L are variable occurrences that attach to quantifiers within a formula; interpret dependence in terms of scope. Then if the occurrence a is within the scope of the occurrences b and c, then either b and c are the same occurrence or one is within the scope of the other.

Let $\langle L, < \rangle$ be a dependency structure. We call a sub-structure $\langle L', <' \rangle$ of $\langle L, < \rangle$ *quasi-closed* if a,b $\in$ L', a $\ll$ b and a $\ll$ c imply c$\in$L'. (Here $\ll$ is the relation of immediate dependence, *i.e.* a $\ll$ b if a < b and a < c < b for no c$\in$L). In a quasi-closed sub-structure we need not fully specify the dependency status of a letter; but if we list one immediate dependee, we must list them all.

Say that one dependency structure $\langle L, < \rangle$ *embodies* another $\langle L', <' \rangle$ if some quasi-closed sub-structure of $\langle L, < \rangle$ is isomorphic to $\langle L', <' \rangle$; and say that a derivation D in tree form *embodies* $\langle L', <' \rangle$ if it is associated with a dependency structure $\langle L, < \rangle$ that embodies $\langle L, < \rangle$. We then have the following result:

Theorem 8
Let S be a system of natural deduction that is classically sound and complete. Let $\langle L, < \rangle$ be a regular dependency structure. Then some derivation (in tree form) permitted by S embodies $\langle L, < \rangle$.

In other words, the dependency structure of letters in a derivation must have a reasonable degree of complexity if a system of natural deduction is to be sound and complete. Note that nothing is said concerning the odd question of what is required for the derivation of all valid sequents within an unsound system.

The proof of this theorem is long and involved, and we shall here merely present a light sketch. As an example of a regular dependency structure, consider:

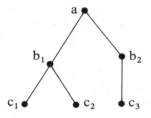

Associate with this structure the formula $\phi_0 = \forall x[\forall y_1(\forall z_1 Fxy_1z_1 \wedge \forall z_2 Fxy_1z_2) \wedge \forall y_2 \forall z_3 Fxy_2z_3]$. (It should be clear from this example what formula, in general, should be associated with a regular dependency structure). Choose variables u, v_1, v_2, w_1, w_2, w_3, all distinct from x, y_1, y_2, z_1, z_2, z_3; and let ϕ_1 be the result of replacing x,

y_1, y_2, z_1, z_2, z_3 respectively, in ϕ_0, with $u, v_1, v_2, w_1, w_2, w_3$.

Let S be a classically sound and complete system. Then we show:

(*) Any tree form derivation of the sequent ϕ_0/ϕ_1 permitted by S embodies the above dependency structure.

This claim is proved on the basis of two further propositions. We define a certain formulation CQ* of the maximally sound system CQ and a certain conception of normality for tree form derivations of CQ*. We show:

(1) Any normal derivation of ϕ_0/ϕ_1 in CQ* embodies the given dependency structure;

(2) Any derivation D in CQ* reduces to a normal derivation D' that embodies no dependency structure that is not already embodied by D.

The claim (*) then follows from (1) and (2). For let D be a tree form derivation of the sequent ϕ_0/ϕ_1 in S. Since S is sound, D (or something very like it) will be a derivation in CQ* too. Let D' be the normal derivation of (2). By (1), D' embodies the given dependency structure; and by (2), so does the original derivation D.

The proof of (2) calls for a considerable modification to the techniques of Prawitz [65]. One of the major difficulties is the presence of the rule EI and an unorthodox form of the rule UG. For example, we have the following non-normal derivation of Fb from Fa:

$$\frac{\dfrac{Fa}{\exists x\, Fx}}{Fb}$$

It is impossible to find a normal derivation of Fb from Fa. Instead what we must show is that, in the proof of sequents that do not involve A-letters, such sequences of steps as the one above are not required.

Another major difficulty is that the reduction steps described in Prawitz [65] may increase the complexity of the dependency structure. Consider the following sub-derivation:

$$\frac{\dfrac{\dfrac{\Sigma(a)}{\phi(a)}}{\forall x\, \phi(x)}}{\phi(b)} ,$$

where a is an A-letter that does not appear in the assumptions of $\Sigma(a)$. This is replaced with:

$$\frac{\Sigma(b)}{\phi(b)}.$$

But in making the replacement, the dependency structure of the whole derivation may increase in complexity. For b may depend upon much more than a does. Suppose now that there is an application of EI within $\Sigma(a)$ in which c is the instantial term and a the side term. Then in making the substitution $\Sigma(b)$, c will come to depend upon b rather than a and the complexity of the dependency structure may thereby be increased.

This difficulty is overcome by supposing that we have a new rule that enables us to infer $\phi(t)$ directly from $\phi(a)$ when before we might have inferred $\phi(t)$ indirectly from $\phi(a)$ through the intermediate step $\forall x \phi(x)$. But the presence of this rule then complicates the proper formulation of the other reduction steps.

The details of the proof tie in with two other topics that I hope to consider elsewhere. The first is the analysis of what one might call the fine structure of dependency relations: which dependency relations are required for the derivation of which results. The second is the formulation and investigation of systems that dispense entirely with quantifiers in favour of reasoning about the dependency relations of arbitrary objects. It seems plausible that the above theorem should have a proof in terms of a sophisticated use of the generic semantics; but I am not sure how it should go.

Further results along the lines of Theorem 8 can be proved. It may be supposed that the rules for either the universal or existential quantifier are excised from the system. A comparable result may then be proved for the ensuing systems. However, it is far from clear that the stated necessary condition is also sufficient, and it would be of interest to obtain a necessary and sufficient condition for a system to be classically sound and complete.

16
Further Conditions

The effect of imposing other conditions on a system may profitably be considered.

We here list some new conditions and, for convenience, restate some of the earlier ones. The cases given are only intended to be examples of the kind of condition that might be considered and are not intended by any means to be exhaustive.

Classical Soundness
Suppose that (Δ, ϕ) is a sequent containing no A-letters. Then (Δ, ϕ) is classically valid if it is derivable.

Classical Completeness
Suppose that (Δ, ϕ) is a sequent containing no A-letters. Then (Δ, ϕ) is derivable if it is classically valid.

Closure under Re-lettering
Suppose the derivation type τ belongs to S. Let ρ be a permutation of the set of all A-letters. Then $\rho[\tau]$ also belongs to S.

Closure under Subderivation
Suppose that the derivation type τ belongs to S. Let τ' be an initial segment of τ. Then τ' also belongs to S.

According to this condition, errors in derivations are irredeemable; a derivation that is incorrect remains incorrect throughout all continuations.

Closure under Reduction
Suppose that the derivation type τ belongs to S. Let τ' reduce τ in the sense previously defined. Then τ' belongs to S.

Closure under Re-ordering of Lines
Suppose that τ belongs to S. Let τ' be the result of re-arranging the terms of τ in any order (minimally adjusting the last components of τ's terms where necessary). Then τ' belongs to S.

Suppositional Indifference
Let $\tau = \tau_1 \ldots \tau_n$ and $\tau' = \tau'_1 \ldots \tau'_n$ be two derivation types such that, for each $i = 1, \ldots, n$, τ_i and τ'_i agree on all but possibly their fourth terms. Then τ belongs to S if τ' does.

Local Determination
There is a set L of line-types such that a derivation type τ belongs to S iff each term of τ agrees with a member of L in all but possibly its last component.

Appendage
If τ and τ' belong to S then so does $\tau\tau'$ (minimally adjusting the last components of its terms where necessary).

Each of these conditions is one that may, for one reason or another, be found desirable. Some, such as classical soundness and completeness, are essential to the purpose of setting up a formal system in the first place. Others, such as Closure under Subderivation, seem intrinsic to the nature of a derivation. And yet others, such as Suppositional Indifference or Local Determination, may be required for certain special purposes.

In the case of each condition or each combination of conditions, there are various questions we may consider. First, are there any systems satisfying the conditions? If there are, we get an example of what is called a *possibility result;* and otherwise, we get an example of an *impossibility result*.

In the case of a possibility result, there are various more refined questions we might ask. Is there a unique system satisfying the conditions? Is there a maximal system? A minimal system? What is a general characterization of the systems satisfying the conditions?

Uniqueness results are of special interest. We may wonder what motivates the adoption of one system rather than another. If we can show that a certain system is the one and only one to satisfy certain

FURTHER CONDITIONS 169

desiderata, then the adoption of the system can be grounded in the commitment to the desiderata.

Maximality and minimality results can be regarded as special kinds of uniqueness result. We may suppose that we want certain desiderata and that, compatibly with those desiderata being satisfied, we want the restrictions on the rules to be either as tight or as loose as possible. A maximality or minimality result then shows that one's choice of a system is thereby uniquely determined.

As an example of an impossibility result, we have:

Theorem 9
There is no system satisfying the conditions of Classical Soundness, Classical Completeness, Closure under Re-lettering and Local Determination.

Proof
By looking at the previous normalisation techniques it may be shown that any classically sound and complete system S must contain a derivation type τ with a term τ_i of the form $(\exists, a, R, S, T)$, with R non-empty. Given that S is locally determined, τ_i, or rather a line type τ_i' agreeing with τ_i on all but its last component, must belong to the set L of line types from which the members of the derivation types in S are obtained. Choose a b∈R. Since S is classically sound, b≠a. Let ρ be the permutation in which b and a are interchanged. By Re-lettering, $\rho[\tau]\in S$, and so a line type τ_i^* that agrees with $\rho[\tau_i]$ on all but its last component belongs to L. Since τ_i', $\tau_i^*\in L$, it follows by Local Determination that the derivation type $\sigma = \tau_i \rho[\tau_i]\in S$. But this type σ is readily shown to be unsound.

This result means that for classically sound and complete systems that are closed under re-lettering, the correctness of a derivation cannot be checked on a line by line basis but calls for some sort of global survey of the derivation. This result is in striking contrast to the situation for systems with a rule of existential elimination. We there have, in the example of G, a system that satisfies the other conditions and enjoys a local criterion of correctness for its derivations.

It should be noted that it is essential to this result that the system S be closed under re-lettering. Pick some ω-ordering of the A-letters as their alphabetic ordering. Let L consist of all line types (q, a, R, S, T) for which a is alphabetically later than each member of R; and let S be the system whose derivation types are those with terms drawn from L. Then S is locally determined by definition and is readily shown to be classically sound and complete. Indeed, S is essentially the same as Quine's system Q, but subject to his 'rule of thumb' concerning alphabetic ordering.

As an example of a maximality result, we have our previous result concerning CQ, but we also have the following result for Q:

Theorem 10
Q is the maximal system to satisfy the conditions of classical soundness and suppositional indifference.

Proof
Clearly, Q does satisfy the two conditions. Suppose now that the system S satisfies the conditions and that τ belongs to S but not Q. Then the dependency relation for τ, as defined for Q, is not irreflexive. Take τ to be of the form $\tau_1 \ldots \tau_n$. For each term $\tau_i = (q, a, R, S, T)$ of τ, let $\tau'_i = (q, a, R, T, T)$; and set $\tau' = \tau'_1 \ldots \tau'_n$. It is readily seen that the dependency relation for τ', as defined for CQ, is the same as the dependency relation for τ, as defined for Q, and that it is therefore not irreflexive. So τ' is an unsound derivation type. But by suppositional indifference, $\tau' \in S$ – contrary to the classical soundness of S.

I have no significant examples of minimality or uniqueness results. But it would be of interest to characterize the various standard systems both in terms of their minimal satisfaction of certain conditions and also in terms of their unique satisfaction of conditions that make no reference to either minimality or maximality.

17
Genericity Generalized

Just as we may set up a general framework for discussing the various restrictions that may be imposed upon the rules of a system of natural deduction, so we may set up a general framework for dealing with the various generic interpretations that may be given to the resulting derivations.

By a *generic interpretation* $\Im$ for a system of natural deduction S we mean a class of pairs of the form (D, $\mathfrak{M}^*$), where D is a derivation permitted by S and $\mathfrak{M}^*$ is an A-model for the language $\mathfrak{L}^+$ (and is endowed, one should recall, with a denotation function d from the set of A-letters of $\mathfrak{L}^+$ into the set of A-objects A). Intuitively, (D, $\mathfrak{M}^*$)$\in\Im$ just in case the A-letters of D may be interpreted in accordance with the specification of $\mathfrak{M}^*$. Since, for given D, $\mathfrak{M}^*$ may range over many A-models, we should allow that $\Im$ may be a proper class in the sense of NBG.

Let us now state various conditions that may be imposed upon an interpretation $\Im$.

Generic Soundness
For any (D, $\mathfrak{M}^*$)$\in\Im$, $\mathfrak{M}^*$ (case-to-case) validates the sequent established by D.

A stronger condition is obtained by requiring that $\mathfrak{M}^*$ should validate any sequent established by an initial subderivation of D.

Generic Completeness
Let D be a derivation permitted by S. Suppose that the sequent (Δ, ϕ) is validated by $\mathfrak{M}^*$ whenever (D$^+$, $\mathfrak{M}^*$) is in $\Im$ for some continuation

D^+ of D. Then some continuation of D that is permitted by S establishes (Δ, ϕ).

Say that a derivation D is *interpreted by* $\Im$ *over* the classical model $\mathfrak{M}$ if, for some $\mathfrak{M}^*$, $(D, \mathfrak{M}^*) \in \Im$; and say that D is *interpreted by* $\Im$ if it is interpreted by $\Im$ over some classical model $\mathfrak{M}$.

Interpretative Completeness
Each derivation permitted by S is interpreted by $\Im$.

A stronger condition is:

A Prioricity
Each derivation permitted by S is interpreted by $\Im$ over any classical model $\mathfrak{M}$.

According to the first of these conditions, each correct derivation gets interpreted. According to the second, the interpretability of each correct derivation is guaranteed a *priori*; it exists regardless of the state of the world (the classical model $\mathfrak{M}$).

Both conditions may be weakened somewhat. In place of the first, we may say that for any derivation D permitted by S there is a continuation D^+ of D that is permitted by S and interpreted by $\Im$. In place of the second, we may say that for any derivation D permitted by S there is a continuation D^+ of D that is permitted by S and interpreted by $\Im$ over any classical model $\mathfrak{M}$.

Closure under Isomorphism
If $(D, \mathfrak{M}^*) \in \Im$ then $(D, \mathfrak{M}') \in \Im$ for $\mathfrak{M}'$ isomorphic to $\mathfrak{M}^*$.

Uniqueness
If $(D, \mathfrak{M}^*), (D, \mathfrak{M}') \in \Im$ then the restrictions of $\mathfrak{M}^*$ and $\mathfrak{M}'$ over the set of designated A-objects are isomorphic.

Restriction
If $(D^+, \mathfrak{M}^*) \in \Im$ then $(D, \mathfrak{M}^*) \in \Im$, for D^+ a continuation of D.

Extendibility
If $(D, \mathfrak{M}^*) \in \Im$ and D^+ is a continuation of D permitted by S, then, for some $\mathfrak{M}'$, $(D^+, \mathfrak{M}') \in \Im$ and the restrictions of $\mathfrak{M}^*$ and $\mathfrak{M}'$ to the A-objects denoted by the A-letters of D are identical.

According to the last but one of these conditions, each interpretation of a derivation must already have been admitted by the sub-derivations. According to the last, each interpretation of a derivation must be extendible to its continuations.

A somewhat weaker condition than Restriction can be obtained by adding to its antecedent the requirement that D be interpreted by $\mathfrak{J}$. And similarly, a somewhat weaker condition than Extendibility can be obtained by adding to its antecedent the requirement that D^+ be interpreted by $\mathfrak{J}$. Also, for Extendibility, we might only require that $\mathfrak{M}^*$ and $\mathfrak{M}'$ are identical over the A-objects denoted by the instantial terms of D.

These two conditions are related to our previous principle forbidding retrospective interpretation. If there is a retrospective interpretation of certain A-letters, then either that interpretation was not admitted by some subderivation containing those A-letters or some other interpretation for the subderivation cannot be extended to the given derivation.

Instantial Determination
Let D and D' be two derivations permitted by S, and suppose that they contain the same A-letters and the same applications of EI and UG (paying regard to what the suppositions are). Then $(D, \mathfrak{M}^*) \in \mathfrak{J}$ iff $(D', \mathfrak{M}^*) \in \mathfrak{J}$.

Non-suppositional Determination
Let D and D' be two derivations permitted by S; and suppose that they contain the same A-letters and the same applications of EI and UG (without regard to what the suppositions are). Then $(D, \mathfrak{M}^*) \in \mathfrak{J}$ iff $(D', \mathfrak{M}^*) \in \mathfrak{J}$.

As with the case of the conditions on restrictions, we may attempt to establish results on the satisfaction of different combinations of conditions. We may also consider hybrid combinations, containing both conditions on restrictions and conditions on interpretations, and we may consider the relation between the two kinds of conditions.

These are not questions I shall pursue here. But we should note that their answers should provide us with a better general understanding of systems with a rule of existential instantiation and that they should provide us, in particular, with a rigorous foundation for those informal considerations that have been thought to favour the adoption of one system over another.

PART IV

NON-STANDARD SYSTEMS

In this part I deal with a certain class of non-standard systems of natural deduction. These systems are distinctive at both the semantic and the syntactic level. At the semantic level, they are distinguished by the feature that the terms arising from applications of EI are given a categorical, not a conditional, interpretation. If $\exists x\phi(x)/\phi(a)$ is an application of EI, then a is taken to be the arbitrary object that ϕ's, not the arbitrary object that ϕ's if anything ϕ's. At the syntactic level, they are distinguished by the feature that conditional proof and other discharge rules do not hold without restriction. In order for a line to be legitimately inferred, it is necessary that certain presuppositions to the terms in the inference shall be among the suppositions to the line. The two features are connected: for under the categorical interpretation of the ∃-instantial terms, the extendibility of the A-objects mentioned in an inference is not automatically guaranteed; and it is in order to guarantee their extendibility that the restrictions are placed on the presuppositions to an inference.

These systems have both an informal and a formal interest. The informal interest resides in their connection with ordinary reasoning. It seems to me that in informal applications of EI the instantial terms are given a categorical interpretation. Therefore these systems provide a better approximation to ordinary reasoning than those which embody a conditional interpretation of the instantial terms.

The formal interest of the systems resides in their connection with other, more familiar, systems of natural deduction – with systems, such as G, that employ a rule of existential elimination and with certain systems of subordinate proof. They also provide a method for formalising inclusive (or 'free') logic and intuitionistic logic that avoids some of the pitfalls arising from the adoption of the rule of existential instantiation.

The present part is in four chapters. In Chapter 18, I lay out the basic presuppositional modification of the system C. In Chapter 19, I consider variants to this basic modification – variants in presentation, in the role of presupposition, and in the underlying system. In Chapter 20, I explore the connection of the presuppositional systems to the system G and to the systems of subordinate proof of Kalish and Montague and of Belnap and Klenk. In the final chapter, I consider how inclusive and intuitionistic logic may be formalised within the presuppositional framework.

The whole topic of presuppositional systems calls for a much more thorough treatment than is given here. I can only hope that I have said enough to indicate its potential interest.

18
Restricted C

The basic idea behind the construction of the system RC is that no ∃-instantial term can be used unless the assumptions upon which its introduction depended are still in force.

For the purposes of a formal definition, it will be convenient to use a formulation of the system C in which an assumption may rest on assumptions other than itself. Thus the characteristic form of an assumption line will be:

   ... (n) ϕ Ass.

where ... is a list of numbers that must include n but may also include the numbers of previous lines. It should be noted that in a Fitch-style system of subordinate proof the artificiality of multiple listings to the left of assumption lines could be avoided.

Now let D be a derivation of the system C, as thus formulated, a an ∃-instantial term of D, and $\exists x\phi(x)/\phi(a)$ the application of EI by which the term a was introduced. (Note that, by the flagging restrictions, there will be exactly one such application.) We say that an A-letter *presupposes* the (assumption with) number m if the A-letter is an ∃-instantial term a as above and if m appears to the left of the premiss of the inference, *i.e.* if it is the number of an assumption upon which the premiss of the inference rests. Given an A-letter a of D, let the *presupposed assumptions* PA(a) *of* a be $\{m:$ a presupposes the assumption $m\}$. Note that PA(a) is empty if a is not ∃-instantial.

Let D be a derivation of the system C and (n) a line of D with assumptions (or rather, assumption numbers) Δ and conclusion ϕ.

We say that an A-letter of Δ or ϕ is *sanctioned by* line (n) if every presupposition of a is a supposition to (n), *i.e.* if PA(a) ⊆ Δ. And we say that the line (n) itself is *legitimate* if it sanctions every A-letter occurring in its suppositions or conclusion.

The derivations of the restricted system RC are now simply those derivations of C in which each line is legitimate.

What effect does the requirement of legitimacy have on the application of the rules? For the rule of assumptions, it is required not only that the assumption itself be listed to the left but also the assumptions presupposed by the ∃-instantial terms occurring in assumptions to the left. We now see why we insisted on a formulation of C in which redundant assumptions were allowed to appear to the left of assumption lines; for without this admission, no assumption involving an A-letter with presuppositions could be made.

For each of the rules ∧ I, ∧ E, ⊃ E, UG and EG, our requirement imposes no additional constraint; for no assumption gets discharged and any A-letter occurring in the conclusion to the inference also occurs in one of the premises. For EI, again no further constraint is imposed, though for a different reason; the new A-letter occurring in the conclusion is one whose presuppositions are automatically assumptions to the inference.

For ∨ I, it is necessary to require that no ∃-instantial term occur in the new disjunct whose presuppositions are not included in the assumptions to the inference. And for each of the other rules, which are all discharge rules, it is necessary to ensure that legitimacy is not lost in the discharge of assumptions. In an application $\psi/\phi \supset \psi$ of ⊃ I, for example, we must be sure that no ∃-instantial term of ψ or of the remaining assumptions Δ has the assumption ϕ as a presupposition.

A characteristic difference between C and RC may be brought out by considering the derivation of the theorem ∃x(∃xFx ⊃ Fx). In C, the derivation can go as follows:

(1) ∃xFx   Ass
(2) Fa   1, EI
(3) ∃xFx ⊃ Fa   1, 2, ⊃ I
(4) ∃x(∃xFx ⊃ Fx)   3, EG

However, this derivation will not go through in RC, since line (3) is illegitimate. Instead, the derivation is forced to take the following more devious route:

RESTRICTED C 179

1	(1)	$-\exists x(\exists xFx \supset Fx)$	Ass
2	(2)	$-\exists xFx$	Ass
2	(3)	$\exists xFx \supset Fa$	2, TF
2	(4)	$\exists x(\exists xFx \supset Fx)$	3, EG
1	(5)	$--\exists xFx$	2, 1, 4, $-$I
1	(6)	$\exists xFx$	5, $-$E
1	(7)	Fa	6, EI
1	(8)	$\exists xFx \supset Fa$	7, TF
1	(9)	$\exists x(\exists xFx \supset Fx)$	8, EG
	(10)	$--\exists x(\exists xFx \supset Fx)$	1, 9 $-$I
	(11)	$\exists x(\exists xFx \supset Fx)$	10, $-$E

Without any further annotation, it is somewhat awkward to test for legitimacy. However, a slight change to the dependency diagram yields a simple and convenient test. As each ∃-instantial term makes its appearance in the dependency diagram, enclose in brackets to its side a list of the numbers of the assumptions which it presupposes. At any line of the derivation we can then consult the diagram to see that legitimacy is maintained.

We have the following simple result on presuppositions:

Lemma 1
Let D be a derivation of RC. If a depends upon b in D, then PA(a) ⊇ PA(b).

Proof
Clearly, it suffices to prove the result in the case where a immediately depends upon b. But in that case, a is introduced into the derivation through an inference of the form $\exists x\phi(x, b)/\phi(a, b)$. Let the assumption numbers to the lines of the inference be Δ. Then by the legitimacy of the lines, PA(b) ⊆ Δ; and by definition, PA(a) = Δ.

A semantics for the system RC can be given on the basis of the categorical, as opposed to the conditional, interpretation of ∃-instantial terms. An A-model $\mathfrak{M}^*$ is now *suitable for* a derivation D of RC if:

(i) $a \neq b$ for distinct A-letters a and b of D;

(ii) a is unrestricted for each A-letter of D not ∃-instantial in D;

(iii) if the non-vacuous inference $\exists x\phi(x)/\phi(a)$ occurs in D, then a realizes the definition $(a, \phi(x))$ in $\mathfrak{M}^*$.

Associated with the derivation D is the system of definitions $\mathfrak{S}$ consisting of (a, ϕ(x)) for each non-vacuous application $\exists x\phi(x)/\phi(a)$ of EI in D and of (a, Λ) for each a in D that is not $\exists$-instantial. A model will then be suitable for a derivation just in case it realizes the associated system of definitions. Note that an $\exists$-instantial term from the inference $\exists x\phi(x)/\phi(a)$ is interpreted as denoting the arbitrary ϕ-er and not the arbitrary thing that ϕ-s if anything does.

Given this interpretation of the $\exists$-instantial terms, there is a difficulty in proving generic soundness in the usual way. For a suitable A-model may not be extendible over the class of designated A-objects and so there will be no guarantee that classical reasoning still holds.

We overcome this difficulty by appealing to a simultaneous induction. If D is a derivation of RC and $\mathfrak{M}^*$ is a suitable model for D, then we show, for each line of the derivation, that:

(1) if the line has assumptions Δ and conclusion ϕ, then $\mathfrak{M}^*$ (case-to-case) validates the sequent (Δ, ϕ);

(2) if also the line is obtained by an application of EI with instantial term a, then, whenever $v \in V$ is a value-assignment defined on the closure of $A_{\mathrm{PA}(a)}$ for which $\mathfrak{M} \models v(\mathrm{PA}(a))$, the A-object a is totally defined in $\mathfrak{M}^v$.

From (2), Lemma 1 and Theorem I.2, it follows that:

(3) if Δ is a set of assumptions from the RC-derivation D, $\mathfrak{M}^*$ is a suitable model for D, and $v \in V$ is a value-assignment with closed domain for which $\mathfrak{M} \models v(\Delta)$, then $\mathfrak{M}^v$ is extendible over the set of A-objects $\{a: \mathrm{PA}(a) \subseteq \Delta$ and $a \notin \mathrm{Dm}(v)\}$.

Proposition (3) can then be used in establishing (1) in the case in which the line is obtained by the application of a proper classical inference rule.

The additional restrictions on the derivations in RC are posited in order to ensure that the proofs of (1) and (2) will go through. Suppose, for example, that we allowed the standard derivation of $\exists x(\exists x Fx \supset Fx)$, as previously displayed. Then the derivation would be correct up to line (3). But the inference to line (4) would be erroneous, since the A-object a might be null.

At the more informal level, we can see the restrictions on RC as motivated by a philosophical distinction between presuppositions and suppositions, and an attendant view on the presuppositions of A-terms. A presupposition is a condition for the intelligibility (or proper interpretability) of a sentence or of the terms in it; while a supposition is merely a condition for the truth of the sentence. So it might be held, for example, that it is a presupposition of any definite description of the form 'the ϕ-er' that exactly one thing ϕ-ed. (Of course, this is not the only view; I merely use it for the purposes of illustration.)

Given that certain terms have presuppositions, it will be a natural requirement on their use that they only appear in contexts in which the truth of their presuppositions has been assumed or established. So, on the previous view of definite descriptions, a definite description could only be used if the appropriate uniqueness claim had been made out.

This requirement iterates. The presuppositions to a term may involve terms with further presuppositions; these presuppositions may involve terms with yet further presuppositions; and so on. Before any presupposition can be made out, it will be necessary to make out the presuppositions to its terms, the presuppositions to the terms of those presuppositions, and so on. In any given context, therefore, there will be a hierarchy of presuppositions, with the intelligibility of any one presupposition depending upon the truth of prior presuppositions. One definite description, for example, may contain others; these may contain yet others; and so on. Before therefore the intelligibility of the given description can be made out, it will be necessary to make out, successively, the intelligibility of these other descriptions.

The system RC can be seen to be the result of applying these general considerations to the system C, under the proviso that the presuppositions of an $\exists$-instantial term are the assumptions upon which its introduction rests. However, in this case it is somewhat hard to see in what the intelligibility or proper interpretability of an A-term is meant to consist. Very roughly, we want to say that the A-terms must be interpreted as denoting totally definable A-objects. But this will not quite do. If I assume $\exists xFxb$, then I may deduce Fab, even though the total definability of a is not thereby guaranteed. In assuming $\exists xFxb$, I am taking the value of b to be fixed. So what I really want to say is that the A-object must be totally definable relative to a fixing of the values of the A-objects mentioned in the suppositions. This is the informal counterpart to our formal requirement (2) above.

As far as I know, there has been no other attempt in the literature to construct presuppositional systems of the sort described here, despite their naturalness and their obvious relevance to key positions on how certain kinds of sceptical or transcendental argumentation are to be formalised. Perhaps the closest one gets is with the axiomatic systems for ι- and η- terms in Hilbert and Bernays [34], where it is a requirement on the introduction of an ι-term (*resp.* an η-term) into the language that the appropriate uniqueness claim (*resp.* existential claim) be established as a theorem. It would therefore be of interest both to develop further presuppositional systems and to investigate the general properties of such systems. I might add that the usual objection to the approach of Hilbert and Bernays, *viz.* that the class of well-formed terms thereby becomes non-effective, is of dubious value. It is a simple matter to reformulate the systems in such a way that the class of theorems remains the same and yet no non-effective restriction is placed on the well-formed terms; and even without this reformulation, it is not at all clear what significance attaches to the requirement that the class of well-formed terms be effective.

19
Variants

We take a brief look at some variants of the system RC. There are three kinds of variant that we shall consider in all: those in presentation; those in the underlying account of legitimacy; and those in the underlying system of logic.

Variants in Presentation

For different purposes, it is helpful to consider somewhat different presentations of the presuppositional system.

First, it is possible to formulate the derivations of RC without explicitly indicating the presuppositions to a given line. Thus the derivations of RC will look like those of C, but there will be a different account of assumption. The *explicit* assumptions to a line will be those listed to its left. The *implicit* assumptions are those that must be supposed to be present if the presuppositional requirements on a derivation are to be met. Of course, a rigorous and detailed account of the implicit assumptions could be given. This is not something we shall bother to do. But two general points should be noted. (1) The implicit assumptions of one line may be inherited from another line, even though they are not required by the use of the A-letters in the suppositions and conclusion of the given line. (2) The restrictions on the application of UG must make reference to both the implicit and the explicit assumptions. The presence of the instantial letter, or a letter depending on it, in the *implicit* assumptions is enough to make the application of the rule fail.

Second, the derivations of RC may be given the kind of presentation in tree-form that is familiar from the work of Prawitz [65]. However, the proper formulation of the rules, once the transition to tree-form is made, is not completely straightforward. Three major difficulties arise. The first difficulty arises from the circumstance that in a tree-form derivation a given formula occurrence never gets used more than once. Consider now the following linear derivation of RC:

1	(1)	∃xFx	Ass
1	(2)	Fa	1, EI
1	(3)	Fa ∨ p	2, ∨I
1	(4)	Fa ∧ (Fa ∨ p)	2, 3, ∧I

If we put it in tree-form, we obtain:

$$\frac{\dfrac{\exists xFx}{Fa} \quad \dfrac{\dfrac{\exists xFx}{Fa}}{Fa \vee p}}{Fa \wedge (Fa \vee p)}$$

But then the flagging restriction is violated, since a is used as the instantial term to two applications of the rule EI.

We may get round this difficulty by an appropriate weakening of the restriction. Let a and b be two occurrences of ∃-instantial terms in a tree-form derivative of RC. So a and b both occur within the context of two given sub-derivations:

$$\begin{array}{cc} \vdots & \vdots \\ \exists x \phi(x) & \exists y \psi(y) \\ \phi(a) & \psi(b) \end{array}$$

We say a and b are *duplicates* if these two sub-derivations are identical in shape (in particular, $\phi(a)$ and $\phi(b)$ are occurrences of the same formula). The flagging restriction then takes the form:

> No two occurrences of ∃-instantial terms are occurrences of the same letter unless they are duplicates.

The second difficulty arises from the circumstance that in a tree-form derivation the discharge of assumptions is not explicitly indicated. This difficulty may be solved, as in the case of standard systems, by so defining the assumptions at a given line that they are the minimum required for the derivation to go through. However, in the present case, we must ensure that the presuppositional requirements are met and so we should follow the previous account in including both the implicit and the explicit assumptions.

The third difficulty arises from the circumstance that derivations in tree-form need not be linear. Consider the following tree-form derivation:

$$\frac{\dfrac{\dfrac{Fb}{\exists xFx}}{Fa} \quad \dfrac{\dfrac{Ga}{\exists xGx}}{Gb}}{Fa \wedge Fb}$$

This derivation conforms to the obvious formulation of the Novelty restriction for tree-form derivations; and yet it is impossible to present it in linear form in such a way that the standard Novelty restriction is satisfied.

How then should Novelty for tree-form derivations be stated? Say that one A-letter a *immediately precedes* another b in a tree-form derivation D if b is an ∃-instantial term in D and if a occurs above the instantial occurrence of b. Let *precedence* be the strict ancestral of immediate precedence. Then Novelty should take the form:

The relation of precedence is irreflexive.

It can be seen that this restriction is exactly what is required for a tree-form derivation to have a linear version that conforms to the standard Novelty restriction.

A third variant presentation of the system is one in which the presuppositions and suppositions to a line in a derivation are somehow kept apart. The numerals for the presuppositions might be underscored, for example. However, it must be allowed that a given formula might serve both as a presupposition and as a supposition. With a more sophisticated annotation, one might even mark off the presuppositions to presuppositions, the presuppositions to presuppositions of presuppositions, and so on.

The big advantage in such a presentation is that it enables us to distinguish between the roles of suppositions and presuppositions. The usual roles of discharge will apply to suppositions without any special restriction. But there will be a rule that will enable us to convert a presupposition to a supposition in case no A-letter from the line presupposes it.

Variants in Legitimacy

Different accounts of legitimacy and hence different accounts of the restrictions on an underlying system S can be given. I shall here rest content with indicating some of the possibilities, without attempting to be systematic or overly rigorous. It would certainly be useful, however, as part of the general study of presupposition systems, to investigate the different kinds of restriction that might be imposed and the relationships that then obtained between the resulting systems.

The present restrictions on C are about as strict as can reasonably be permitted. There are, however, at least three respects in which these restrictions might be relaxed. One arises from distinguishing the roles that may be played by different occurrences of the same A-letter. Consider the following derivation:

1	(1)	$\exists xFx$	Ass
1	(2)	Fa	1, EI
1, 3	(3)	p	Ass
1, 3	(4)	p ∨ Ga	3, ∨I
1, 3	(5)	Fa ∧ (p ∨ Ga)	2, 4, ∧I

The definition of legitimacy requires that (1) be an assumption to line (4) and hence to line (3). But it is not until line (5) that we need identify the roles of the 'a' in line (4) and the 'a' in line (2). An alternative definition would therefore impose no special requirement on occurrences of an A-letter that did not emanate from the instantial occurrence. As a consequence, the following version of the previous derivation would be correct:

1	(1)	$\exists xFx$	Ass
1	(2)	Fa	1, EI
3	(3)	p	Ass
3	(4)	p ∨ Ga	3, ∨I
1, 3	(5)	Fa ∧ (p ∨ Ga)	2, 4, ∧I

In the semantics for such systems, of course, one will need to assign different interpretations to the same A-letter according to its role.

A further form of relaxation is obtained by allowing that an ∃-instantial term may be used not only when its presuppositions are among the given assumptions but also when they may be established on the basis of those assumptions. Consider the following derivation:

1	(1)	∃xFx	Ass
1	(2)	Fa	1, EI
3	(3)	∀xFx	Ass
3	(4)	Fb	3, UI
3	(5)	∃xFx	4, EG
3	(6)	Fa	3, UI

The derivation is correct under the proposed relaxation, since the assumption (3) to line (6) is one from which the presupposition to a has been derived. However, under the original restrictions, the derivation is faulty, since the presupposition (1) to a is not itself an assumption to line (6).

The third, and most significant, relaxation in our restrictions is obtained by letting an ∃-instantial term occur in an assumption without the support from its presuppositions. There is a general issue here, that may be illustrated in the case of definite descriptions. Suppose one takes descriptions to have presuppositions. Then can one make a supposition involving a description without assuming or establishing its presupposition? One view is that any use of a description requires the support of its presupposition. Another view is that in making a supposition involving a description one is implicitly assuming the truth of its presupposition and so there is no need to state it as a separate assumption.

If one takes the latter view, then not only will the use of descriptions in suppositions not require any presuppositional support. The use of descriptions in suppositions will also provide independent support for their use in a conclusion. If ever a description or other term is used in a supposition, it may be used in a conclusion derived from that supposition; and given that the use of the term may presuppose the intelligibility of other terms, those other terms may also be used in the conclusion.

Applying these ideas to the case of ∃-instantial terms, we obtain the following modification in the definition of legitimacy. Let D be a derivation of C and (n) a line of D with assumptions Δ and conclusion ϕ. Then line (n) is *legitimate* if, for each A-letter occurring in ϕ, either (i) $PA(a) \subseteq \Delta$ or (ii) there is a term a^+ identical to or dependent upon a that occurs in Δ. Note that, under clause (ii), we allow not only a to occur in Δ but also any A-letter a^+ dependent upon a. This is because the use of a^+ already presupposes the intelligibility of a.

The difference between the present and the original definition of legitimacy may be explained in terms of the sanction for an expression. What before sanctioned the use of a term was the presence of its presuppositions among the suppositions of a line. What now sanctions the use of a term is either the presence of the presuppositions among the suppositions or the occurrence of that term or one of its dependents in the suppositions.

Let R^+C be the system that results from the present definition of legitimacy. Then a categorical semantics can be given for R^+C along the lines already indicated for RC. There is, however, a subtle difference in the semantic potential of the two kinds of system. Suppose we had a discharge rule that allowed us to infer a given conclusion from a disjunct of a disjunction when it had been inferred from the disjunction itself. Such a rule would allow us to go from the sequent $\Delta, \phi \vee \psi/\chi$ to either of the sequents $\Delta, \phi/\chi$ or $\Delta, \psi/\chi$. Now such a rule would be validity-preserving on the previous semantics, but not on the present semantics; for just because we had a v for which $v(\Delta)$ and $v(\phi)$ were true but $v(\chi)$ was false, we would have no assurance that such a v could be extended to the A-letters in ψ. This potential difference results in no actual difference between the systems RC and R^+C, since none of the usual discharge rules are ones in which a supposition or part of a supposition gets 'lost'.

Corresponding to Lemma 1 for RC, we have:

Lemma 2
Let D be a derivation of R^+C. If a depends upon b in D, then either $PA(a) \supseteq PA(b)$ or, for some b^+ identical to or dependent upon b, b^+ is an A-letter of $PA(a)$.

It may also be shown that, in the definition of legitimacy, we may allow under clause (i) that $PA(a^+) \subseteq \Delta$ for some a^+ dependent upon a at the line in question, without any alteration in the resulting class of derivations.

The difference between the systems RC and R^+C can be brought out by considering how $\exists y(Fy \vee Gy)$ is to be derived from $\exists x(Fx \vee Gx)$. In R^+C the derivation may go as follows:

1	(1)	$\exists x(Fx \vee Gx)$	Ass
1	(2)	$Fa \vee Ga$	1, EI
3	(3)	Fa	Ass
3	(4)	$Fa \vee Ga$	3, $\vee$I
3	(5)	$\exists y(Fy \vee Gy)$	4, EG

6	(6) Ga	Ass
6	(7) Fa ∨ Ga	6, ∨I
6	(8) ∃y(Fy ∨ Gy)	7, EG
1	(9) ∃y(Fy ∨ Gy)	2, 3, 5, 6, 8, ∨E

However, in RC, the lines (3), (4), (6) and (7) are not legitimate. The derivation is therefore forced into the following form:

1	(1) ∃x(Fx ∨ Gx)	Ass
1	(2) Fa ∨ Ga	1, EI
1, 3	(3) Fa	Ass
1, 3	(4) Fa ∨ Ga	3, ∨I
1, 3	(5) ∃y(Fy ∨ Gy)	4, EG
1, 6	(6) Ga	Ass
1, 6	(7) Fa ∨ Ga	6, ∨I
1, 6	(8) ∃y(Fy ∨ Gy)	7, EG
1	(9) ∃y(Fy ∨ Gy)	2, 3, 5, 6, 8, ∨E

Although the requirements on legitimacy are so much stricter for RC than for R^+C, there is a close connection between the derivations of the two systems. Roughly speaking, the derivations of RC may be obtained from those of R^+C by adding the implicit presuppositions as further assumptions.

To make this connection precise, we need some terminology. Given a derivation D of R^+C, say that one assumption *presupposes* another if some A-letter of the one presupposes the other; and let *hereditary presupposition* be the (non-strict) ancestral of presupposition. Given a set of assumptions Δ, let the *closure* Δ^+ *of* Δ be the set of assumptions hereditarily presupposed by the assumptions in Δ.

Given a derivation D of R^+C, let its *expansion* be the result of replacing the set Δ of assumptions listed to the left of any line with its closure Δ^+. The concept of expansion may be illustrated by reference to the two previous derivations of ∃y(Fy ∨ Gy) from ∃x(Fx ∨ Gx); the derivation in RC is an expansion of the derivation in R^+C.

Call a derivation of R^+C *regular* if PA(a) never contains an A-letter upon which a does not depend. Intuitively, no A-letter should rest, for its intelligibility, on the use of an A-letter upon which it does not depend; and it is, in fact, an easy matter to convert an irregular derivation into a 'comparable' regular derivation.

We now have:

Theorem 3
Let D be a regular derivation of R^+C. Then its expansion is a derivation of RC.

Proof
By an induction on the construction of D.

The restriction to regular derivations is somewhat inelegant. Its use is required to ensure that the correctness of applications of UG is preserved under expansion. Its use might be avoided if the systems were given a presentation that distinguished between the roles of suppositions and presuppositions; the standard restrictions on the role UG would then apply only to the suppositions.

Two other variant accounts of legitimacy may be considered, somewhat different from the others. The first is obtained by letting terms in both the suppositions and conclusion to a given line carry their presuppositions with them. This approach may be related to the previous one by treating all derived sequents Δ/ϕ as if they were of the form $\Delta, -\phi/\bot$. From a semantical point of view, this approach is the simplest; since it is only required of each derivable sequent that it be case-to-case valid, and no additional requirement is imposed to ensure the conditional extendibility of its A-letters. From a syntactic point of view, the approach gives a 'maximal' system, one with the largest number of permitted derivations.

However, the formulation of the rules for such a system is somewhat unnatural and unintuitive. We can no longer superimpose on the usual formulation of the rules a general requirement of legitimacy on the lines resulting from the application of those rules. Instead, we must impose a general requirement of legitimacy on the application of the rules themselves. This is that any term 'lost' in the inference should be properly sanctioned in the concluding sequent. If, for example, we go from $\phi \wedge \psi$ to ϕ, then we have to be sure that any A-letter in ψ is properly sanctioned by the suppositions to the conclusion ϕ.

Within this system, the standard derivation of $\exists x(\exists xFx \supset Fx)$:

```
1   (1) ∃xFx                Ass
1   (2) Fa                  1, EI
    (3) ∃xFx ⊃ Fa           2, ⊃I
    (4) ∃x(∃xFx ⊃ Fx)       3, EG
```

is blocked at the last step, since a is lost at line (4) without its presupposition being regained. It is amusing to note that we can now fault this derivation at each of its three steps: if one adopts the system G, the inference from line (1) to (2) is incorrect; if one adopts a standard presuppositional system, such as RC or R⁺C, then the inference from (2) to (3) is incorrect; and if one adopts the present presuppositional system, then the inference from line (3) to (4) is incorrect.

The second variant account is obtained by admitting into the language a predicate D with the sense 'is defined'. In the terminology of Chapter 2, such a predicate would be classical as opposed to generic. Terms attached to the predicate would be exempt from the usual strictures concerning presuppositions. On the other hand, the presence of Da among the suppositions would sanction the general use of a.

Variants in the Underlying System

The kinds of restriction imposed upon the system C can also, with appropriate modifications, be imposed upon other classical systems of natural deduction with a rule of existential instantiation. We may, for example, take Quine's system Q as our basis. The ∀-instantial terms must then also be seen as a source of presupposition and the definition of legitimacy modified accordingly.

Of special interest as an alternative basis is the system C^+ (in which Irreflexivity replaces Novelty as a condition on ∃-instantial terms). Since the first use of an A-letter may precede its use as an ∃-instantial term, it is necessary to exercise some care in formulating the appropriate restrictions on derivations.

Let D be a derivation of C^+, (n) a line from D with assumptions Δ and conclusion ϕ, and D' the subderivation of D that terminates in the line (n). Then the line (n) is said to be *legitimate* if, for any ∃-instantial term a of D that occurs in Δ or ϕ, PA(a)⊆Δ and a is ∃-instantial in D'. Note the extra condition that a be ∃-instantial in D'. For C this condition is superfluous, since if a occurs in Δ or ϕ it must already have been introduced as an ∃-instantial term. But for C^+ the condition is not superfluous. It suffices, for example, to exclude the following inference:

1 (1) ∃xFx   Ass
1 (2) ∃xFx ∨ Ga   1, ∨I
1 (3) Fa   1, EI

It is clear that the additional condition is reasonable; for if a term is to be used at a given stage of a derivation, it is necessary not only to have established its presuppositions but to have established that these *are* its presuppositions.

Although the system C^+ contains many more derivations than C, the restricted system RC^+ contains the same derivations as RC; for if every line of a derivation of C^+ is legitimate, then Novelty, as well as Irreflexivity, must be satisfied.

To formulate the system R^+C^+, take D, (n), Δ, ϕ and D' as before. Then the line (n) is now said to be *legitimate* if, for any A-letter a occurring in ϕ, either (i) $PA(a) \subseteq \Delta$ and a is ∃-instantial in D' or (ii) there is a term a^+ identical to or dependent upon a in D' that occurs in Δ. For the same reasons as before, it is necessary to add to clause (ii) the condition that a^+ be dependent upon a in the subderivation D'.

Analogues of Lemmas 1 and 2 may be established for RC^+ and R^+C^+ respectively. It may also be shown that in the definition of legitimacy for R^+C^+ we may allow, under clause (i), that $PA(a^+) \subseteq \Delta$ for some a^+ dependent upon a by the line in question, without any alteration in the resulting class of derivations.

The relationship between R^+C^+ and R^+C is more complicated than the corresponding relationship between RC^+ and RC. The derivations of the two systems do not exactly coincide; but they do coincide over a certain natural and representative sub-class.

To define the sub-class, we need some further terminology. Let D be a derivation from R^+C^+. We say the A-letter a presupposes b if b is an A-letter of PA(a). The presupposed A-letters are those directly involved in explaining the intelligibility of a given A-letter. Let *hereditary presupposition* be the strict ancestral of presupposition. The hereditarily presupposed A-letters are those involved, either directly or indirectly, in explaining the intelligibility of a given A-letter. An A-letter a is *circular* if it hereditarily presupposes itself. Intuitively, a circular A-letter is one whose intelligibility cannot be explained without circularity. The derivation D is then said to be *circular* if it contains a circular A-letter. In a sense, a circular derivation is illegitimate; for there is no proper way of making out the meanings of all its terms.

Now say that a derivation D of R^+C^+ is *essentially of* R^+C if some re-ordering of the lines of D results in a derivation of R^+C. For example, the following derivation:

1	(1) Ga	Ass
2	(2) ∃xFx	Ass
2	(3) Fa	2, EI

is essentially of R^+C, since upon re-ordering its lines we obtain the following actual derivation of R^+C:

2	(2) ∃xFx	Ass
2	(3) Fa	2, EI
1	(1) Ga	Ass

Of course, upon re-ordering the lines, they will no longer be numbered consecutively. The consecutive numbering of lines must therefore be regarded as an inessential feature of the derivations of R^+C. However, it will still be important that the justification of a given line refer only to previous lines.

Next, say that a derivation D from R^+C^+ is *connected* or *of a piece* if no line other than the last line can be dropped, *i.e.* if the loss of any line other than the last line destroys the correctness of the derivation. For example, neither of the two previous derivations is connected: for in the first, we may drop line (1); and in the second, we may drop line (2). A connected derivation is one in which all lines are used in establishing the last line. When it is written out in tree-form, it terminates in a single formula occurrence. We say that a derivation D is *complete* if it is both finished (*i.e.* contains no ∃-instantial terms in its final sequent) and connected; and we say that D is *completeable* if some correct continuation of it is complete.

The connection between the systems R^+C and R^+C^+ is now given by the following result:

Theorem 3
For any derivation D of R^+C^+, the following conditions are equivalent:

(i) D is essentially a derivation of R^+C;
(ii) D is non-circular;
(iii) D is completeable.

The proof of this result is long and detailed, and is therefore omitted.

Within the context of the presupposition systems, this theorem provides an interesting motivation for the Novelty condition. For the condition can be seen to be exactly what is required to obtain the independently desirable features of non-circularity and completeability.

20

Connections

There are some fairly simple transformations, of a structural sort, that show the derivations of RC and G and of RC and certain systems of subordinate proof to be substantially the same.

Let us deal first with the connection between RC and G. It will here be convenient to present the derivations of either system in tree form. In regard to the system G, we shall adopt the tree-form presentation of Prawitz ([65], pp. 23–24) and, but for obvious modifications, we shall adopt his terminology and notation. In regard to the system RC, we shall adopt the tree-form presentation described in the previous section.

Let D be a tree-form derivation which contains an application of ∃E, as displayed:

$$\frac{\exists x\phi(x) \quad \begin{array}{c}[\phi(a)]\\ \vdots \\ \psi\end{array}}{\psi}$$

We call D′ an *immediate transform* of D if it is the result of replacing the given application of ∃E by the following applications of EI:

It is understood that the derivation of $\exists x\phi(x)$ is placed above each occurrence of the assumption $\phi(a)$.

Let D be a tree-form derivation of G. We may successively replace each application of $\exists$E with an application of EI in the manner described until no more applications of $\exists$E remain. (There will, in general, be many ways in which this can be done). The resulting derivation D* will be called a *transform* of D. Note that as we go through the replacements, the intermediate derivations will contain applications of both $\exists$E and EI.

Recall from Prawitz ([65], pp. 28–29) the concept of a derivation (or deduction) that has *only pure parameters*. We shall say instead that the derivation is *pure*. Intuitively speaking, a pure derivation is one in which the parameters (or A-letters) are not needlessly identified; in terms of the terminology of Chapter 15, we do not have distinct quasi-letters without having distinct letters. It is readily shown that any derivation of G can be converted, by re-lettering, into one that is pure (Prawitz [65], p. 29).

We now have the following connections between G and RC:

Theorem 4
Let D be a pure derivation of G from Δ to ϕ. Then some transform D* of D is a derivation of RC from Δ to ϕ.

Theorem 5
Let D* be a finished derivation of RC from Δ to ϕ. Then it is the transform of a derivation D of G from Δ to ϕ.

The proofs of these results are somewhat long and involved; I shall therefore not go into details. The basic idea is to set up a transitional system RC-G that combines features of both RC and G. In particular, it contains both a rule $\exists$E of existential elimination and a rule EI of existential instantion. We then show that: (1) the derivations of RC-G not containing an application of EI are essentially the derivations of G; (2) the derivations of RC-G not containing an application of $\exists$E are essentially the derivations of RC; (3) any derivation D' of RC-G that contains an application of EI is the immediate transform of some derivation D of RC-G; (4) any derivation D of RC-G that contains an application of $\exists$E has an immediate transform D' that is a derivation of RC-G. Under (3) and (4), it must also be shown that there is no gain in assumptions in going from D' to D or D to D'.

It is important to appreciate that the results under (3) and (4) are not at all trivial and are very sensitive to the properties of the underlying systems. Suppose we start off with an application of ∃E:

$$\frac{\exists x\phi(x) \quad\quad \begin{matrix}[\phi(a)]\\ \vdots\\ \psi\end{matrix}}{\psi}$$

Then in going to the application(s) of EI:

$$\begin{matrix}\vdots\\ \exists x\phi(x)\\ [\phi(a)]\\ \vdots\end{matrix}$$

the application of the rules in the second part of the derivation may be invalidated by the presence of additional assumptions in the first part. On the other hand, in going from the application(s) of EI to an application of ∃E, the application of the rules in the right-hand part of the derivation may be invalidated by the presence of the additional assumption $\phi(a)$ and, moreover, assumptions that were originally discharged in the second part of the given derivation may no longer be discharged in the resulting derivation. It is this last difficulty that is critical; and it is the one for the solution of which the presuppositional character of RC is essential.

The present results put the rules of existential elimination and existential instantiation in a new light. Instead of being regarded as alternatives, either can be regarded as a disguised version of the other. The original intention behind the presuppositional systems was that they should provide an appropriate formalisation for the categorical interpretation of the ∃-instantial terms. It is therefore remarkable that they should also yield those restrictions appropriate for establishing the equivalence on the two kinds of rule for the existential quantifier.

Let us turn now to the connection between RC and certain systems of subordinate proof. I have in mind the systems of Kalish and Montague [64] and of Belnap and Klenk (Klenk [83]). The reader may refer to the respective books for full details, but we may here review some salient features.

The Belnap-Klenk system BK is a system of subordinate proof in the style of Fitch. With the exception of UG and EI, the rules are standard. The rule for UG may, in our symbolism, be schematically presented as follows:

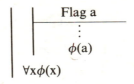

There are the usual stipulations concerning the relationship between $\phi(a)$ and $\forall x \phi(x)$. Note that the application of UG requires that one starts off a new subordinate proof in which the instantial term is 'flagged'.

The rule for EI is schematically given by:

$$\exists x \phi(x)$$
$$\vdots$$
$$\phi(a) \qquad \text{Flag a}$$

No new subordinate proof is begun for an application of EI, but the instantial term is flagged to the right.

There are two general restrictions on flagging. The first is that no flagged letter can occur *above* the step where it is flagged. The second is that no flagged term can occur *below* the subproof where it is flagged.

The system KM of Kalish and Montague is a system of subordinate proof in the style of Jáskowski, with boxes taking the place of lines. Quite apart from the use of boxes, the presentation of subordinate proofs is somewhat special. A subordinate proof is prefaced with the statement:

Show ϕ

where ϕ is the formula to be shown. Once the subordinate proof is done, it is boxed and the given occurrence of 'Show' is cancelled. So what, in a Fitch-style system, would look as follows:

$$\begin{array}{|l} \phi \\ \vdots \\ \psi \end{array}$$
$$\phi \supset \psi$$

in the Kalish-Montague System becomes:

CONNECTIONS 199

Show $\phi \supset \psi$

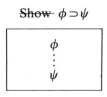

ϕ
$\vdots$
ψ

But for the modifications required by this approach, all of the rules, with the exception of UG and EI, can be standard. For ease of presentation, it is preferable to have discharge roles that discharge only one assumption at a time. Kalish and Montague therefore dispense with the usual rule of $\vee$-elimination and use certain proper sentential rules in its place.

The role UG may be given the form:

Show $\forall x \phi(x)$

$\vdots$
$\phi(a)$

And the rule EI takes the form:

$\exists x \phi(x)$
$\vdots$
$\phi(a)$

Note that, again, the application of UG requires a new subordinate proof, while an application of EI does not.

The restrictions on the $\forall$-instantial and $\exists$-instantial terms are somewhat different. For $\forall$-instantial terms, it is required that they not occur in lines *antecedent to* the given statement (*i.e.* to lines that are then 'available for use'). For $\exists$-instantial terms, it is required that they not occur in lines *preceding* the given instantial line.

We should also require that no $\forall$-instantial letter be identical to an $\exists$-instantial (or, at least, an 'available' $\exists$-instantial letter). Kalish and Montague do not make a typographic distinction between free and bound variables. By insisting that the $\forall$-instantial term a be identical to the variable x of quantification, they are able to avoid the need for a separate flagging restriction.

Superficial inspection reveals a close affinity among the systems RC, BK and KM. Consider, for example, the following attempted derivations of $\exists x(\exists xFx \supset Fx)$ in BK and KM (annotations are omitted):

1 | $\exists xFx$
2 | Fa
3    $\exists xFx \supset Fa$
4    $\exists x(\exists xFx \supset Fx)$

1   ~~Show~~ $\exists xFx \supset Fa$

2 | $\exists xFx$
3 | Fa

4    $\exists x(\exists xFx \supset Fx)$

Both systems allow one to derive Fa from $\exists xFx$ and yet disallow the inference to the conditional $Fa \supset \exists xFx$ in a way that is reminiscent of the workings of the system RC.

Further inspection confirms that these systems are, indeed, very close. Let me not present the details, but merely the basic ideas behind the correspondence.

First consider the transition from BK to RC. Any derivation D of BK (or of any other system of subordinate proof) may be written out in linear nonsubordinate form D' in an obvious manner. (There are certain details concerning iterations and nested assumptions that we need not go into). Let us call D' the *transcription* of D.

It can now be established that the transcription D' of any derivation D of BK is a derivation of RC. Two basic facts need to be verified. The first is that the Independence restriction on the rule UG is satisfied. But this follows readily from the observation that b occurs before a in a derivation whenever a depends upon b. The second fact is that an ∃-instantial term cannot occur without its presuppositions. But this is almost an immediate consequence of the requirement that an ∃-instantial term not occur below the subproof in which it is flagged.

This result does not quite hold for the system KM. Consider the following derivation of KM.

CONNECTIONS

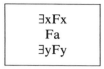

Show ∀yFy

| ∀xFx | |
| Fa | Premiss |

(∃xFx ⊃ ∃yFy) ∧ ∀yFy

Its transcription is not a derivation of RC or even of C^+, since the flagging restriction is violated.

The difficulty arises from the presence of unrelated occurrences of the same A-letter. It may therefore be avoided by relettering the derivations of KM in such a way that two occurrences of the same A-letter are always related.

The transitions in the other direction are more involved. Let D^* be a derivation of RC. Suppose that we are allowed to perform the following operations on a derivation, as long as the final line and its assumptions remain the same.

(1) *Repositioning*

A line may be repositioned as long as the annotation is adjusted accordingly and the resulting derivation remains correct.

(2) *Differentiation*

Two uses of the same line may be differentiated

For example, the derivation:

1	(1)	p	Ass
	(2)	p⊃p	1, 1, ⊃I
1	(3)	p∧(p⊃p)	1, 2, ∧I

may be re-written as:

1	(1)	p	Ass
1'	(1')	p	Ass
Λ	(2)	p⊃p	1', 1', ⊃I
1	(3)	p∧(p⊃p)	1, 2, ∧I

(3) *Re-lettering*
A derivation may be re-lettered so as to ensure that unrelated occurrences of a letter are never occurrences of the same letter. Call D′ a *transform* of D* if it can be obtained from D* by successively applying these operations. Then it can be shown that any derivation D* of RC has a transform D′ that is the transcription of a derivation D of BK. Since KM is essentially a more liberal system than BK, a similar result holds for KM.

It is again remarkable that systems which are so differently motivated should be so closely connected.

One aspect of the transition from RC to BK deserves special mention. Let us ask how the flagging restrictions for ∃-instantial terms are made to hold in the derivation D. Consider an application of EI in D:

$$
\begin{array}{ll}
\vdots & \\
\exists x\phi(x) & \\
\vdots & \\
\phi(a) & \text{Flag a} \\
\vdots &
\end{array}
$$

By Novelty for D′, the letter a will not occur above the line in which it is flagged. So it remains to show that a does not occur below the given subordinate proof (*i.e.* below and 'to the left'). Consider the two typical ways in which this could happen:

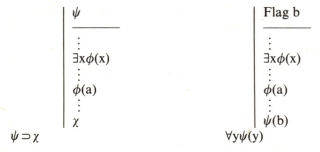

In the first case, we can arrange the derivation D′ in such a way that ∃xφ(x) would not occur under the supposition ψ in D′ unless ψ were a presupposition of a in D′; but then the presuppositional requirement on ∃-instantial terms guarantees that a cannot occur in ψ ⊃ χ. In the second case, we can arrange the derivation D′ in such a way that a would not occur in the subordinate proof headed by 'Flag b' unless a depended upon b; but then the dependency requirement on ∀-instantial terms guarantees that a cannot occur in $\forall y \psi(y)$.

We therefore see that the presuppositional and dependency requirements come together in the flagging restrictions; what are disparate conditions in RC are aspects of a single unitary condition in BK.

It should also be remarked that the above results, both those for KM and BK and those for G, can very probably be improved. It has been shown that certain systems coincide, modulo certain structural transformations. It would be desirable to tighten the control over these transformations and, in particular, to limit or totally remove the application of re-lettering, which is not properly a structural rule at all; and it should then be possible, by mutually adjusting the details of the different systems, to prove tighter results of this sort.

Semantics for the systems BK and KM may be developed along the lines of the categorical semantics for RC. It is interesting to note that there is also a very simple and simply applied ambiguous-name semantics for the system BK. This semantics associates a class X_n of 'suitable' models with each step of a derivation D. When $n=0$, X_n is the class of *classical* models that assigns a denotation to every A-letter other than those flagged in D. Suppose now that $n > 0$. Let m be the number of the first line in the same subproof as line (n) to precede line (n); and let m be 0 if there is no such line. We then let $X_n = X_m$ unless line (n) introduces a supposition or a flagged term. If the line introduces the supposition ϕ, then $X_n = \{\mathfrak{M} : \mathfrak{M} \in X_{n-1}$ and $\mathfrak{M} \models \phi\}$. If the line introduces the ∀-instantial term a, then $X_n = \{\mathfrak{M}' : \mathfrak{M}'$ extends a model $\mathfrak{M}$ of X_{n-1} by assigning any individual i from its domain to a$\}$. If the line introduces the ∃-instantial term a via the formula $\phi(a)$, then $X_n = \{\mathfrak{M}' : \mathfrak{M}'$ extends a model $\mathfrak{M}$ of X_{n-1} by assigning an individual i for which $\mathfrak{M} \models \phi[i]$ to a$\}$.

We now prove by a simultaneous induction on $n > 0$ that:

(1) If $\mathfrak{M} \in X_n$ and ϕ is the formula at line (n), then $\mathfrak{M} \models \phi$;

(2) If line (m) is the first line in the same proof as line (n) to precede line (n), then, for any model $\mathfrak{M} \in X_m$, there is a model $\mathfrak{M}' \in X_n$ that is either identical to or an extension of $\mathfrak{M}$.

Classical soundness then readily follows.

If we examine the proof of (1) and (2), we see that the inductive hypothesis for (2) is required to establish (1) both for the case in which φ is obtained by discharging a supposition and for the case in which it is obtained by an application of UG. The proof therefore reveals a certain affinity in the roles of suppositions and flaggings. It may be that a more thorough exploitation of the generic semantics would provide a deeper explanation of this affinity (somewhat along the lines of the Heyting interpretation for intuitionistic logic). We may see constant terms and sentences alike as designating objects, with terms designating individuals and sentences designating truth-values. And just as we take schematic terms to designate arbitrary objects whose values are individuals, so we may take schematic sentences or formulas to designate arbitrary objects whose values are truth-values. We may now think of an ∀-instantial flagging as indicating that every expression within its scope (be it a term or a formula) designates an arbitrary object that depends upon the arbitrary object designated by the flagged term. And we may likewise think of a supposition as indicating that every expression in its scope designates an arbitrary object e dependent upon the arbitrary object s designated by the supposed formula. But in this case the dependence is rather special; for e will fail to take any values when s takes the value f and it will take its values according to the usual stipulations when s takes the value t. In this way, flaggings and suppositions are seen to play identical roles and the dependence of a conclusion upon a supposition is seen to be a special case of the dependence of one arbitrary object upon another.

However, intriguing as this extension of the generic semantics may be, it is not a matter that we shall pursue here.

21
Inclusive and Intuitionistic Systems

We briefly indicate how the idea of presuppositional backing can be helpful in formulating systems of natural deduction that are based upon either an inclusive or intuitionistic logic and employ a rule of existential instantiation. The topic deserves a much more thorough treatment than I am able to give it here.

An *inclusive* logic is one that is meant to be correct for both empty and non-empty domains. There are certain standard difficulties in formulating a system of inclusive logic. If, for example, we have the usual rules of UI, EG and conditional proof, then the following derivation of the theorem $\forall xFx \supset \exists xFx$ goes through:

1	(1) $\forall xFx$	Ass
1	(2) Fa	1, UI
1	(3) $\exists xFx$	2, EG
	(4) $\forall xFx \supset \exists xFx$	1, 3, $\supset$I

But the formula $\forall xFx \supset \exists xFx$ is not valid in the empty domain; the antecedent is true, while the consequent is false.

There are also certain special difficulties that arise from the use of the rule of existential instantiation. Suppose that we have the usual rules of EI, EG and conditional proof. Then the following derivation of the theorem $\exists x(\exists xFx \supset Fx)$ goes through:

| 1 | (1) $\exists xFx$ | Ass |
| 1 | (2) Fa | 1, EI |

(3) ∃xFx ⊃ Fa   1, 2, ⊃I
(4) ∃x(∃xFx ⊃ Fx)   3, EG

But again, the formula ∃x(∃xFx ⊃ Fx), like any other existential formula, is not valid in the empty domain.

We had doubts before over the correctness of the above derivation. But these doubts arose from our insistence that the interpretation of the ∃-instantial terms be categorical; with a conditional interpretation, they disappear. In the present case, the doubts have a more fundamental source in the possibility that the domain is empty; for when the domain is empty, the A-object a will be empty regardless of how it might be interpreted.

But although the source of the difficulties is different in the two cases, the solution to them can be the same. We can insist that whenever certain terms are used in a derivation they should have an appropriate presuppositional backing.

We must now insist, however, that all A-letters, and not just the ∃-instantial terms, have this presuppositional backing; for given that the domain may be empty, we want to be sure that even the unrestricted A-objects mentioned in a derivation are not null. We may therefore take the presupposition of an A-letter that is not an ∃-instantial term to be any existential formula. (The presupposition is, in a certain sense, disjunctive: it must be an existential, but any existential will do. If we had a propositional constant in the language with the meaning 'something exists' and if we had appropriate rules in the system for this constant, then we could take it to be the standard presupposition of the A-letters in question.)

The presuppositions of ∃-instantial terms can vary. If we adopt a categorical interpretation, then we should take their presuppositions to consist of the suppositions upon which their introduction depended – just as in the case of the exclusive or classical systems. If we adopt a conditional interpretation, then we should take the presuppositions of ∃-instantial terms to be the same as for the other A-letters – either an arbitrary existential or the standard existential.

Different systems of inclusive logic can now be obtained by adopting different accounts of legitimacy. According to the strictest standard, a line with suppositions Δ and conclusion ϕ is not legitimate unless every term, in either Δ or ϕ, has a presuppositional backing in Δ. According to a more liberal standard, it is only required of terms of ϕ which do not occur or have a dependent in Δ that they should have a presuppositional backing in Δ. A more liberal standard still is to allow the use of any term that is not ∃-instantial (or ∃-instantial with a categorical interpretation) to sanction the use of any other such term. A fourth account is obtained by letting each term carry its own presuppositions; and a fifth account is obtained by introducing a predicate D for 'defined'. Of course, these options are all independent of the possibility of distinguishing between different uses of the same A-letter and of allowing the presuppositions to be indirectly established.

It should be noted, though, that there is very little difference between requiring an arbitrary existential to be derivable from the suppositions and also allowing, instead, that an arbitrary A-letter occurs in one of the suppositions; for if an A-letter occurs in a supposition, an existential may immediately be derived by EG.

It should also be remarked that we can obtain presuppositional variants of the system G in the same way. Since in this case there are no ∃-instantial terms, there will be the following three accounts of legitimacy corresponding to the first three accounts above: (1) whenever an A-letter occurs in the suppositions or conclusion to a line, an existential has been derived from the suppositions; (2) whenever an A-letter occurs in the conclusion to a line, either it occurs in the suppositions or an existential has been derived from the suppositions; (3) whenever an A-letter occurs in the conclusion, then either an A-letter occurs in the suppositions or an existential has been derived from the suppositions.

If we adopt the fourth account, then we must restrict the derivations in such a way that whenever all A-letters are 'lost' in making an inference, then an existential has been derived from the remaining suppositions. This yields a maximal system of inclusive logic, that is the natural deduction counterpart to the sort of system proposed by Mostowski [51]. Finally, by adopting the fifth account, we may exploit the possibility of relating our systems to those which use an existence-predicate or something corresponding to it. It is interesting in this regard to note that Jaskowski [34] requires that no formula shall be assumed unless its free variables are also 'assumed'.

It seems to me that the first three of these systems have various advantages over the standard formulations of inclusive logic. (The reader may consult Schock [68] for a survey of some of the standard approaches). First, it seems to me that they correspond well to how we actually reason in the empty domain. Take a Fermat number to be a counter-example to Fermat's Last Theorem; and let n be an arbitrary Fermat number. Then in ordinary reasoning with n, it seems that we presuppose that there are Fermat numbers.

Second, they allow us to retain the usual rules of quantificational reasoning and, in particular, do not require the use of an existence-predicate for their formulation. It might appear as if there were a restriction on the rule UI; for one cannot infer $\phi(a)$ from $\forall x \phi(x)$ unless an appropriate existential has been derived from the suppositions to the inference or unless an appropriate term occurs in those suppositions. But this is best regarded not as a restriction on the rule UI as such but as a global restriction on the use of the letter a.

There are also complications arising from the vacuous application of UI and EG. If $\forall x \phi$ is so interpreted as to be always true and $\exists x \phi$ so interpreted as to be always false in the empty domain, then the application of UI and EG must be restricted; it must be subject to the same restriction as the use of an $\forall$-instantial term in a conclusion. On the other hand, the vacuous cases of $\forall x \phi$ and $\exists x \phi$ may be so interpreted as to be always equivalent to ϕ, even when the domain is empty. In this case, there is no need to restrict the vacuous application of UI and EG, although it will be required that the previous existential presuppositions should be non-vacuous.

Third, the systems allow one to give uniform proofs of results that hold good both in the empty and in the non-empty domains. Indeed, many derivations that are correct in an exclusive system will remain correct, upon minimal adjustment, in the inclusive systems. Consider, as an example, the sequent $\exists x Fx, \forall x Gx / \exists x (Fx \wedge Gx)$. The standard derivation of this sequent in a system with EI goes as follows:

1	(1)	$\exists x Fx$	Ass
2	(2)	$\forall x Gx$	Ass
1	(3)	Fa	2, EI
2	(4)	Ga	2, UI
1, 2	(5)	$Fa \wedge Ga$	3, 4, $\wedge$I
1, 2	(6)	$\exists x (Fx \wedge Gx)$	5, EG

By making lines (2) and (4) also dependent upon assumption (1), we obtain a derivation that is correct in the inclusive systems.

Although I have not gone into the question of semantics, it should be clear how generic semantics for these inclusive systems might be developed.

Let us now look, if only very briefly, at systems of intuitionistic logic that embody a rule of existential instantiation. In such a system, the propositional rules must, of course, be appropriately modified. But this is not enough. For, as we have seen, the rule EI, along with EG and CP, allow us to derive $\exists x(\exists xFx \supset Fx)$ as a theorem, even though this formula is not intuitionistically valid. (As far as I know, Lemmon [65] was the first to appreciate this point. Borkowski and Słupecki ([58], p. 98) overlooked it; and their error was noted in Smirnov [76].)

The semantical reasons for the breakdown in the standard derivation should be clear. Classically, we are assured, by the logical truth of $\exists x(\exists xFx \supset Fx)$, of a non-null A-object a that conforms to the steps of the derivation. But intuitionistically, we can have no such assurance and we can only define an A-object whose non-nullity is dependent upon the truth of the supposition $\exists xFx$.

In the light of this breakdown, logicians have experienced some difficulty in setting up a reasonable system for intuitionistic logic with a rule of existential instantiation (See Smirnov [76] and the references contained therein for details). But if we take the presuppositional route, there should, as far as I can see, be no essential difficulties in setting up a simple, natural and well-motivated system of this sort. It should also be possible, by constructing the generic semantics over a forcing model, to give a semantics for such systems.

Bibliography

(References in the text are given by author and year of publication, save that for works published in the 20th century the digits '19' are omitted.)

Barth, E.M.
   1974 *The Logic of the Articles in Traditional Philosophy*, Reidel: Dordrecht-Holland.

Bell, J.L.
   1977 *Boolean-valued Models and Independence Proofs in Set Theory*, Oxford: Clarendon Press.

Berkeley, G.
   1710 *A Treatise Concerning the Principles of Human Knowledge.*

Borkowski, L. and Słupecki, J.
   1958 'A Logical System Based on Rules and its Applications in Teaching Mathematical Logic', *Studia Logica* vol. 7, pp. 71–106.

Church, A.
   1956 *Introduction to Mathematical Logic* vol. 1, Princeton University Press: New Jersey.

Cohen, P.J.
   1966 *Set Theory and the Continuum Hypothesis*, Benjamin: New York.

Copi, I.
   1954 *Symbolic Logic*, Macmillan: New York, First Edition.
   1956 'Another Variant of Natural Deduction', *Journal of Symbolic Logic* vol. 21, pp. 52–5.
   1965 *Symbolic Logic*, Macmillan: New York, Second Edition.

Fine, K.
   1982 'The Problem of Non-Existents I – Internalism', *Topoi* vol. 1, pp. 97–140.

1983 'A Defence of Arbitrary Objects', *Proceedings of the Aristotelian Society* Supplementary Volume 57, pp. 55–77. Also in E. Landman and F. Veltman (eds.), *Varieties of Formal Semantics* (Foris Publications, Dordrecht-Holland, 1984), pp. 123–42.
1984 Review of Parsons *Non-Existent Objects*, *Philosophical Studies* vol. 45, pp. 95–142.
1985 'Natural Deduction and Arbitrary Objects', to appear in *Journal of Philosophical Logic*.

Fitch, F.B.
1952 *Symbolic Logic*, The Ronald Press: New York.

Frege, G.
1893, 1903 *Grundgesetze der Arithmetic*, 2 volumes, Jena: H. Pohle. Translated in part by M. Furth as *The Basic Laws of Arithmetic* (University of California Press: Berkeley and Los Angeles, 1964).
1970 *Philosophical Writings of Gottlob Frege* (trans. P. Geach and M. Black), Blackwell: Oxford.
1979 *Posthumous Writings* (ed. H. Hermes *et al.*), Chicago: University of Chicago Press.
1980 *Philosophical and Mathematical Correspondence* (trans. H. Kaal, ed. B. McGuinness), Chicago: University of Chicago Press.

Gentzen, G.
1934 'Untersuchungen über das Logische Schliessen', *Mathematische Zeitschrift* vol. 39, pp. 176–210.

Gumin, H. and Hermes, H.
1956 'Die Soundness des Pradikalen Kalküls auf der Basis der Quineschen Regeln', *Archiv. fur Mathematische Logik und Grundlagen Serschung* vol. 2, pp. 68–77.

Gupta, H.
1968 'On the Rule of Existential Specification in Systems of Natural Deduction', *Mind* vol. 77, pp. 96–103.

Hailperin, T.
1957 'A Theory of Restricted Quantification', Part I, *Journal of Symbolic Logic* vol. 22, pp. 19–35, Part II, *Journal of Symbolic Logic* vol. 27, pp. 113–129.

Hardy, G.
1914 *Pure Mathematics*, Cambridge University Press, Second Edition.

Hendry, H.E.
1975 'Another System of Natural Deduction', *Notre Dame Journal of Formal Logic* vol. 16, pp. 491–5.

Hilbert, D. and Bernays, P.
1934 *Grundlagen der Mathematik* Volume I, Berlin: Springer.

Jaskowski, S.
1934 'On the Rules of Suppositions in Formal Logic', *Studia Logica* No. 1.

Kalish, D.
1967 Review, *Journal of Symbolic Logic* vol. 32, p. 254.

Kalish, D. and Montague, R.
1957 'Remarks on Descriptions and Natural Deduction', *Archiv. für Mathematische Logik und Grundlagen Forschung* vol. 3, pp. 50–64 and 65–73.
1964 *Logic: Techniques of Formal Reasoning*, Harcourt, Brace & World: New York.

Kleene, S.C.
1952 *Introduction to Metamathematics*, Van Nostrand: Princeton.

Klenk, V.
1983 *Understanding Symbolic Logic*, Prentice-Hall: Englewood Cliffs.

Leblanc, H.
1965 'Minding One's X's and Y's', *Logique et Analyse* vol. 8, pp. 209–10.

Lemmon, E.J.
1961 'Quantifier Rules and Natural Deduction', *Mind* vol. 70, pp. 235–238.
1964 'Existential Specification in Natural Deduction' (Abstract), *Journal of Symbolic Logic* vol. 29, p. 220.
1965 'A Further Note on Natural Deduction', *Mind* vol. 74, pp. 594–7.
1967 *Beginning Logic*, Nelson: London.

Lewis, D.
1972 'General Semantics', in D. Davidson and G. Harman (eds.), *Semantics of Natural Language* (Reidel: Dordrecht-Holland, 1972), pp. 169–218.

Luschei, E.L.
1962 *The Logical Systems of Lesniewski*, North Holland: Amsterdam.

Mackie, J.L.
1958 'The Rules of Natural Deduction', *Analysis* vol. 19, pp. 27–35.
1959 'The Symbolizing of Natural Deduction', *Analysis* vol. 20, pp. 25–37.

Menger, K.
1979 *Selected Papers in Logic and Foundations, Didactics, Economics*, Reidel: Dordrecht-Holland.

Mostowski, A.
1951 'On the Rules of Proof in the Pure Functional Calculus', *Journal of Symbolic Logic* vol. 6, pp. 107–111.

Parry, W.T.
1965 'Comments on a Variant Form of Natural Deduction', *Journal of Symbolic Logic* vol. 30, pp. 119–122.

Parsons, T.
1980 *Non-existent Objects*, Yale University Press: New Haven and London.

Prawitz, D.
1965 *Natural Deduction: A Proof-Theoretical Study*, Almqvist & Wiksell: Stockholm.
1967 'A Note on Existential Instantiation', *Journal of Symbolic Logic* vol. 32, pp. 81–2.

Quine, W.V.O.
1950 'On Natural Deduction', *Journal of Symbolic Logic* vol. 15, pp. 93–102.
1952 *Methods of Logic*, Routledge & Kegan Paul: London.

Rescher, N.
1969 *Topics in Philosophical Logic*, Reidel: Dordrecht-Holland.

Rosser, J.B.
1953 *Logic for Mathematicians*, McGraw-Hill: New York.

Routley, R.
1969 'A Simple Natural Deduction System', *Logique et Analyse* vol. 12, pp. 129–152.

Russell, B.
1903 *The Principles of Mathematics*, Allan & Unwin: London.

Schagrin, M.
1963 'A Dilemma for Lemmon', *Mind* vol. 72, pp. 584–5.

Schock, R.
1968 *Logics Without Existence Assumptions*, Almqvist & Wiksell: Stockholm.

Slater, J.G.
1966 'The Required Correction to Copi's Statement of UG', *Logique et Analyse* vol. 9, p. 267.

Smirnov, V.A.
1976 'Theory of Quantification and E-Calculi', in J. Hintikka *et al.* (eds.), *Essays on Mathematical and Philosophical Logic* (Reidel: Dordrecht-Holland, 1976), pp. 41–7.

Suppes, P.
1957 *Introduction to Logic*, Van Nostrand: Princeton.

Tarski, A.
1965 *Introduction to Logic*, Oxford University Press: Oxford.

Tennison, B.R.
  1975 *Sheaf Theory*, Cambridge University Press, Cambridge.

van Fraassen, B.C.
  1966 'Singular Terms, Truth-value Gaps, and Free Logic', *Journal of Philosophy* vol. 63, pp. 481–95.

Wang, H.A.
  1963 *A Survey of Mathematical Logic*, North-Holland: Amsterdam.

General Index

(Technical terms are italicized. Usually, only a reference to their place of definition is given. A compound expression is often identified by its head. So 'interpretative completeness', for example, is listed under 'completeness'.)

abstraction, 8, 12, 44–5
A-letter; see *A-name*
A-model:
    actual, 24; *extendible*, 31;
    parametrized, 27; *possible*, 23;
    standard, 35; *sub*, 27; *suitable*, 62,
    92, 99, 111, 152, 179
A-name, 41; *A-instantial*, 105, 110, 129;
    circular, 192; *duplicate*, 184; *∃-instantial*, 105, 110, 129; *given*, 53,
    82; *instantial*, 82; *occupied*, 75, 116;
    preceding, 185; *quasi*, 163; *related*,
    163; *restricted*, 151; *sanctioned*, 178;
    vacant, 75, 116; see also *dependence*
A-object; 23; *dependee*, 23; *dependent*,
    18, 24; *higher-order*, 30, 44;
    independent, 18, 24; *level*, 25; *null*,
    24; *occupied*, 75; *restricted*, 24;
    totally defined, 31; *universal*, 24;
    unrestricted, 24; *vacant*, 75; *value-restricted*, 24; *value-unrestricted*, 24
arbitrary (A-):
    domain, 23; *frame*, 24; *model*, 23;
    object, 23; *structure*, 24
attribution, generic, 9, 42, *et passim*

basis:
    canonical, 37; *of model*, 23; *of set*, 36
Bell, J. L., 45
Belnap, N., 176, 197
Berkeley, G., 9, 44, 137

Bernays, P., 2, 61, 182
bivalence, 11, 45–6
Borkowski, L., 110, 111, 209

Carnap, R., 141
Church, A., 5
circularity: *of definitions*, 55; *of derivation*, 192; *of term*, 192
classical: *completeness*, 67, 161;
    conditions, 13–16, 29–30, 43–44,
    191; *soundness*, 66, 167; *validity*, 48, 50
closure: *condition*, 116; *of set*, 24, 189;
    under isomorphism, 172; *under reduction*, 168; *under re-lettering*,
    167; *under re-ordering*, 168; *under subderivation*, 167
Cohen, P. J., 45
coherence, 9–15, 78, 116
completeness; 161–166, 167; *classical*,
    67, 161, 167; *generic*, 96–103, 171;
    interpretative, 172; *of derivation*,
    193; *of systems of definitions*, 54
condition: *classical*, 13–16, 29–30, 43–44,
    191; *defining*, 53; *generic*, 13–16,
    29–30, 43–44
condition of *Anti-symmetry*, 84;
    Appendage, 168; *Aprioricity*, 172;
    Classical Completeness, 167;
    Classical Soundness, 167; *Closure*,
    116; *Coherence*, 78, 116; *∃-ordering*,
    106; *Existence*, 33; *Extendibility*,

31, 172; *Flagging*, 82, 184, 198; *Foundation*, 24; *Identity*, 34; *Independence*, 103; *Instantial Determination*, 173; *Interpretative Completeness*, 172; *Irreflexivity*, 85; *Local Determination*, 168; *Local Restriction*, 82; *Multiplicity*, 34–35; *Non-Suppositional Determination*, 173; *Novelty*, 104; *Ordering*, 83; *Partial Extendibility*, 31; *Piecing*, 25; *Restriction*, 24, 172; *Suppositional Indifference*, 168; *Uniqueness*, 172; *Weak Flagging*, 105 Also see *closure, generic, rule connection*, 162–163, 193
Copi, I., 2, 59, 63, 81, 104–121, 123, 150
Cut, 52
Czüber, 15, 18

definite description, 181, 182
definition, 53; *defined terms of*, 53; *defining condition of*, 53; *given terms of*, 53; implicit, 45; *on*, 24, 42; *over*, 24, 42; *predicate*, 30, 191, 207; *realizations of*, 54; *system of*, 54, see also *system*; total, 57, 58
dependence, 17 *et passim*; direct 28; ∃-dependence, 105; *immediate*, 54, 82, 105, 163; mutual, 28; predicate for, 29; *relation of*, 23; *structure*, 163; syntactic, 54, 83, 105; see also *A-object* and *diagram*
derivation:
  circular, 192; complete, 193; completeable, 193; connected, 193; connections in, 162–3; essentially of R⁺C, 192; expansion of, 189; immediate transform, 194; normalised, 103; potential, 82; pure, 196; regular, 189; transcription, 200; transform, 196, 202; tree form, 162; type, 148; unsound, 154; well motivated, 102–3; see also *system*
determination: instantial, 173; local, 17, 168; non-suppositional, 173
diagram
  appropriate, 86, 107; dependency, 85–89, 107–111, 179

epsilon calculus, 2, 140
equivalence: generic, 56; type 148;
existence:
  conditions 33; of A-objects 6–8, 20, 33; theorems 36–40
existential: elimination, 67; generalisation, 81; instantiation, 81; introduction, 67.
extendibility, see *A-model, condition*

Fine, K., 2, 45, 55
Fitch, F. B., 78, 198.
flagging, 82, 105, 184, 198
formula: A- 41; I- 41; pseudo 41
free logic, 78, 138, 176, 205–208
Frege, G., vii, viii, 5, 15–21, 61–2, 139

generalisation, vii, 1, 62, 78, 81, 116
generic: attribution, 9, 42, *et passim*; completeness, 96–103, 171; equivalence, 56; interpretation, 171; language, 13; semantics, 122–126 *et passim*; set, 45; soundness, 171; truth, 42; validity, 48; see also *A-model, A-object, condition*
Gentzen, G., 59, 61, 67–8, 121
Gupta, H., 131

Hailperin, T., 2
Hardy, G., 142
Hendry, H. E., 160
Hilbert, D., 2, 59–67, 182

identity: of A-objects, 7–8, 16–19, 34, 96, 115; predicate of, 153; rules of, 153;
independence: condition, 103; *of A-object*, 24
individual (or I-):
  domain, 23; *formula*, 41; *model*, 23; *name*, 41, 136–7; *object*, 23
inference, 49; improper, 69; proper, 69; see also *logic, reasoning*
infinitesimal, 43
instantiation, 1 *et passim*; see also *A-name, rule of*
intuitionistic: logic, 46, 176, 204, 208–9; models 28, 43, 209

INDEX

isomorphism, 96; closure under, 172; generic, 56

Jaskowski, S., 78, 198, 207

Kalish, D., 2, 78, 81, 104, 123, 124, 150, 176, 197, 198
kinds, 43
Kleene, S. C., 75
Klenk, V., 176, 197
Kripke, S., 141

Leblanc, H., 123
Lemmon, E. J., 61, 67, 209
Lesniewski, 6
Lewis, D., 6
liberation, 79, 116
line: legitimacy, 178, 187, 191; soundness, 63; type, 148
list, 76, 115
logic, see free, intuitionistic, semantics, systems of logic
Luschei, E. L. 5.

Mackie, J. L., 137
Meinong, A., 44–5
Menger, K., 6
model: Boolean-valued, 45; classical, 22 et passim; forcing, 28, 43; generic, see A-model; sheaf, 46; underlying, 23
Montague, R., 78, 176, 197, 198
Mostowski, A,, 207

name, schematic, vii, 138–143; see also A-name, I-name
novelty, 104

object, see A-object, I-object
occupancy, 75, 116; list, 76, 115

Parry, W. T., 123
Parsons, T., 44
piecing, 25 et passim
possible: models, 23; worlds, 28, 35, 141
Prawitz, D., 2, 69, 81, 104, 123, 126, 149, 162–163, 165, 184, 195, 196
presupposition, 2, 177–209, 206–7;
assumptions, 177; hereditary, 189, 192; relation, 177, 189
principle, see rule of
programming language 2, 75
pronouns, 6

Quine, W. V. O., 2, 5, 59, 63, 81–103, 104, 119–121, 123–124, 126, 150
realism, in regard to A-objects, 6–8
realization, of definitions, 54
reasoning, informal, 1–2, 68–80, 127–46, 175 et seq; instrumentalist view of, 66, 126, 131–132; mathematical, 2, 6, 19–20, 142–143
reduction: of A-objects, 7, 40; of types, 155
Rescher, N., 6
restriction: class, 148; see also A-name, A-object, condition, value-assignment
Rosser, J. B., 123
Routley, R., 140
rule: Cut, 52
improper, 69; informal, 127; proper, 69; soundness, 63
rule of, abstraction 12, 44–5
bivalence, 11, 45
Cut, 52
existential elimination, 67
existential generalisation, 81
existential instantiation, 81
existential introduction, 67
generalisations, 62, 79, 116
generic attribution 42
identity, 153
liberation, 79, 116
modus ponens, 62
universal elimination, 67
universal generalisation, 81
universal instantiation, 81
universal introduction, 67
see also condition
Russell, B., 5

Schock, R., 207
semantics, see completeness, generic, model, soundness, truth, validity
sequent,
see inference

sheaf, 46
Skolem functions, 46, 136
Slater, J. G., 123
Słupecki, J., 110, 111, 209
Smirnov, V. A., 209
soundness, 123–124, 150–160, 167, 171; *classical*, 66, 167; for BK, 203; for C, 111-115; for CQ, 152–3; for G, 69; for H, 62–7; for Q, 90–96; generic, 171; *line*, 63; *line-to-line*, 63; *maximal*, 153–159; *rule*, 63
Suppes, P., 111, 131, 136
supposition, 68–80, 115, 128–129, 134–5, 168, 180–1, 185, 203–4
supervaluations, 45
system of definitions, 54; *complete*, 56; *defined terms*, 54; *given terms*, 54; *realization of*, 54; *refinement of*, 54; *unequivocal*, 54; *well-founded*, 55
systems of logic, 148;
 BK, 197–8, 199–200, 202–203; C, 105–126, 150–152, 178, 181; C^+, 106–115, 150–152; CQ, 150–160, 170; G, 67–80, 169, 176, 195, 203; H, 62–86; KM, 198–199, 200–203; Q, 81–104, 122–126, 150–152, 170; RC, 177–191, 195; R^+C, 188–190; R^+C^+, 192–194

Tarski, A., 5
Tennison, B. R., 46
term, see *A-name*, definite description, definition, *I-name*, name

theory: inconsistent, 8; logical, 66; of A-objects, 6–21
total: function, 39; *defined A-object*, 31; *definition*, 57, 58
truth: *absolute*, 42; *classical*, 42; *relative*, 42
type: derivation, 148; *equivalence*, 148; *line*, 148; *reduction*, 155; *unsound*, 154

universal: elimination, 67; *generalisation*, 81; *instantiation*, 81; *introduction*, 67; *object*, 24

validity: case-to-case, 51; *classical*, 48, 50; *generic*, 48; *relative*, 48, 76, 97, 115; *truth-to-truth*, 49–50
vacancy, 75, 82, 115–119;
 value, 77
vagueness, 11
value, 5, *et passim*; dependence, 24; independence, 63; *range*, 24; *-restricted*, 24; *-unrestricted*, 24; *vacancy-* 77; see also *value-assignment*.
value-assignment, 23; *admissible*, 23; *basic*, 36; *conforming*, 57; *possible*, 23; predicate, 29–30; *regular*, 39; *restriction*, 24
van Fraassen, B. C., 45
variable, 6, 19–20, 41, 61–62, 75, 110, 132–133, 139, 142; see also *A-name*, *A-object*, name

Index of Symbols

$\mathfrak{M}$	classical model, 22
$\mathfrak{L}$	classical first-order language, 22
I	domain of individuals, 23
A	domain of A-objects, 23
$\prec$	relation of dependence, 23
V	family of value assignments, 23
$\mathfrak{M}^+$	A-model, 23
VR	value-range, 24
[ ]	closure, 24
| |	strict closure, 24
V_B	value assignments on B, 24
VD	value dependence, 24
l	level, 25
$\mathfrak{M}^v$	parametrized A-model, 27
$\mathfrak{L}^*$	extended language, 41
d	designation function, 42
$\mathfrak{M}^*$	extended A-model, 42
$\models$	truth-predicate, 42
A	A-objects of, 42
$\models$	validity predicate, 48
$\gg$	immediate syntatic dependence, 54, 82, 148, 150–1
$>$	syntactic dependence, 54, 83, 148
H	Hilbert system, 62
MP	Modus Ponens, 62
Gen	Generalisation, 62
G	Gentzen system, 67
$\forall$E	universal elimination, 67
$\forall$I	universal introduction, 67
$\exists$E	existential elimination, 67

INDEX OF SYMBOLS

∃I	existential introduction, 67
Q	Quine system, 81–2
UI	universal instantiation, 81
UG	universal generalisation, 81
EI	existential instantiation, 81
EG	existential generalisation, 81
LR	Local Restriction, 82
F	Flagging, 83
O	Ordering, 83
AS	Anti-symmetry, 84
I	Irreflexivity, 85
C	Copi System, 104–5
C^+	Modified Copi System, 106
CQ	Copi-Quine System, 151
PA	Presupposed Assumptions, 177
RC	Restricted C, 177–8
R^+C	Variant of RC, 188
R^+C^+	Variant of RC^+, 192
BK	Belnap-Klenk System, 197–8
KM	Kalish-Montague System, 198–9